everyone everywhere. At the heart of the master's gift to his apprentice is the insight that 'our overarching priority must be to become the kinds of people who dream dreams worthy of our lives.' It is their gift to us now, the master and his apprentice together. Theirs is a conversation with consequences, for now and forever."

—Steven Garber, founder and principal of The Washington Institute and author of *Visions of Vocation: Common Grace for the Common Good*

"*Preparing for Heaven* opens up new vistas in how we see God's life for us not only after death but also here and now in this moment. Our crabbiness and pettiness fade as we gaze wide-eyed into the 'glorious riches' of joining God in the cosmic plan of the renewal of all things."

—Jan Johnson, coauthor of *Renovation of the Heart in Daily Practice* and *Hearing God Through the Year*

"*Preparing for Heaven* is a powerfully formative and tender book that is intellectually and spiritually profound while also emotionally stirring. Gary Black Jr. has invited us into his unique and enlightening conversations with Dallas Willard during the last stages of Dallas's earthly life. Their discussions on the life to come will alter your present life and carry you to a hope and joy in Jesus that is palpable and transformative. Enjoy this heavenly delight!"

—Keith J. Matthews, professor of Spiritual Formation and Leadership at Azusa Pacific Seminary

"If you wonder what heaven will be like, and especially if you wonder what your reaction might be the unmitigated presence of God . . . you need to read this book. Gary Black Jr. and his discussions with Dallas Willard are a sound guide for exploring the afterlife."

—Todd Hunter, author of *Christianity Beyond Belief*

PREPARING FOR HEAVEN

What Dallas Willard
Taught Me About Living,
Dying, and Eternal Life

Gary Black Jr.

HarperOne
An Imprint of HarperCollinsPublishers

HarperOne

Unless otherwise noted, all biblical quotations are taken from the New Revised Standard Version, copyright 1989, National Council of Churches of Christ in the U.S.A.

HarperCollins books may be purchased for educational, business, or sales promotional use. For information please e-mail the Special Markets Department at SPsales@harpercollins.com.

HarperCollins website: http://www.harpercollins.com

Photograph on page 293 courtesy of Dieter Zander.

FIRST EDITION

Library of Congress Cataloging-in-Publication Data

Black, Gary, Jr.
Preparing for heaven: What Dallas Willard taught me about living, dying, and eternal life / Gary Black Jr.—first edition.
pages cm
ISBN 978–0–06–236552–1 1. Future life—Christianity. 2. Heaven—Christianity. 3. Willard, Dallas, 1935–2013. I. Title.
BT903.B53 2015
236'.24—dc23
2015018079

15 16 17 18 19   RRD(H)   10 9 8 7 6 5 4 3 2 1

To Susan Jean Black—The Kingdom of Heaven comes ever closer when you are near.

Were a star quenched on high,
For ages would its light,
Still traveling downward from the sky,
Shine on our mortal sight.

So when a great man dies,
For years beyond our ken,
The light he leaves behind him lies
Upon the paths of men.

—HENRY WADSWORTH LONGFELLOW, "CHARLES SUMNER"

Contents

Foreword

I thank God for *Preparing for Heaven*. We can be grateful that Gary Black Jr. has been able to bring to us the penetrating insights of Dallas Willard on the subject of death and the life to come. And Gary does it all with exceptional skill and sensitivity. Dallas made a wise choice in asking Gary to bring this material into published form.

I consider it providential that God would bring a world-renowned philosopher and a bright, young theologian together in a unique working relationship for the final years of Dallas's earthly life. Their prolonged discussions about life in the Kingdom of the Heavens (beginning now and continuing on into eternity), especially as Dallas was facing his own death, make for riveting reading.

I was particularly moved when, in the midst of their work on several writing projects, Dallas emphatically insisted to Gary, "You must immediately stop flattering me." After Gary recovered from the shock of this statement, Dallas went on to challenge Gary that he must be willing to "take apart every one of my ideas, hold it up to the light, scrutinize every word, as if the truth itself hangs in the balance. . . . You've got to be hard on me and my ideas. I'll have it no other way." After Gary agreed to this new arrangement, Dallas declared, "Okay, let's start. Where do you think I am wrong?"

I am so glad for this turn of events. Following this crucial conversation, the relationship between them changed from a starstruck student trying to faithfully record the words of the master teacher into a collaborative search for truth. And it was by "talking tough," as Dallas would sometimes put it, that the insights found here began to emerge. Good for Dallas. Good for Gary.

The genesis for this book grew out of extensive material Dallas had written down for a course he taught at the University of Southern California on death and immortality. And now, with Dallas's own impending death, the issues became highly focused and personal. Here is someone who had read, studied, and thought long and hard over the philosophical, religious, and theological dimensions of death and the life to come and who now was himself preparing to make this very transition.

Many will be taken by the moving conversations the two of them had in the final weeks and even hours of Dallas's earthly life. And they are moving indeed! But there is more, so much more. Together, they wrestle with thorny questions such as: "Is there an intermediate heavenly state before the final resurrection?" and "Is there work for us to do in heaven?"

Perhaps for me, the most striking aspect of this book is Gary and Dallas's contention that we will continue to learn and grow and even increase in personal character formation following our bodily death. They take deadly aim at the popular notion that at the moment of death, every ounce of sin is simply erased as if it never existed and that we will become perfectly completed, whole, and finished. Dallas called this the "cosmic car wash" view of heaven. He clearly understood how devastating this approach was to any serious transformative change in this present life. Given this approach, character development and the transformation of heart, mind, and soul into Christlikeness could then be viewed as nonessential or simply a luxury in the

Christian life, certainly having no actual connection with the life to come. In contradistinction, Dallas saw a deep connection between the spiritual formation we are developing now in this life and the formation we will continue to experience into eternity. Our life and death and the life that is to come are delicately and deliberately interconnected. With laser-like insight, Dallas perceived that we would need to grow, develop, learn, and mature in character if we are "to endure the eternal realities of the Kingdom of Heaven."

In these pages, Gary explores what Dallas expected would likely be the course of human existence in heaven. Black writes, "If you are looking for a grand vision of the type and quality of life that lies far beyond the reach of the current imaginings . . . if you are looking for a purpose that is worthy of devoting your life to, if you are wondering about the enduring reality of heavenly existence and its eternal call, this book is for you."

At this point, if you are anything like me, you are wondering exactly what biblical evidences or rational justifications there might be for such convictions. Well, friend, you will want to read *Preparing for Heaven* and then judge for yourself.

Richard J. Foster
May 2015

Eternity in a Peach Box

T he genesis of this book was a series of initially un-
planned conversations during Dallas Willard's final
few months on earth. Beginning in January 2013, Dallas and I spent a good deal of time together working diligently to
finish *The Divine Conspiracy Continued*. When we started our
research, Dallas was reasonably hopeful he would recover from
his cancer, if not fully, at least enough to finish a few lingering
writing projects. He was optimistic about having at least several
months, perhaps even years, of life still ahead. This hope was
justified by a cautiously optimistic prognosis.

He talked about his outlook for the future one chilly winter
morning as we walked through the garden toward his library.
The library was located in a little white house that sits on a lot
adjacent to the Willards' home, which at the time was filled to the
rafters with books and boxes of all shapes, conditions, and sizes
full of a myriad of subjects. Forrest Gump's momma used to say,
"Life is like a box of chocolates. You never know what you're
gonna get." The same was true of the bookshelves and boxes
in the Willard library. One never knew what treasure could be
found packed away in some lonely corner. It was a perfect space

for quiet study and contemplation, where I routinely got lost for hours in deep and meaningful reflection.

Dallas was in good spirits that day. Having recovered from a recent chemotherapy treatment, he shared with me his excitement about starting our new project together. With deliberate movements, he took his time finding the books and papers we needed. We found a collection of used grocery boxes, high atop a row of bookshelves, full of notes and teaching materials he had used in his philosophy classes at the University of Southern California (USC). Many of the subjects covered in *The Divine Conspiracy Continued* originated from the notes and lectures gathered in an old Brawny paper towel box labeled "Professions." Next to it was a Del Monte peaches box labeled "Death and Immortality."

"Death and Immortality? What's that?" I asked.

"Oh, that's something I taught now and again. Not a class for the faint of heart," he quipped with a chuckle.

He asked me to take both boxes down from the bookshelf. As I worked through the Brawny box, he began to thumb through the Del Monte box. He continued thumbing for quite a while—long enough that I got him a chair so he could sit while he rummaged. It was a surprise for me to discover a subject he had thought so deeply about but had never published. More importantly, in suffering through his illness, and considering the prospects of a terminal diagnosis, Dallas was now experiencing firsthand some realities he had previously only considered in theory. He was facing his own mortality, and immortality was now closer than ever before. It was a poignant moment for me to watch Dallas read over his now aged, faded notes and ideas on the subject of death and eternal life. The emotions on his face ranged from surprise, thankfulness, and irony as he engaged in an internal conversation with an earlier version of himself. The box of insights acted as a time capsule of sorts opened at just the perfect moment. He spent a couple of intensive hours silently skimming his writings and reflections.

Finally, after I had organized my stacks of material, I asked, "Do you want to do some work on that?" He took a while to answer.

"Maybe so. If we have time." Those words floated ominously in the air. "If." That was the operative word. Neither of us knew if he would be *given* the time. As we were about to leave the library, he suggested I look through the box of material on immortality as well. He gave it to me with a casual "Just see if you can make anything of it."

I spent the long Presidents' Day weekend sorting through large portions of his notes and lectures. The box also contained a few books covering a range of philosophical arguments for or against the continuation of personal spiritual existence after physical death. Dallas primarily used the course to investigate how death affects the human condition, what unites and sustains the human personality before and after death (including whether one could or should infer the continuation and integration of personhood after death), and what religious and nonreligious viewpoints exist regarding the survival of the person, or soul, beyond bodily death (immortality). The last section of the course dealt with the meaning of life in light of death and with what kinds of human existence are implicated in worldviews that either accept or reject the concept of the immortality of the soul. There were also several pages on the subject of near-death experiences.

Dallas used several different core texts in the class. Since I am trained as a theologian and not a philosopher, only a few texts were well known to me: C. S. Lewis's *The Great Divorce*, Peter Kreeft's *Heaven: The Heart's Deepest Longing*, and Saint Augustine of Hippo's *The City of God*. I was surprised and delighted to find Richard Matheson's book *What Dreams May Come*. I only skimmed through the other texts, choosing instead to spend a fair amount of time reading through Dallas's very thorough syllabus. Some sixty pages into the syllabus, I came across a reference to Mitch Albom's book *Tuesdays with Morrie*. The title leaped off the page. *Tuesdays with Morrie* describes the life lessons journalist Mitch Albom learns from regular meetings with his former sociology professor, Morrie Schwartz, who is in the process of dying of ALS. A heartrending premonition began to loom over me.

I returned to the faded Del Monte box and found a well-marked copy of Albom's book. Dallas used *Tuesdays with Morrie* as a modern-day example to highlight the classic concept of a good death and to illustrate the significance and goodness in the lives and deaths of other historical figures such as Socrates and Jesus. Dallas suggested that Albom's description of Schwartz's life and death demonstrated the moral goodness available even in the process of dying. For Dallas, dying *with* principles was as significant an accomplishment as dying *for* principles.

Yet that was not what caused a lump to grow in my throat and a knot to twist in my stomach. As I thumbed through *Tuesdays with Morrie*, looking at Dallas's highlights and underlined passages, it was as if I were gaining a bird's-eye view of the very situation Dallas and I were in, and the fog of my denial slowly began to lift. The more I realized the harsh probabilities of Dallas's future, the more overwhelmed with grief I became. All the hope and energy I was giving to our book projects had blinded me to the harsher reality of Dallas's illness. Albom provided something of a guidebook for navigating whatever time I had left with Dallas, and I began to realize I must follow Albom's lead.

That afternoon, a significant weight began to settle across my shoulders. It felt like equal parts burden and blessing. Even as I sit to write these words, I feel the same mixture of duty to represent Dallas's life and thoughts well and a deep sense of gratitude for having the opportunity to know him as a friend and learn from him as a mentor.

It wasn't until a few days later that Dallas and I had a chance to discuss the subject again. Dallas was not feeling well that day. He was weaker and uncertain whether he was going to be able to maintain some important speaking engagements. We were all praying for a miracle. He asked, "So do you think we can make anything out of that mess of material in the box?" He was always so humble.

I laughed. Tongue in cheek, I answered, "Yeah. I think there might be just a few ideas that matter in there, like maybe the whole meaning of life thing. That might be interesting to a few people."

He looked down at his feet with a chuckle and nodded his head. "Well . . . if you think so." Dallas was simply one of the most brilliant, secure, and unassuming men I have ever met.

It was that interaction that proved to be the spark that set this book into motion. Over the next several weeks, we discussed many more subjects. We covered why and how to convey some key insights on the subjects of heaven, death, and discipleship in light of the nature and realities of heavenly existence. We discussed what he believed was most important, what to focus on, and what should be avoided on the subject and why.

Dallas and I also talked about how we believed Matheson was on to something very important about the human will. In *What Dreams May Come*, Matheson depicts Chris and Ann, a married couple who are deeply devoted to each other but become tragically separated when Chris is suddenly killed in an auto accident. Much of the book focuses on the process of learning and growth Chris experiences as he navigates the new realities of life after death. Dallas saw the biblical parallels found in Jeremiah 29:13, John 15:7, and Matthew 6:33 and 7:7 as fairly straightforward and easy to discern. Perhaps eternal life is a place where our "dreams," if we can define them as manifestations and envelopments of our strongest desires, can come true. Perhaps eternity is the place where what we deeply desire eventually becomes a reality, for better or worse. If this is so, Dallas suggested that our overarching priority must be to become the kinds of people who dream dreams worthy of our lives, people who know that what we seek after is both good and best.

Much of Dallas's work was dedicated to explaining and teaching the idea that we were made to do good by first becoming good people through lifelong apprenticeship to Christ. This is what it means to willfully inhabit, reflect, and share the glory of God. The weightiness, the gravitas, of God is found in his unstoppable goodness, which is sourced by his unending love. So how do our dreams reflect God's goodness? Are we, or are we becoming, the kinds of people who dream the kind of godly dreams that would benefit us and others should they become a reality?

Dallas also appreciated the habitual power of the will, and thus, he understood the necessity for an authentic representation of God's never-ending, life-giving sufficiency to progressively invade, and then transform, our hearts and minds. Grasping any paradigm-shifting message requires a clear-eyed, cost-counting, and well-reasoned vision of God, which is especially true for grasping enlightening visions of the Kingdom of God and the Church. People need a compelling vision of the good that lies at the center of Jesus's good news. The sheer power of such goodness alone carries the potential to subsume all other competing and counterfeiting motives, thoughts, and actions. When this good is tasted and seen, we progressively become willingly and joyfully capable of trusting our entire being to the transforming light of the Spirit of God, who is able to eradicate darkness, fear, and pride from our hearts and minds.

This is the divine effect of the knowledge of God that Dallas reveled in and loved to share with those who desired to live in the realm of God's love and grace. He knew that knowledge of God, as God is, was the full measure of the easy yoke that binds us to Christ and his loving ways (2 Pet. 1:3). Dallas encouraged us to seek, knock, and ask because God's grace blesses the pursuit of the "with-God" life and opposes only a prideful attitude connected to earning favor. Blessing and goodness are not earned, but they must be sought. This book endeavors to help us rethink and reimagine our lives in light of God's design and desire for human flourishing, both now and throughout all eternity. There are ways, and God has made those ways available to us, that we might become increasingly transformed into the likeness of his Son. This opportunity for experiencing life from above has been made available to us by Christ. We can enter into an eternal life that starts now and never ends.

Many of my conversations with Dallas over the years were revolutionary for me, and the subjects we began to cover became even more poignant and profound during his illness. But we never specifically discussed Albom's book. In fact, I avoided it. At times now, I deeply regret not discussing the similarities between *Tuesdays with Morrie* and what Dallas and I experienced as he died. Perhaps it was my own insecurity at work. I didn't want to be caught presuming too much, either of his illness or of our relationship. I rationalized that I didn't want to focus his energy on something so sentimental. Plus, what if I was wrong? What if God was planning on healing him and his death remained years away? What if the Albom connection only existed in my imagination? I concluded that mentioning the Albom-Schwartz relationship didn't serve any higher purpose, and therefore, I would hold these thoughts to myself.

I can't know if that was the right decision or not, but I am deeply grateful for making the connection between our time together and *Tuesdays with Morrie*. Looking back, I realize that it prepared me, both mind and heart, to act as a sponge in retaining as much of my experiences and our conversations as possible. You could say that day I was given the gift of recognizing the need for an "eternal suitcase" to pack every precious artifact I would encounter and to store them deeply within my heart and mind. Hopefully, one day I'll be able to forge these gifts just as deeply into my character.

Since Dallas's death, I have often wished I had recorded all of our conversations in those last few months. Much of our time together over the years was spent with a recorder nearby. But in the last few weeks, so many of our discussions were spontaneous and personal and a little bit random or unpredictable. Often I would visit with Dallas to work on the book and would end up profoundly surprised at the enlightening and meaningful turns our conversations would take. A few times, I managed to pull out my phone and record a few words, but most of the time, I just didn't think of recording our conversations. In some ways, I'm glad I didn't. Sitting next to Dallas's bed listening to his thoughts on these subjects, as he was encountering them for the first time, was a different experience than that of conversations we'd had before. Many of these moments were simply too raw, too poignant, sometimes revealing his soul in all its frail authenticity. Sometimes, when I thought of setting a tape recorder beside the bed, it seemed it would have infringed upon the sacredness and privacy of those moments. Other times, I wish I had recorded more.

Instead, I remained intentional about treating every interaction as instruction, not just as a casual relation but rather as a window of opportunity into something essential and purposeful for both me and perhaps others as well. I began to engage Dallas as if I were going to lose him sooner than I wanted, and I considered every moment precious because it might have been our last. I now realize that for a few short months I had the opportunity to treat Dallas the way I should treat everyone all the time. Our time was precious to me, he was precious to me, and my actions followed suit.

By March, we learned of his terminal prognosis. Shortly thereafter, sitting in his backyard enjoying the warm sunshine of a springtime afternoon, Dallas and I talked about what lay ahead. I fumbled through a few words of sympathy, appreciation, and sorrow and finally got around to asking how he was bearing up under such distressing news.

That afternoon, in the garden, Dallas certainly had not given up hope of surviving, believing God could heal him, if God chose, and Dallas was continuing to ask for as much. We discussed how his surgery and recovery had been very difficult over the past several months. He said that he felt if he wasn't meant to regain his strength, he was willing to continue his life in eternity rather than being left to linger with his ailments and their limitations. He was growing weary of the fight for his life on earth. Yet with a sparkle in his eye, he looked up into a cloudless sky and said, "Either way, whatever is best. I am at peace. I am confident things will work out just fine."

It came as no surprise to me that he was very much at peace placing supreme confidence for his eternal destiny in God's hands. What was surprising to me was how powerfully that peace manifested itself in him, and on him, and by extension, on me as well. There was a certain level of sorrow that hung in

xxii *Prologue*

the air between us. At times like that, it is easy to realize how imposing and violent death is to the entire human experience. In years past, I had heard Dallas speak about how easy it is for us to forget that death is a foreign invader into the eternal designs and character of God. Death was never part of God's overarching plan for humanity. And when it shows its bony face, death's finality and mystery can sneak up on us in unsuspecting and terrifying ways.

But not for Dallas. Mixed with the tears of loss, there was an unmistakable gleam of anticipation in his eyes as well. I can only describe it as a childlike excitement, and despite the pain and weakness of the disease, and the temporary loss of connection to his loved ones, his expectant joy was unquenchable. He knew he was shortly to experience what he had long dreamed of and hoped for. He was soon to come face-to-face with his dearly beloved Lord and friend, Jesus. That reality carried with it a power that was sustaining us both, allowing us to rise just above all other cares and concerns of this world. I learned that day, like never before, how highly contagious knowledge and faith can be, as can be the joy and peace they produce.

Even though I knew, perhaps even expected, this joy to be a natural product of Dallas's intimate relationship with Christ, it was an immeasurable gift to witness firsthand the effects of his trusting faith in action. I watched him stand at the precipice of the greatest of unknowns, what some call the void, where knowledge fades and we are susceptible to the dread of a cold, empty, dark, and solitary nothingness. For so many, perhaps most of us, the journey of death and dying is a haunting one through unblinking fears born from the expectation of an unforeseeable measure of suffering and loss. Such gut-wrenching questions and their potential realities did not escape Dallas, nor was he immune to their power for fanning doubt into dread. But his vast experience of God's goodness, attained throughout the many years he walked with Jesus, dug a reservoir of truth that swallowed such fears, engulfed them, and transcended them, while never needing to deny their presence or potential. His knowledge of God's loving care produced a joy strong enough to cast dread as far from his heart and mind as the east is from the west. As a result, Dallas faced the beginning of his heavenly existence with a welcoming expectation of engaging and sharing in an even more abundant supply of love, peace, and hope than that he had experienced during his life on earth. To live was Christ. To die was gain. He endured a good death because he chose and lived the good life.

Those last months with Dallas helped me to begin learning that the eternal significance of a good life and a good death are inseparably interwoven, interdependent, and mutually reinforcing. The degree to which my choices, my thoughts, my relationships, my desires, my fears, my pride, and my faith affect my experience of the eternal kind of life, both now and into eternity, remains perhaps the most altering and fulfilling lesson Dallas ever taught me. A lesson and insight, I am still, and will be forever, working to master.

Characteristically, that afternoon it didn't take long for Dallas's thoughts to focus on those around him. He talked about how good his life had been because of those who loved him best. How proud he was of his children and granddaughter. How wonderful his life had been with his wife, Jane. And he made a point of making sure I was committed to accepting his charge to complete this book. I admitted that I had a significant lack of confidence in my ability to successfully carry his words and ideas forward without him. To which he replied, "God is with us in this work. And we have to look for him and expect his help in these things. He will help you as he certainly helped me." Dallas had a wonderful way of recognizing, yet never validating, fear, so that a growing confidence in God's enabling grace was the result.

We reminisced for a while longer. When a chilling breeze began to blow through the trees, we decided to return to the house. For the first time since he had taken ill, he gently took my arm to steady himself as we walked across the yard and into the family room, where he settled down into the comfort of his favorite recliner. He then asked me when I would be back. I told him I would return the next day and that we could start right where we left off. "Good," he said. "That's a good plan." Before I turned to leave, he took my hand in his and with his other hand gently tugged at my elbow, pulling me down closer to where he could look into my eyes and whisper with a smile, "You're going to do just fine." Somehow I was able to hold my emotions in check until I said my good-byes to Jane and was back in my car. I wept most of the way home.

The most honorable thing I can say about Dallas was that he believed in the truth and lived what he believed. And his last few months on earth were certainly no exception to that rule. In large measure, the reason why Dallas was able to manifest in deed what he professed in word came from what he knew by experience. He understood better than anyone I have ever known what a pivotal role our ideas play in how we live our lives and navigate our world. This was never clearer to me than when I was able to both watch and listen to how Dallas integrated a few key ideas about eternity into the reality he faced during his own demise. It is these ideas, and their impact, that he hoped would be a great blessing to those endeavoring to grasp the larger canvas of God's enduring plan for life to the full in God's Kingdom. This book seeks to illustrate and critically engage those ideas.

Over the years, I've often caught myself realizing how amazing it was to be sitting in Dallas's living room, enjoying a meal together, listening to him lecture in the classroom, or sitting at his bedside as he described his experiences of and wisdom on any number of subjects, and I've wished there were a way others could listen in on and learn from his unique perspectives and wisdom. I'm certain I am not alone in the longing to share these moments with as many as would benefit from his insights and encouragements. Many of Dallas's friends and students have conveyed identical yearnings for their friends, family, and colleagues. One of these strongest beliefs and keenest insights centered on the critical and definable role eternity should play in the life of a disciple of Jesus. As Dallas and I discussed these subjects, and what lay ahead for him personally, along with the ideas we had gathered from the Del Monte box, it became increasingly obvious to us how catalytic such insights could be for inspiring Christians to fulfill their potential for living holistically within the realm of God's love, power, and grace.

The end of Dallas's life followed in step with the one ultimate motivation he carried for both his life and work. He desired to experience for himself, and to point others in the direction of, the wonderful, majestic person of Jesus the Christ and the eternal reality available for life and living in his Kingdom. That was Dallas's—and remains my—highest hope and objective for this book.

Like no other person I have known, Dallas had a special manner of intentionally conveying wisdom and beauty in ways that they became forever lodged deep in the hearts and minds of those around him. He also had a way of so thoroughly demolishing a bad idea that I never had to think such thoughts again. Likewise, I pray that God can use these pages to present the beauty and grandeur of the "with-God" life, as Dallas called it, both now and throughout eternity. Living in the reality and knowledge of God and his peace allows us to summon the courage, the will, the desire to take seriously the need for taking captive every thought, preparing, experiencing, and packing away the eternal qualities of faith, hope, and love that are essential for the abundant, eternal life with God. Amen.

Preparing for Evermore

I don't like to pack. It's one of the least enjoyable things I do. Perhaps it's because I don't like to fold. Never have. The ever-present wrinkles in my shirts and jeans are a testament to my lack of enjoyment of what feels to me like fashion origami. Another reason I loathe the chore of packing is the inescapable requirement to find things. I can rarely find the things I need when I need them, but packing requires me to try nonetheless. Further, my personality tends to lean more toward the spontaneous than the methodical, and packing requires me to plan ahead, another of my enduring weaknesses. Despite my best efforts to properly prepare for my travel, I invariably arrive at my destination only to discover, far too late, that I've forgotten to pack something essential. This is why I have drawers full of cheap Windbreakers, umbrellas, and phone chargers I've purchased on innumerable street corners in cities across the country. Once while traveling to Milwaukee in February, I didn't think to pack my winter gear and nearly froze while ruining a good pair of leather-soled loafers trudging through calf-high salted snowdrifts in a rental-car parking lot. (Think Steve Martin in the movie *Planes, Trains and Automobiles*.) Of course my parka and insulated boots were hidden safely someplace in my closet. I think.

My most loving wife knows how packing challenged I am, and one of the amazing gifts she will often give me is to pack my things when I am traveling to a short one- or two-day seminar or conference. If I lay out my things on the bed, she will graciously fold and tuck my things away as if she's piecing together a jigsaw puzzle. It's a sublime experience for me to watch. Yet on longer trips, especially family trips where we are gone multiple days and are engaging in multiple activities like bike riding, fishing, swimming, and the granddaddy of all packing assignments, snow skiing, she leaves me to the mercy of my own skills and focuses her gifts on getting the rest of the family organized. I'm not very pleasant to be around during the several hours such endeavors require late at night the evening before we leave. Attila the Hun may have been more congenial.

It may feel ironic, after enduring my packing diatribe, to find out that I very much enjoy traveling. Travel can begin to wear on me if I do too much of it, but I mostly enjoy experiencing new places, eating local cuisine, meeting interesting people, seeing enlightening vistas, and experiencing all the unique tastes, cultures, histories, stories, and dreams of a certain time and place in the world that others call home. However, I can't get to what I really enjoy about travel without first preparing myself to endure the trip. I have to pack. I have to be intentional in thinking through what is important, what can be left behind, what is too heavy, what I should expect upon arrival, the original purpose of my journey, and what I hope to achieve. All of which leads us to the topic of this book.

See, my wife, Susie, has developed a wonderful system of packing. She starts a week, sometimes two weeks before her departure. She lays her luggage in a corner of our bedroom, out of the way, and as she goes about her day, as things come to mind that she needs to pack, she starts looking for them, finding them, washing them if need be, replacing certain items, getting new items, and so on. She also goes online to find a weather report and search out nearby historical sites or museums. All the while her excitement and anticipation of the trip grows, and the packing and preparation are not stressful but enjoyable. As a result, she's ready, prepared, and excited about her adventure. She keeps the end in mind, always. She prepares; I just throw items into a suitcase and hope things will work out.

If there's anything we should all be preparing for, it's eternity. Yet most of us are more like me in this sense than like my wife. We expect that we'll just throw it all together and be ready at the last minute. Other than simply planning our destination, we believe that what's happening day-to-day in our pre-travel lives has very little to do with our upcoming trip. Unfortunately, the opposite is true. If we are unintentional about our day-to-day movements, we are left highly susceptible to the gale-force winds of our circumstances to the point where we only stop to think about what is crucial in our lives when we run aground and our progress comes to a jarring halt. We're busy, very busy, scattered, and distracted and therefore don't give much forethought to our overarching purpose, where we are headed, and what we need to achieve. The thrust of this book is meant to encourage us to slow down long enough to reconsider and redirect this increasingly popular, haphazard, off-the-cuff way we go about spending our lives.

For What Do You Dream?

Part of our trouble comes from a few foundational cultural beliefs that underpin our lives. Western society can appear at times to be rushing headlong toward the precipice of total collapse. The never-ending 24/7 media cycle has self-diagnosed contemporary generations as anxious, youth-worshiping, rights-demanding, truth-avoiding, photoshopped, "reality" TV–obsessed, debt-riddled, politically polarized, desire-addicted, angry, morally obtuse, and epidemically depressed. If the essence of these reports is even partly true, we should be very concerned about how these factors reveal the ultimate, underlying motivations that fuel our lives. How did we get here, and what keeps us in such a state? We should think deeply about what foundational beliefs lie at the base of what we hope and strive for in our lives, and the degree to which we either suffer or flourish as we reap the consequences of what we value and dream of. These factors carry huge repercussions, not only now but throughout all eternity.

The unavoidable decision that each of us must face, then live with for eternity, is what kind of human beings we choose to become. God has given us the freedom and responsibility to make such a choice. And God has also given us all the means by which we can make the best choice possible. Our task in this book is to investigate what this most consequential and eternal choice entails, and what eternal life amounts to.

Such a task requires us to first better understand the nature of human existence and of eternal life while also seeking to better understand what kinds of people will naturally benefit from the quality and character of a life sourced only from above. Perhaps then we could grasp a clearer vision of how all of this must play a crucial role in how we prepare ourselves to dream dreams worthy of the gift of life itself. We have the ability, and a mandate, to grow and mature into the kinds of people who glorify God and enjoy the nature of his Kingdom and character, right now, precisely where we are, long before we leave this earth. Therefore, I hope to help us better grasp how the lives we live, and the characters we "pack" and carry forward within our timeless souls—both now and in the afterlife—greatly define whether, and to what degree, we will achieve the flourishing we all so desperately seek on our journey through life. Forming our eternal lives begins now and lasts forever. This is your life, your one and only life. Are you the person you want to be?

A helpful illustration comes from Richard Matheson's *What Dreams May Come,* a novel that eventually became the 1998 motion picture of the same title.[1] Although the visual images of the film are stunning and worth seeing in their own right, the book delves more deeply into the internal troubles and triumphs of human relationships and the impact our lives, together and separately, have on the eternal condition of our souls. In the story, Chris and his beloved wife, Ann, are separated after he is killed in an auto accident. Much of the book focuses on Chris as he learns while exploring life after death. Fortunately, Chris has a teacher and guide, his previously deceased cousin, Albert, who is committed to mentoring him in understanding the new, heaven-like realities of Summerland.

Chris's thoughts and devotions, however, remain tethered to his living wife, who is suffering from the overwhelming loss of her husband. Chris's choice to dwell on the pain of Ann's despair and grief keeps him from living fully in the fruits of his Summerland existence. When Ann succumbs to her grief and commits suicide, Chris decides to leave the bliss of Summerland and risk the dangers of the hellish realms in an attempt to rescue her.

Of course, I don't endorse all the theology the story advocates. In one sense, Matheson has written a fictional story loosely tied to Dante Alighieri's poem *Inferno,* and it should be treated as such. There are several theological claims that would not stand up to the tenets of the scriptures, but there is no reason to assume Matheson ever intended his story to be held to such a standard. Dallas was, however, deeply intrigued by Matheson's depiction of heaven and hell as states created by the limitation or lack of maturation of one's mind, experience, desires, and character cultivated on earth. Matheson suggests that if the deceased would simply choose a flourishing existence—marked not by despair and darkness but instead by joy, peace, and goodness—they would be able to achieve that condition in the afterlife. For Matheson, one's eternal reality is constructed either as an experience of severe limitation (bondage) or unbridled potentiality (freedom), depending only on the power of the will to conceive of, then pursue, one state of being over the other.

To illustrate this point, Matheson describes Ann's descent into the "lower realm" after her suicide not as an act of punishment, but simply as a result of her patterned unwillingness to accept the fact that a quality of life that transcended her pain and despair was available to her if she chose to pursue it while she was alive. Instead, the habitual devotion to her suffering resulted in the decision to end her own life. For Matheson, in order for Ann to experience any degree of redemption and transformation, she must willfully reject the originally flawed and distorted rationale, ideology, or belief used to justify her suicide. Acceptance of the truth of her life is necessary before she can live in the reality that surrounds her. She must choose to adapt to the irrepressibility of truth, which consequently alters her thoughts, shapes her experiences, and eventually transforms her entire existence.

Dallas believed Matheson was making a crucial argument about how the nature and quality of our afterlife is largely affected by the lives we lead on earth. Matheson holds the idea that whether or not our dreams are sustained or become a reality in the afterlife is determined by what dreams, hopes, values, and beliefs consume our lives before we die. In the end, Matheson believes that a significant determiner of our eternal existence is preestablished by the quality of the life we live and the choices we make while on earth. Dallas argued that the overarching moral of the book is based on the assumption that what our heart most desperately seeks or desires determines what we eventually find. The book and the movie illustrate both the potential and the consequences of such a proposition.

I've often heard it said, "You never see a U-Haul being pulled by a hearse." The idea is that we don't take anything with us after we die. That's actually not true at all; we enter eternity as the people we have become. We take our "selves" with us—our memories, our characters, our personhoods, our spirits, our souls. Our entire, holistic beings carry on into eternity. This is similar to what happens when we move from one house or apartment to another. We tend to box up only our most treasured, valuable, or useful possessions with us and get rid of the rest through garage sales or thrift store donations. Likewise when we each enter eternity, we only take one thing with us, and it's the most valuable asset we ever possess: the sum of our life. The question is, What kind of people will we be when we enter the eternal state? Other questions should naturally follow: Have we done our part in transforming our characters in such a way that our lives are filled with the fruit of a life lived in the power, peace, wisdom, and love of God? Are we preparing our lives, filling our days, and directing our minds and bodies toward the good life Jesus offers us that begins right now and extends throughout eternity? What is it that we will carry forward in the "suitcase" or "boxes" of our lives? Are we prepared to live and experience the abundant life both now *and* forevermore?

This is not your normal book on heaven. I didn't die or come back or receive a divine vision of the afterlife that I am retelling here. Make no mistake: Dallas believed, as do I, that near-death experiences can be real, even though not all of what we read or hear about these events might be credible. This book is about the nature of eternal life, lived in the Kingdom of Heaven, that has already started and will continue for eternity. Jesus reveals to us that eternal life, or what Dallas defined as the "with-God" life, offers us a type and quality of existence that we don't have to die to experience. It's available right now, it's within arm's reach, and it is literally at hand. What we probe in this book is the nature of what human life is intended to be, one long (eternal) existence that has a very distinct and discernible quality to it. The key questions this book seeks to answer are: What does this eternal kind of life amount to? What is it that we can expect to experience as a result of living in and by the Kingdom of Heaven? And perhaps more important, Would I like or could I endure the reality of heaven, and if so, what am I doing now to prepare for that possibility?

What I learned from Dallas, especially as he was entering the end of this life and beginning the next phase of his eternal existence, was that the degree to which I live in the reality of the Kingdom of Heaven now, will have a huge impact on what it will be like after my physical death. What I also learned is that what we call near-death experiences are actually mislabeled. We shouldn't think of these experiences as representing what it means to be close to death at all, but as just the opposite. We should call them near-life experiences because it is at these times when we are nearer to true life than we may ever have been before. Learning that fact changed everything about how I look at and approach my life here on earth, and it also changed my view of eternity. The truth is that we can find and live the abundant life to the full long before we die. This fact can and should shape our view of eternal life. It has mine.

Of course, the apostle Paul tried to convey this message nearly two millennia ago when he said, "Set your minds on things that are above" (Col. 3:2). It wasn't until I heard Dallas say those exact same words to me the day before he entered heaven that my eyes began to open up to the reality of what eternal life really has in store for us. Hopefully, I can help you see what too many of us ignore for much too long. Heavenly existence has already started for those whose life is now hidden in Christ (Col. 3:1–4).

In the following pages we will begin engaging with some of the reasons for, and the benefits of, purposefully focusing our time, thoughts, and energies on preparing our character for what the New Testament describes as a life based on the wisdom "from above" (James 3:17), which is demonstrated in the life of Christ (1 Cor. 1:22–25; James 3:13–18). Matthew's Gospel describes this life as one lived in the Kingdom of the Heavens. What Jesus argues over and over again is that we can begin now to intentionally practice living our lives in light of this truth. Heaven is actually closer than we have previously imagined. For it is not luggage we carry into our journey through timeless infinity; it is the sum total of ourselves, accumulated into our character, which will largely define not only our experience of life now, but ultimately, the nature of our eternal destinies.

Our first hurdle is to better understand at least some of the crucial implications, phenomenal opportunities, and potentially tragic consequences we face in light of the reality that human existence is eternal. Each of us faces both a timeless destiny as well as an inescapable reality. The heavenly reality already exists, but construction on our destiny in that reality has begun and remains fluid and dynamic in the moment-to-moment decisions we make. In total, our choices forge the character of the person we become (Deut. 30:19). This is paramount when we stop to consider the unalterable reality that as human beings we will never cease to exist. Therefore, we can only be awed at the fact that we are always going to be someone. The question is,

Who? In light of the truth that you will live forever, who do you want to be?

Among the greatest assets we have in this quest to understand the essence of eternal life that comes from above are the unique perspectives and valuable lessons, which I'm still learning, from Dallas. In the chapters that follow, I will share some of the key moments that marked the beginning of Dallas's ultimate voyage into eternity. During his illness, I was also able to see how Dallas and others benefited from his lifelong preparation for entering eternity. He had long ago packed away several crucial truths and treasures into the depths of his own soul. Each chapter to follow will reveal the nature of one of those treasures. I too am attempting to pack away these truths into my own life, and therefore, I will offer some of my own thoughts and reflections regarding the implications of Dallas's views on these essential, yet often misunderstood or overlooked, treasures of Christian living. Hopefully you can benefit from both Dallas's insights and my stumbling journey in coming to grips with these essential realities in order to prepare for evermore: ever more life, love, grace, peace, wisdom, and power.

A second important goal of this book is to bless those who may be struggling with facing the reality of their own physical death or perhaps the loss of someone dear to them. Finally, I pray this work provides encouragement and wisdom to everyone longing to live their real life, right where they are, in full view of the eternal realities available in God's Kingdom, which has already begun and extends forevermore.

The Problem

What We Misunderstand About Heaven

"If you read history you will find that the Christians who did most for the present world were just those who thought most of the next. . . . It is since Christians have largely ceased to think of the other world that they have become so ineffective in this."

—C. S. Lewis, *Mere Christianity*

One

Beyond the Cosmic Car Wash

O ne of the most powerful and life-altering insights I gained from Dallas rests in the idea that what God receives out of our life, and what we receive from our lives as well, is the person we become.[1] We often talked about that one concept for hours on end. Eventually, these conversations would land on either a tragic or heroic character from history or from our personal experiences whose life was dramatically affected by either the knowledge or ignorance of this simple but profound idea. Both who we are now and what we will become carry eternal consequences that have already begun to play out in our daily existence.

One prominent example of this truth, and someone Dallas and I discussed at length, was my paternal grandmother. During the years my wife and I were in seminary, throughout the period of completing my doctoral dissertation, my grandmother lived just a few miles away, and our family visited her at least once a week. We attended a church close to where she lived and were able to spend most Sunday afternoons together. During these visits, she often questioned me about the contents of the sermon we had heard. (I think she was quizzing me to see if I was paying attention.) Yet I cherished our talks. Not only did they help me to get to know my grandmother better, but those often difficult, tumultuous conversations helped me better realize how my Christian faith was shaped and how important it is to think deeply about the kind of person I am becoming in order to intentionally seek real life—life to the full.

For all the time I knew her, my grandmother remained a deeply religious woman. I can't overemphasize the word *deeply*. She came from an impoverished background, having been raised in a very rural environment deep in the hills and valleys of the Ozark Mountains of southern Missouri. Her father died from diabetes when she was only twelve years old, leaving his wife and five children to scratch out a meager existence during the worst of the Great Depression. I've never heard anyone say anything positive about my grandmother's mother (my great-grandmother.) The best they could say was that she was a "hard" woman. To suggest my grandmother's upbringing was unstable is to risk omitting the harsh fact that she regularly did not know where the next meal would come from.

During our Sunday afternoon chats my grandmother told me of how she struggled as a young mother, trying to raise her only child, my father, with very few parental skills passed on from her mother. She was left largely alone with mounting insecurities to raise a toddler, feeling ill equipped and uneducated for the task.

During this trying time, she was invited to attend the services of an itinerant revival preacher visiting a small country church some fifteen miles outside of town. That night she remembered experiencing something that neither she nor anyone around her had ever seen or could imagine. She described the experience as an overflowing of emotion, an ecstatic awakening somewhere deep within her that caused her to express herself without concern for appearances. The preacher explained this was a "filling of the Holy Spirit," and some sixty years later, my grandmother would recall that event with tears of joy and expectation in her eyes. It was then, for the first time, that she began to believe that Jesus was real and that his love for her was all encompassing. That event changed my grandmother forever, and she longed for others to experience that same sense of utter peace and goodness that first flooded her heart that fateful evening.

That, however, is not the end of the story. My grandmother then began to attend church every time the doors were open. In truth, she developed something of an addiction to Christianity. She talked about Christianity all the time. She tried to persuade others to convert. She interpreted her life's situations and the life events of others around her in light of the last sermon she heard. She quoted scripture. She read Christian magazines and cut out little articles to tape around her kitchen. She hung pictures of Jesus on her walls. Her entire life centered around and was consumed by Christian-ese.

Here's the deal: None of her family would have had a problem with any of that. It may have been mildly annoying at times, and it did appear as if there were significant lacks of balance to her interests. But the problem wasn't with my grandmother's devotion to her faith; the problem was with her character. She was predictably mean, angry, vengeful, and bigoted. She stubbornly held on to clearly inaccurate and detrimental opinions. For instance, she could never appreciate or fully respect any minister, preacher, or teacher of scripture who was not connected to her particular denomination. Her friends and family also watched her ungratefulness go unchecked for decades. When my mother and father attempted to look after every financial, emotional, physical, and spiritual need she expressed, her response was not gratitude, but bitterness and complaint. Her gossip could rise to the level of a flamethrower. There were times she would start in on a member of the family or a neighbor, and my wife would have to take our children out of the room. There was a brutal side to my grandmother that was very disturbing.

It was also true, however, that she and I could talk for hours about some deep and meaningful truths about the Bible, salvation, or the Church. It's something we did more and more after she received her terminal cancer diagnosis, and I loved those conversations. Yet right in the middle of our dialogue, she could exhibit an unbelievable level of arrogance, anger, bitterness, or vengeance. The best way I can describe it is like a unique form of spiritual Tourette's. In the middle of a conversation about God's love, grace, or forgiveness, she could, suddenly and without irony, start describing a situation or memory in which she displayed a total absence of love, forgiveness, or grace.

The close proximity of her hypocrisy to her stated ideals and beliefs left me and others dumbfounded. She would criticize others for being critical, condemn others for being condemning, and preach to others about not presuming to preach to others. Her lack of self-awareness was nearly maddening for those around her, but more to the point, it was deeply confusing to my children. On the way home from a visit, my daughters would ask, "Why is Great-Grandma like that? Why is she so angry? Why doesn't she do what she says?" Those were tough questions for me to answer because my daughters knew—in fact, everyone knew—what my grandmother said she believed. The problem was they didn't see evidence of those beliefs in her life. So in asking why, my daughters were also inquiring if what she professed belief in—and thus, what they professed belief in—matters at all. It was a very good question.

I can't, of course, catalog the entirety of my grandmother's life here, but it is important to say there were some amazing qualities to her life as well. Like all of us, she was a mixed bag. In addition to a very dark shadow side she most often revealed to her immediate family, there was also a side that was completely the opposite. There may be friends of my grandmother who are right now thinking I have completely misled you because in their experience my grandmother was the most caring, generous, and sweet lady they had ever come across. I don't dispute those facts at all. Our family heard those reports by the dozens. Several of her friends tell wonderful stories about my grandmother giving or saying something or standing up for someone in a way that genuinely touched them. I'm grateful for the help and blessings she was able to give to others, but I know that wasn't the full story, that such acts were a struggle for her and often resulted in increased bitterness and frustration rather than growing levels of joy, peace, patience, kindness, and mercy.

There are three primary reasons why I've chosen to tell part of my grandmother's story here. First, I believe, and we will discuss in more detail later, that my grandmother is now in a place where the reality of her life and choices is something she is no longer able or willing to cover up or hide from. Second, we need to learn some lessons from her life. And third, in no way do I believe my grandmother is an anomaly. In fact, Dallas and I often discussed the fact that her life may well represent the norm. That is why spending her last four years together was such a gift. One can learn a lot about how to live life from following the example of others. But we can also learn just as much, and sometimes more, about how not to live our real lives by watching and learning from the mistakes of others who are caught simply in a state of being alive, largely missing the opportunity to fully experience the abundant life. My grandmother's life taught me both lessons.

My grandmother was miserable most of her life for one simple reason: she was tormented by the reality that she was not who she thought she should be, yet she never knew how to change or that change was actually possible. She served in her church, she cooked meals, she watched other women's children, even taking in a little girl and raising her as her own for a while. She taught Sunday school, gave money she didn't have for causes that didn't really need her money. She tried desperately to do genuinely good works in an effort to prove to herself she was "acting like a Christian." Yet when push came to shove, or when the rubber hit the road, it was a struggle, a fight, for her to do good. It was hard for her to be nice, it was an effort to serve, and she was bitter about having to give away what little she had.

For example, for many years, she and my grandfather rented out a small house my grandfather had built. And I never heard her say anything good about any of their tenants. Bitter gossip flowed routinely about their comings and goings. Yet at the same time, I also know she was routinely generous and merciful when it came to allowing late payments or even forgiving back rent altogether. Still, such acts of mercy and generosity seemed only to increase bitterness, not joy. It was as if she believed these acts of service were making her into some sort of victim, but she couldn't say no to such opportunities of service out of her sense of obligation to her Christian commitments. She was literally damned if she did and damned if she didn't. As a result, she lived most of her adult life deeply disappointed both in herself and in those around her.

After my grandfather's death, and because of her mounting discontent, my grandmother actually looked forward to dying, and testified to as much long before she became ill. She hoped she would be able to leave all of her disappointments, failures, poor choices, faults, and misgivings behind. She had become exhausted by her life. Why? Because she couldn't do enough, nor had she become the person she knew she should be, nor could she will herself to want to do more. That, in my mind, is a form of hell. Her Christian convictions and beliefs told her she should be full of grace, joy, and peace. But she wasn't. And all of this combined to form a level of discontentedness and futility that would boil over in anger and resentment.

In the months that led up to her death, I sat by her bedside and listened to my grandmother tell her "real" testimony, and things began to open up for me. I heard huge numbers of assumptions, dogmas, doctrines, traditions, wives' tales, and superstitions that littered her Christian faith. I heard descriptions of God, interpretations of scripture, and applications of teachings that, when blended together and tempered with time, had created a religious system that resembled an endless maze of dead-end alleyways. Probably the most difficult conversation we had involved her understanding of God's wrath poured out on sinners for all eternity in a conscious, torturous hell. In those conversations, I saw her own sense of righteous indignation against all those who had wronged her, against the wounds of a desperate childhood, against her fears of a fatherless, rudderless life. It was a wrath fueled with decades of pain and neglect, and in some ways, she had justified keeping her scorn boiling because she believed, and had been taught, that God too felt precisely the way she did about sin and sinners.

Eventually I realized why my grandmother spent the final twenty years of her life with the primary yearning to go home to heaven. I'd want to escape all her deep disappointments, anger, and pain too. I also came to realize I had many of these same fundamentalist, judgmental, and condemning theological ghosts in my own heart and mind. And if I didn't change, there was a good chance I would end up in the same state as she: bitter and ungrateful—all while drifting aimlessly in the sea of "Christianity." Her discontent was not in spite of what she believed, but largely because of what she believed. Her God, and thus, her life, was centered on a belief and experience of legalism, condemnation, and judgment. Her religion acted as a sledgehammer that sought to destroy the knowledge of sin and sinfulness within the heart of the sinner. The experience of God's love became connected to the experience of feeling the hammer of conviction, followed by the euphoria of mercy. The threads of what we now understand as cyclical abuse are impossible to miss. She loved Jesus and knew him as her friend. But God the Father was someone to be wholly and completely afraid of. Her compartmentalized view of God was as undeniable as it was necessary for the survival of her professed belief in the goodness of Jesus.[2]

I remember telling Dallas about these conflicting accounts regarding my grandmother's life and faith. As was his habit, he often looked down at the ground when he was listening reflectively and intently. He took his time to respond. When he did, he said two very piercing and profound words: "whitewashed tomb." That was it. As Dallas so often did, he hit at the very core issue. Good deeds on the outside; troubled heart on the inside.

I never heard my grandmother speak of spiritual transformation or of becoming more Christlike in an intentional discipling relationship with Jesus. She desired to be Christlike. She just didn't know how to do it. Actual change, becoming a different person, with different motives and actions was not on her radar. Instead, she struggled through a gritted-teeth obedience produced primarily out of fear. Such a life is not easy or light. It is a heavy burden produced by the deadening yoke of futility.

This was something Dallas and I began to discuss at great length while I was writing my dissertation on his theology. He knew better than most what I was describing, and what my grandmother had experienced. Ironically they grew up not 100 miles from one another in the poverty-stricken mountains of rural Missouri. He had encountered many like my grandmother whose vision of life as a "good" Christian had become so twisted that they believed their faith required them to endure a deep level of misery, not due to persecution or suffering, but simply as a necessary accompaniment to holiness itself. The more miserable she was, the more holy my grandmother assumed she was becoming. Joy was reserved primarily for life after death. Dallas called this "miserable sinner Christianity" and much of his ministry stemmed from recognizing and addressing how such misery actually sprung from within many of our systems of belief. Thus, he worked tirelessly to illuminate how what we think and believe about God is tied to what vision we have of our eternal life with God and to illuminate why our understanding of the gospel becomes so eternally significant.

So it's important to ask the *why* and *what* questions. Why was my grandmother's view of Christianity so ineffective? What is the whitewash veneer of Christianity? What are the beliefs that so many Christians still employ today that lead them, good people with good desires, to struggle and scratch their way toward the Kingdom of God only to have passage through the Kingdom's gates elude them in their experience of this life?

The Religious Myth of a Cosmic Car Wash

Dallas recognized better than anyone I have ever known why my grandmother and countless other Christians like her find it so difficult to experience the change they desire in their lives and their characters. Dallas understood how religious views and opinions can sometimes result in disastrous consequences if applied uncritically without sound, scriptural wisdom, teaching, and judgment. Dallas told me, on more than one occasion in reference to many different contexts, "That is just part of being caught up in 'the systems of the world.'"[3] One of the more embedded systems of belief we discussed relates to an often unconscious yet powerful assumption found within many brands of Christianity regarding the nature of eternal existence in heaven. This common assumption inaccurately accepts as fact that transformative change during earthly life is nonessential or something of a luxury. Such a belief rests on the supposition that a person's entire character will be miraculously and holistically transformed into a completely perfected state the very instant a saved soul enters heaven.

Let me try to illustrate these ideas as clearly as possible. Imagine the eternal soul of a disciple of Jesus as represented by a perfect circle, with one quarter of the circle shaded black to represent the part of the soul that has been captured or controlled by the darkness of sin. The common assumption for most people is that, immediately upon dying, the circle representing the soul will go through what Dallas called a "cosmic car wash" and emerge in heaven free of the black stain of sin. In other words, many Christians assume that, at the moment of our death, every ounce of sin is simply erased as if it never happened. And what we end up with is a perfectly completed, or whole and finished, soul. "It won't be like that," Dallas said of this assumption.

Perhaps a more accurate illustration would be to visualize our souls entering eternity as a misshapen circle, more oblong than round, or as a pie with a significant slice missing. Dallas argued that a disciple's soul enters heaven completely sinless, but not complete, not flawlessly round, not whole. Our sin is removed, but incompleteness remains. Part of the problem we face in thinking about this idea comes from our confusion centered on the two words *perfect* and *complete*. We enter heaven perfect, meaning without sin, but we are not complete. We are not finished, nor is God finished with us. As an example, Dallas would say often that a small tree sprout could be perfectly developed at every stage of its maturation while remaining incomplete. Likewise, as we learn to choose to live and walk with Jesus in the intermediate state of paradise, he is able to complete the work he first began in us, bringing us to our fullness in Christ. Eventually God will finish the work he started in us (Phil. 1:6; 1 Thess. 5:23–24). But this will take some effort, time, and grace.

Dallas and I kidded that the concept of instant character transformation at death may even mean that the more stubborn among us will need more than a car wash. Perhaps there will be a celestial auto body shop to straighten, replace, or refinish every flaw, dent, and ding in our character. Dallas simply thought that the myth of a cosmic car wash is inconsistent with the biblical witness, with what we know about human life, life with God, the power of the human will, and human spiritual transformation.

To be clear, the myth at the crux of the cosmic car wash ideology is the belief that as our last breath leaves our physical body, so too, we leave all of the results or effects of our sin behind. Thus, the assumption goes, we begin eternity, from the very moment we "open our eyes" or "wake up" in heaven as shiny, new spiritual beings, utterly whole, lacking in nothing, in a state as if our sin and its effects have left no impact on our lives or perhaps never existed at all. Such a belief system drains much, if not most, of the motivation away from engaging in the difficult, slow, and patient process of spiritual transformation and character development while on earth. Instead, all the cosmic car wash requires is for us to hang on by our fingernails, keeping hold of our systems of "sin management" until we die, and the car wash will take care of the rest.[4]

Much of the cosmic car wash theology seems to stem from a misapplication of this section of Psalm 51:

> You desire truth in the inward being;
>> therefore teach me wisdom in my secret heart.
> Purge me with hyssop, and I shall be clean;
>> wash me, and I shall be whiter than snow.
> Let me hear joy and gladness;
>> let the bones that you have crushed rejoice.
> Hide your face from my sins,
>> and blot out all my iniquities.
>
> (Ps. 51:6–9)

This is a beautiful passage full of truth; however, there is no ample or substantive evidence in the teachings of Jesus, or in the scriptures as a whole, to support elevating the metaphors of washing or the whiteness of snow into a theological claim to validate instant, complete perfection at the point of physical death. In fact, the presumption of attaining instant, complete transformation at the moment of death may actually work against at least parts of what scripture describes as the state one assumes in eternity.

Dallas believed that heavenly existence will not be a state wherein it is as if we had never sinned.[5] Instead, we will forever realize and be eternally thankful for the grand mercy and grace of God's love and forgiveness. Such awareness will require an understanding of why we were forgiven, some understanding of what we were forgiven of, and the depths of love that overcame our sin. The constant realization of such huge measures of undeserved favor will be a major cause of our never-ending gratitude and worship of Christ throughout eternity. To erase the memory of sin is to also erase the conscious awareness of God's overwhelming power, grace, love, mercy, and faithfulness.

Yet it is important to state that maintaining a memory of sin does not mean sin continues to have dominion over us. Truly, sin will have no power in heaven. But part of the memory of sin's black stain works to create the eternal backdrop on which the illimitable brightness of God's glorious acts throughout history will shine. And with it, the conscious depth of our gratitude and wonder of God's works will be reflected as well.

As disciples of Jesus we are to be actively developing our ability to reign or rule with God as citizens of heaven (Phil. 3:20–21). This is what my grandmother missed out on during her lifetime on earth. What Dallas came to understand and demonstrated early in his life is that one does not rule in eternity if one chooses not to be ruled in earthly life as an ambassador of the Kingdom of God. The gospel of Jesus teaches we are intended to do both: to rule and be ruled. We live in this world, but we are not from this world. We have the ability to do this now through a discipling relationship with Christ in order to prepare ourselves to accomplish God's plan for our lives both now and into eternity.

Dallas believed not in a car wash that disrupts and separates this life from the next, but in a continuous, interactive, communicative experience and existence that connects this life and the next. I was able to hear him describe exactly this sort of powerful and joyous encounter with the heavenly realms in his last few days, which I outline in detail at the end of the next chapter. Some people define these as near-death experiences. But in reality, watching Dallas in his last few days on earth, I have come to realize these are moments when we have an opportunity to come close to what true life really is intended to be. They become *near-life* experiences because in these moments, death and its sting can seem as if they are as temporary and inconsequential as a mirage or mist (James 4:14).

I realize there are good people with honorable intentions who disagree, hopefully in agreeable ways, on these issues and interpretations, and like Dallas, I think it is important to hold some of these ideas with open and humble hands. Even still, it is important to examine some valid reinterpretations of at least a few of our most commonly used scriptures on the topic and theology of heaven.[6]

The Biblical Case Against the Cosmic Car Wash

Listen, I tell you a mystery. We will not all die, but we will all be changed, in a moment, in the twinkling of an eye, at the last trumpet. For the trumpet will sound, and the dead will be raised imperishable, and we will be changed. For this perishable body must put on imperishability, and this mortal body must put on immortality.

(1 COR. 15:51–53)

Paul's statement in 1 Corinthians 15 regarding being "changed, in a moment, in the twinkling of an eye" is the text most commonly used to support the idea of instantaneous character transformation at death. A careful reading of the text above, however, reveals that Paul does not specifically describe the kind of change he is anticipating, nor what means are used to enact this change, nor what others who have died prior to the "last trumpet" are now experiencing or will experience in the future. Neither does Paul describe when this change will come nor what conditions will exist prior to this last trumpet signal. There is much Paul leaves unanswered about this sort of change.

What we can be assured of from this passage is that we will experience significant and meaningful change. But precisely how or when this transformation will occur or become complete are topics Paul leaves largely undefined.

A second passage often cited to suggest instant character transformation at death is found in Revelation 21:1–6 (ESV):

> *Then I saw a new heaven and a new earth, for the first heaven and the first earth had passed away, and the sea was no more. And I saw the holy city, new Jerusalem, coming down out of heaven from God, prepared as a bride adorned for her husband. And I heard a loud voice from the throne saying, "Behold, the dwelling place of God is with man. He will dwell with them, and they will be his people, and God himself will be with them as their God. He will wipe away every tear from their eyes, and death shall be no more, neither shall there be mourning, nor crying, nor pain anymore, for the former things have passed away." And he who was seated on the throne said, "Behold, I am making all things new." Also he said, "Write this down, for these words are trustworthy and true." And he said to me, "It is done! I am the Alpha and the Omega, the beginning and the end. To the thirsty I will give from the spring of the water of life without payment. . . ."*

As wonderful as this picture is to ponder, and as marvelous as it will be to experience, it seems to be describing what will happen once the events described in Revelation 20–22 come to pass. These verses are regularly quoted at funerals, and rightly so. Yet this passage appears to be referring to the end of "this age" when a new creation—a new heaven and a new earth—is revealed.[7] These ending chapters of Revelation are something of a mirror image of events described in Ezekiel 37–48. There is a pattern to both that follows the resurrection of God's people (Rev. 20:4a; Ezek. 37:1–14), the establishment of a new reigning Kingdom (Rev. 20:4b–6; Ezek. 37:15–28), an ultimate and conclusive struggle (Rev. 20:7–10; Ezek. 38–39), and the finale of a new way of life in a renewed social order overseen and directed by God (Rev. 21:1–22:5; Ezek. 40–48).[8]

Although these passages are often referenced in most of the sermons preached on the subject of heaven, I suggest the time frame referred to in these scriptures most likely describes our final condition. This final state of human existence begins with a "new" or renewed, redeemed heaven and earth. N. T. Wright describes this period as the life we have following our life after death.[9] By this he means there is a form of immortality for humans that lies between physical death and the final heavenly existence we receive after the final resurrection.[10]

To be clear, Dallas believed in, and Wright has provided detailed exegetical scholarship for a biblical understanding of, an in-between time. This is defined loosely as the time beginning just after our physical death on earth and until a point in time still in the future described by Revelation 20–22 and Ezekiel 37–48, known as *the* final resurrection or *the* end of the age when all things are redeemed or recreated. This in-between or intermediate heavenly state—again, a period that starts after the death of our earthly bodies and lasts until the final resurrection, which will also mark the beginning of existence in our new or renewed heavenly bodies—is one where humans continue to exist, live, move, and have being. It is a condition that has drawn some important and significant debates over the centuries.

There are some specific hints we can draw from the scriptures that give us important information about what our existence is like between the death of our bodies and our ultimate bodily resurrection and the renewal of all creation. Similar to Wright and C. S. Lewis, Dallas also believed and taught that immediately after physical death, faithful believers will enter into a state called "paradise," which is identical to the intermediate state, or "in-between" time and place where we are absent from our physical body but present "with the Lord" (2 Cor. 5:8).[11] Jesus seems to say as much in Luke 23:43, where he tells the thief on the cross next to him that they will "be" together, that very day, "in paradise." It seems clear Jesus is indicating that both he and the thief will endure their physical death and that their existence will continue without their physical bodies.[12]

For those who have previously died, this intermediate condition is not the final condition. We will be given new, incorruptible bodies (2 Cor. 5; 1 Cor. 15) at what the Bible calls "the resurrection of the dead," or the time of Christ's return (perhaps these are simultaneous events), or—whenever God decides to make that occur. The timing is not as critical as the event itself. Dallas believed that disciples of Christ can be confident that we will receive a new heavenly body and that our ability to engage with God's creation, which includes the physical and material parts of our world, will be reinstated at the resurrection. At such a time, we will be fully integrated once again—body, mind, spirit, and soul—just as we were intended to live with God at the beginning of creation. Until then, those who have placed their full confidence in Christ are not with their physical bodies; therefore, they are "with the Lord," clothed or robed in his glory, living an eternal type and quality of life, in time, watching at least some, if not all, events as they unfold in history, fully conscious and aware of who and what they are, and who and what they are not.[13]

Lazarus and the Rich Man

Perhaps the most crucial and insightful description of the intermediate state is Jesus's parable of Lazarus and the rich man
(Luke 16:19–31), in which a rich man and a beggar named Lazarus both die. While Lazarus is carried away by angels to be with
Abraham, the rich man is sent instead to hades, where he experiences torment.

The parable carries several important messages, but perhaps
the bigger point that too often goes unexamined is that the parable suggests that wrong attitudes and actions toward others, if
left unexamined and unrepented, continue to have negative effects after death.[14] It is perhaps the single most compelling biblical argument for the continuity of both human existence and
personal character formation extending beyond bodily death
and into eternal life.

Part of the parable's power is in the reversal of fortune that
comes to both the main characters. All of the privileges afforded
the rich man while alive are lost to him in his eternal state. Yet
Lazarus, who was poor in life and lay covered in sores at the rich
man's gate, has every need provided for him in his life after his
death. A clear aspect of the intent of the parable is Jesus's warning that devotion to wealth can bind the heart from compassion
and generosity, and that wealth in life is not a determiner for
wealth or prosperity in the life to come.[15] The dialogue is painful
and tragic, with the outcome seemingly permanent.

The point for us to consider is whether or not the story is
only a parable or if it is also a description of realistic events.
Dallas believed it was both a parable and a realistic example in
large measure because he felt Jesus would not use such a detailed
comparison with such consequential effects on his listeners'
understandings about the afterlife without the story being as

equally accurate as it was parabolic or comparative. It also seems surprising that Jesus would use the settings of heaven and hell simply to illustrate a truth about wealth alone. It seems more likely that Jesus is offering a lesson about both wealth and how our actions and attitudes in the present affect our eternal lives.

There are many ironies or reversals of fortune in this parable. The first twist is that only Lazarus is named, and therefore "known," or personified to Jesus's listeners. In ancient cultures, a name often signified an important aspect of a person's character, behavior, or destiny. In this case, the name *Lazarus* means "God helps" and may have also indicated poverty.[16] The rich man, on the other hand, is left unknown in the parable, and perhaps his destiny is left intentionally unclear or unknown as well. Jesus's choice of names already draws a sharp contrast.

The parable proceeds to describe the results of the life choices of the rich man and how the decisions and values behind his choices formed him and his character while alive and appear to carry forward into his intermediate or eternal state. In contrast, Lazarus enters "Abraham's bosom," sometimes thought of as a gathering place for the patriarchs or faithful followers of God who are the children of God experiencing blessing and fellowship with one another and God after death.[17] The rich man enters hades, or the Old Testament's place of the dead. It is questionable whether Jesus used the Greek word *hades,* but in keeping with the term "Abraham's bosom," he might have likely used the Hebrew term *sheol,* which is often translated into the English words *hades* or *hell.*[18] *Sheol* is the shadow world, the gathering place of the dead. Although part of *sheol* is described as a place to be avoided, even this shadowy side of *sheol* is painted less dramatically than the fiery dungeon of torture common to later descriptions of hell, which emerged not from the Bible but from parts of Dante's *Inferno* and tend to fill our contemporary imaginations with devils sporting horns and pitchforks. It may be surprising to realize that the Hebrew scriptures' concept of *sheol* has both the righteous and unrighteous existing in some proximity, separated only by a partition or chasm of sorts.

In keeping with Luke 13:28, the righteous and the unrighteous in *sheol* are conscious, carry memories from life on earth, have the potential to be in some form of contact, are aware of each other and events on earth, and are alert to their current condition.[19] The rich man knows Abraham as his "father," (Luke 16:24, 27, 30) and likewise Abraham calls the rich man his "son," (Luke 16:25, NKJV) or "descendant child." Further, Lazarus and the rich man maintain their knowledge of each other, indicating memories carried into the eternal state from their previous lives on earth.[20]

Interestingly, the rich man never asks why he is suffering, nor does he argue such a condition is unwarranted or unjust.[21] He is realizing that his religious heritage as son of Abraham, an Israelite, by itself has no salvific power. Yet he remembers and remains stubbornly connected to that previous religious worldview. The rich man also remembers Lazarus, although, despite seeing Lazarus in his new, elevated position over him, the rich man habitually reacts to Lazarus as a lower-class citizen, seeking his service even after death. Hence, the parable describes how the rich man's character, his worldview, and his biases continue after death and affect his experience of eternity. This is precisely the paradigm described by Lewis in *The Great Divorce*.[22]

Key to highlight is that the rich man's wealth itself is not the crucial or pivotal factor. Rather, in this case, his wealth is a sign of his self-indulgence, which, unlike his material prosperity, is carried into eternity. It is not his possessions but his heart that damns him, both during his time on earth and into the next life. While on earth, his self-indulgence caused others anguish. In eternity, this is reversed, and he alone is suffering the pain and grief of his overwhelming and enduring egotism. What was lacking in the rich man's character on earth—generosity, compassion, mercy, goodwill, and humility—is equally lacking in his experience of eternity. He is both reaping what he sowed and suffering the lack of what he did not sow (Luke 16:20–24).

In contrast, Lazarus's suffering has ended, and he is now being "comforted" (Luke 16:25), which has an interesting meaning in the original Greek language. The word is *parakaleitai,* which many may recognize as similar to *parakletos,* the term used for the Comforter or Holy Spirit, carries the concepts of encouragement, advocacy, and peace.[23] Perhaps Jesus is suggesting that Lazarus is experiencing the kind of robust existence that originates directly from life that proceeds from the Spirit of God.

The story ends with Abraham declaring his impotence to build a bridge between the two abodes of *sheol*. The "great chasm" (Luke 16:26) separates both these individuals as equally as it separates their worldviews and existential experiences. In the unfettered light of eternity, the life and ways of the righteous and the ways of the unrighteous do not, cannot, interact. This chasm suggests an irreversible decisiveness that comes as a result of physical death. The way of God, clearly depicted in Micah 6:8–10, has been shown to all humanity. We have been shown, and God can be counted on to show us through Christ, what is good and what God requires.[24] Therefore, to ignore or reject these ways, these rescue attempts, is to forge a manner of being in which one's life course eventually becomes established. One's ideas, decisions, wills, and desires work together, over time, to cast a once pliable, formable, molten soul into a calcification of one's personhood or character. Those whose hearts are fixed toward the knowledge of God and his righteousness will receive and enjoy the peace righteousness affords. Those fixed toward unrighteousness, too, will receive their hearts' desires, and the dissonance will linger in their spirits forever, for they know and desire nothing else.[25]

It would do us good to consider the overwhelming angst that surely accompanies eternal regret. Can we imagine the possibility of never being able to find peace simply because we must forever face our choice to turn a blind eye to the necessity, truth, and power of love, mercy, and justice, thus lamenting their absence forever? The rich man's awareness is as keen as his regret, which fuels an unquenchable flame of despair.[26] The eyes of God search the whole earth for those who desire these qualities (2 Chron. 16:9). Yet if love, mercy, and justice are not desired, God allows these choices as well, along with the grief that is sure to follow, now and into eternity.

In expected fashion, the rich man has formed a character that necessitates engaging in a futile argument with Abraham. Such is the action of a heart hardened and a mind dulled to the truth. The rich man is continuing in the stubborn ways that brought him to the place he is in. He is caught in a cycle of ever-debilitating egotism. Just when he seems ready to break out—thinking of others, asking for warning—he rejects the truth that would save his brothers and himself. He continues to reject, even now. He knows no other manner of being.[27]

We can return to Matheson's novel *What Dreams May Come* to further illustrate this point. To recap, Matheson's novel is what I consider to be a modern-day adaptation of Dante Alighieri's poem *Inferno*. Of course, there are several key differences, but what these two works share is an investigation into what the nature of human character might be like in a place, like hell, without all of the peace, comforts, and buffers of life on earth, which are so often taken for granted and therefore left unappreciated until these common goods or prevenient "graces" are gone.

Matheson creates an opportunity for the reader to imagine what human existence would be like if these "graces" were removed and if we were left only with what we are, what we have packed into ourselves or into our souls.

As the two main characters, Chris and Albert, descend through the different levels or regions of hell, they enter a place that begins to wreak havoc on Chris's mind and spirit that I think may help illustrate more clearly the state where the rich man finds himself in Jesus's parable.

There was an odor in the air; a smell which I can only describe as one of corruption. . . . All I could hear was the scuffing of our shoes on the gray, flinty soil. Off to our right, I saw some people moving aimlessly, others standing motionless, all dressed in shabby clothes. Who were they? I wondered. What had they done—or failed to do—that they should be there? We walked within a few yards of a group of them; several men and women. Even though Albert had said he didn't think that Ann was there, I found myself looking closely at the women. None of the people glanced at us as we passed. "Can't they see us?" I asked. "We're of no interest to them," Albert said. "They're absorbed by their own concerns." I saw some people sitting on boulders and it gave me an odd sensation to realize that those boulders were created by their minds. They sat, heads bowed, hands hanging loosely, staring at the ground, immobile in their desolation. I know that, unless they were deaf, they heard us walking by but none gave any sign of noticing our presence. . . . "They all look so grim," I said. "They are," he replied. "Grim in their preoccupation with themselves." "Were they—are they—all so bad?" I asked. He hesitated before answering my question. Finally, he said, "Try to un-

derstand, Chris, when I tell you that this is nothing com-
pared to what lies ahead. The people you see here may not
be guilty of sins which were, in any way, horrendous. Even
a minor transgression takes on darker aspects when one is
surrounded by those who have committed similar trans-
gressions. Each person multiplies and amplifies the failures
of the others. Misery loves company, is what they say on
earth. It should be: Misery, in company, grows ever worse.
There's no balance here, you see. Everything is negative and
this reverse animation feeds upon itself, creating more and
more disorder. This is a level of extremes—and extremes of
even a lesser nature can create a painful habitat. . . . There
can be no rapport between the people because they're all
alike in essence and can find no companionship, only mir-
ror images of their own shortcomings."[28]

Matheson's fictional account attempts to illustrate what,
in the end, lies at the heart of the rich man's complaint. He is
caught in an unending cycle of blame. Ultimately, he holds God
responsible, not himself. Such a twisted lie stems from the essence of all evil, a wickedness that first blossomed at the base
of the tree of the knowledge of good and evil. The serpent's lie
has remained the same: God isn't good and can't be trusted; you
need more. This is perhaps the greatest evidence of the serpent's
influence or control of the place where the rich man has chosen
to abide. Not even a sign of Lazarus's resurrection will cure such
blindness. It certainly didn't for those who lived in the time of
Jesus.

As is so often the case in his parables, Jesus presents the lis-
tener with a comparative choice. In light of God and his love,
provision, and blessing, are we generous, giving, merciful,
compassionate, and thankful? Or do we live lives that are self-

absorbed, self-seeking, self-sustaining, and self-centered? The answer reveals whether one will be comfortably aligned with or stubbornly opposed to the values and ethos of the Kingdom of God, a reality Jesus suggests exists now and will continue for all eternity, as will those who proliferate or oppose it. To not love and care for others is to not love and care for God, since God's very essence is one of lavish love poured out on others.

> *Those who say, "I love God," and hate their brothers or sisters, are liars; for those who do not love a brother or sister whom they have seen, cannot love God whom they have not seen. The commandment we have from him is this, those who love God must love their brothers and sisters also.*
>
> (1 JOHN 4:20–21)

Who We Are Becoming

The primary point for us to remember here is the idea that what we get out of our lives, and what God gets out of our lives, are the people we become. This is so crucial because if the people we are, the characters we forge, and the lives we lead on earth have little to no significance on our eternal existence, then it stands to reason there is little actual, substantive meaning assigned to our lives until we die. If this is the case, it would also stand to reason that what we encounter, experience, endure, or even decide with regards to eternity becomes suspect as well. The central question then becomes, How could we live our lives best without assigning any eternal meaning and consequence to our earthly lives? If we look at the status of a growing number of people, cultures, and nations around us, this appears to be exactly the driving force behind an ever-increasing state of delusion, demise, and destruction, both personally and collectively. The Bernie Madoff scandal, and so many others like it, before and since, demonstrate how crucial it is for us to place our minds not on earthly things but on things above—those realities, truths, and necessities that are revealed as essential to life and living that come from God alone—and which give meaning to our lives both now and into the future.

The Bible speaks of now and forever as a continuation of a single existence. Consequently, much of the transcendent purpose God has for human life can only be properly discerned in light of eternity. Unfortunately, for an ever-increasing number of us who suffer through the pain and disillusionment of dysfunctional relationships in our families and marriages, of political or social injustice, of physical and emotional abuse, and of mental or psychological disorientation, our lives simply do not, and will not, make sense without eternity as a backdrop on which God can manifest his endless love, redemptive power, and enabling grace. Such a perspective alone has the potential to revolutionize the universe. Without it, the delusion of nihilism can appear a welcome relief.

As he was dying, Dallas realized how even he had been trapped by the traditions and intellectual habits of Christian life and belief, which often erects hurdles to eternal living and tends to encourage maintaining the status quo. Dallas came to better understand that despite even good intentions, the power in our religious traditions can blind us from the truth.

The rest of this book will explore what Dallas expected would likely be the course of human existence in heaven. It is important to note that he did not hold dogmatically to some of these ideas; in fact, at times he held them rather lightly. He didn't want to press some points too far and create controversy or incite another battle in religious circles over interpretations. Instead, Dallas looked at the nature of what was happening around him and at what he believed the scriptures were describing. From that, he inferred or interpreted what he believed was a reasonable, historically valid, scripturally consistent, and experientially sustained understanding of the afterlife. That is what we will attempt to do in this book as well.

For those looking for a reason to hope, who are excited to pursue what may be around the corner, over the distant horizon, or through the wardrobe—if you are looking for a grand vision of the type and quality of life that lies far beyond the reach of the current imaginings of human potential now defined and limited by our cultural contexts, if you are looking for a purpose that is worthy of devoting your life to, if you are wondering about the enduring reality of heavenly existence and its eternal call, this book is for you. Together we will engage what Dallas taught me about what the scriptures teach, hint at, reflect, echo, and foreshadow regarding what is required and what is possible for a life that is unlimited in both quality and quantity. Again, I hope to discuss and challenge you to consider why God chose to create humanity, what purpose God has for us, who we are now, what life with God in eternity may be like, and therefore, what challenges and opportunities such a reality might present to us. We will also consider what changes may be required in the essential nature of our characters in order for life with God in eternity to be not only endurable but also beneficial and joyous.

For some, these ideas will come easily. For others, like me, a paradigm shift may need to occur in order for the weight of these concepts to take full effect. Luckily, our Good Shepherd is patient, loving, and kind. He is willing to go at the speed that is best for us. Take your time. There is no rush. There is nothing to fear. Dallas certainly took his time packing these invaluable ideas and truths into his own heart and mind. Likewise, I pray God sows seeds of eternity in your hearts and minds, as he has mine: seeds that bear the fruits of holiness and love in your life, now and forever more. It is to these ideas and their glorious potential that we now proceed.

Two

A Good Death?

A few weeks before Dallas's last visit to the hospital, I discussed with Jane the possibility of staying overnight a couple of times a week, partly to help give Jane a break and to help with whatever was needed around the house, but also to save time on the long commute and take advantage of whatever energy Dallas found to continue our work. Several days later, Jane and Dallas determined his condition had gotten to the point where they could benefit from some assistance and asked if I was still willing to help. During the drive toward the Willard home that Sunday morning in early May, I sensed I would soon face the loss of my mentor and friend. In some ways, the 70-minute drive allowed me to put on a "game face" in preparation for the difficulty that lay ahead. I didn't know what was coming, but I also had a unique and enlivening sense that the Spirit of God was moving and an important blessing was looming as well.

It was a bright and crisp traffic-less morning as I drove west on the 210 freeway. It wasn't long before I passed the off-ramp sign to the little town of Sierra Madre. I pass this exit fairly routinely, but on this morning, heading to be with Dallas and Jane, my mind drifted back several years, to a moment at the very beginning of the two-week doctoral seminar Dallas taught for Fuller Theological Seminary.

Every other year, Dallas's doctoral seminar convened at Mater Dolorosa Passionist Retreat Center, a converted monastery tucked up on a hillside overlooking the mountains surrounding the Pasadena area. Even now, I can visualize Dallas welcoming his students and cheerfully walking them through some opening formalities. It was a cool, early summer morning, and a refreshing breeze carried the melodies of songbirds through the open window. I was sitting in the back row of a classroom full of eager students with high expectations. Dallas was already well known to the group. He was a prolific Christian author on subjects ranging from spiritual disciplines, prayer, church leadership, apologetics, and discipleship, to the nature of the gospel and the purposes of the church, just to mention a few. His most well-received work, *The Divine Conspiracy,* was *Christianity Today*'s Book of the Year in 1999. He was also an internationally renowned speaker and intellectual, in both Christian and secular academic circles.

Even though he recoiled at the comparisons, some have likened the profundity of his thought to that of Martin Luther, John Wesley, or C. S. Lewis. Although many in the classroom knew of his reputation in Christian circles, probably few sitting at the tables before him that morning understood how deeply respected and well-published Dallas was as a philosopher and academic. It could be argued that the span of his philosophical works is even more prolific and impressive than his Christian writings. We were all greatly anticipating what wisdom he had to share.

Before going through each detail on the course syllabus, Dallas opened our time together with a specific prayer. Not a fan of new technology, he took out a well-used piece of transparency paper and laid the following words on an overhead projector.

Then he closed his eyes, bowed his head, raised both arms with palms pointed forward and spoke these words over his students.

> *I pray that you would have a rich life of joy and power, abundant in supernatural results, with a constant, clear vision of never-ending life in God's world before you, and the everlasting significance of your work day by day. A radiant life and a radiant death.*

I can still recall how I felt the very moment these words first settled on my heart and mind. Dallas's strong baritone carried through the room, and a hush fell over the group. His voice was naturally subdued and gentle, but he also kept a great rhetorical strength in reserve for moments like these.

I sensed from the opening prayer alone that we were just beginning to understand what lay in store for us in the coming weeks. Dallas's manner, his way of being, his peacefulness and gracious confidence were as rare as they were intoxicating, so much so that few people can pinpoint exactly what was so compelling about such a seemingly average, unassuming, and shy man. He certainly wasn't the slick, image-managing, author/speaker/celebrity that has come to typify so many Christian preachers, teachers, and authors today. Instead, his undeniable magnetism came from his relationship with Jesus, which slowly broke the spells of skepticism, egotism, and insecurity toward an obsession with success that so many of us struggle to conquer in our own secret ways. This opening prayer began to reveal the essence of the man who stood before us, and we were beginning to realize that he also possessed what each of us longs for in the depths of our souls. Dallas knew how to live life to the full, to live from eternal, heavenly resources, and he was extraordinarily gifted in his abilities to share what he knew with others.

Then Dallas spoke those last three words, "a radiant death." A radiant what? "Radiant" and "death" went together like a speed bump and the Indy 500 speedway. I was almost offended, as though I had found a wayward hair in an otherwise wonderful bowl of soup. I simply didn't understand how these two concepts belonged in the same sentence. A radiant death? I opened my eyes to sneak a peek at the projector screen just to see if Dallas had misspoken or if there was a typo somewhere on the overhead. Nope. He had read it accurately. A radiant death. What in the world was that?

A Radiant Life and a Radiant Death

For most of my life I've been insatiably curious about deep and difficult philosophical and theological questions, such as: Who is God? What is the meaning of life? Where is heaven? How does eternity work? What happens when we die? Wrestling with these questions has not always been an easy path to walk, especially in a society that has progressively treated these subjects, particularly the subject of death, as something altogether foreign, unwelcome, impractical, and therefore, avoidable.

My particular fascination with death and immortality began when I was very young. One of my earliest memories is of my first funeral. I was three or four years old when my mother and I traveled to rural Kentucky one summer to attend the funeral of one of my grandmother's eleven siblings. The combination of the humid heat and the mandate to be still and quiet made it difficult for my parents and grandparents to keep me from being a disruption in the small country church—that is, until I caught a glimpse of my great uncle's corpse. From then on, all I had were questions. And every answer led to another question.

Why is he sleeping? Why is he in that box? How do you know he is happy? He doesn't look very happy. Why are the flowers all around him? Why is he in the long black car? Why is she crying? Why is he being put into that hole? Where did he go? Will he ever wake up? How will he get out of that hole when he wakes up? Where is heaven? Even though I was to receive many answers to these childhood questions that day, and countless more in subsequent years, too many of the answers I've received have left me with still more questions. At times, I've come away wondering whether I could or would ever satisfy the deep longings these questions first stirred in me.

There have been seasons of my life, some longer than others, when I've backed away from the potential consequences of the answers I've discovered. At times, finding out how wrong I've been has seemed simply too troubling or painful to face. Yet by God's patient grace, at least thus far in the journey, I have been enabled to continue my attempts to apply what I'm learning, though often in fits and starts, and as Paul suggests, "with fear and trembling" (Phil. 2:12). Still, nothing I had encountered previously prepared me for what I experienced with Dallas in his final few months. Perhaps the greatest of these catalytic shifts centered on the concept of a good death.

Before hearing Dallas's opening prayer in that class, I remember being first introduced to the concept of a good death when my wife and I attended the motion-picture adaptation of the book *Legends of the Fall*.[1] In depicting the heroic tale of the main character, Tristan Ludlow (played by Brad Pitt), the director artfully and ironically unveils his take on the legacy of rugged American individualism, all seen through the eyes of a narrator, an aging Cheyenne warrior and lifelong friend of Ludlow's named One Stab. In the final scene, with only a hunting knife and his honor as a defense, Tristan's indomitable fearlessness is memorialized as he embraces death in a blow-for-blow struggle with a mammoth grizzly bear high in the seclusion of the Canadian Rocky Mountains. As the movie fades to black, we hear One Stab's final words of tribute to his friend: "It was a good death."

The audience is left with the idea that only something more wild and untamable than Tristan himself could ever have brought about his demise. Mere mortals could never overwhelm Tristan's unconquerable will. For a Native American such as One Stab, the good in such a death is found in courageously facing what would cause any other man to shrivel and hide. As the echo of those words hung in the theater and the credits began to roll, I remember chuckling at the thought. The concept of a good death was far too romantic and antiquated a notion for me to embrace. Such an idea, I reasoned, was an artifact left over from an ancient warrior culture and, therefore, didn't have much to offer my contemporary life. Still, I remember being jealous of the idea and allured by the possibility.

Over the years that followed, I tried to make some sense of a good, or as Dallas called it, "radiant" death as I watched my grandmother, the one I described in the previous chapter, suffer and die. Yet sitting at her bedside during her last few weeks, watching her slow and painful demise, I couldn't imagine a good and radiant death being anything but an over-romanticized version of something that in "real life" should be avoided at all costs.

Most of us won't die in hand-to-hand combat with the fiercest creatures in the wild. Today I have a better chance of getting hit by lightning or winning the lottery. In our modernized society, the top ten leading causes of death are heart disease, cancer, respiratory diseases (mostly related to smoking), strokes, unintentional accidents (falls, highway fatalities, etc.), Alzheimer's, diabetes, kidney disease, the flu or pneumonia, and suicide. At first glance, none of these means of death seem romantic or lend themselves to the notion of a good death. Some of them even carry a significant degree of self-infliction. We rarely think of the way most of us actually die as carrying the potential power, dramatic effect, or honor depicted in the deaths of, say, Socrates or Jesus. To the degree we think about death at all, a quiet pain-less death is the best we can imagine and hope for, to fall asleep one night and wake up in eternity. Thus, death is perhaps the most universally experienced and least-prepared-for event in all of human existence.

The accounts of valiant deaths on battlefields or those suffered by first responders certainly qualify as heroic deaths, as inspiring and humbling displays of momentous sacrifice and courage. But do we even have a category today that would allow us to label such deaths as "good"? Do we tell the grieving families at funerals that their spouse or parent died a good death? Many in our culture today simply do not have the imagination to conjoin these words or the ideas attached to them.

Fear of Death

Our culture is, and therefore, perhaps we as individuals as well are, becoming increasingly fragmented, individualized, and nar-cissistic, to the point where it is now considered wholly accept-able for people to advocate for a life lived utterly for one's self. The media is full of such stories. And our social institutions, including the church, are slowly acquiescing to the incoming tide of the not-so-silent majority and its "will." Life, liberty, and happiness are now assumed by increasing numbers of Americans to refer only to *my* life, *my* liberty, and *my* happiness. We can certainly choose to live only for ourselves, but for many, the consequence of such a choice is to die alone with only one's trophies, whether real or imagined, from which to seek some measure of comfort or assurance.

To experience significance and meaning in the circumstances of our death, our lives must be devoted to more than our own self-interested desires. Yet like a sand castle facing the ocean tide, a life governed solely by the pursuit of self-satisfaction crumbles when faced with the inescapable reckoning that accompanies even the prospect of one's death. The now common usage of the term *bucket list*, a list of things that a person wants to do before dying, testifies to the proper reflection that comes to bear on one's life when facing death. Did I live a good life? Did I make a difference? Did I make good choices? Did I love others and did others love me? What do I regret? Am I afraid and what am I afraid of? Did I know what was important? Did I do the right thing? How will I be remembered? These are the questions that few of us have the courage to face before we are left with nothing else to face. When the distractions of life become exposed as the petty dalliances they are, only then do we take the time to get our affairs in order.

It is perhaps more critical now than ever to realize how inseparable the answers to these deathbed questions are from the requirements of living a radiant life. Stories such as *Tuesdays with Morrie*, Plato's account of Socrates's death, and even the New Testament description of Jesus's execution demonstrate that our lives largely determine the nature and quality of our deaths. Certainly, some die suddenly and tragically. But thankfully, these events are rare. Because of radical advancements in medical treatments, most of us face the prospect of having fairly clear foreknowledge of the slope of our decline. This is a recent development in human history but one we must come to better terms with.

Prior to sitting with Dallas over the last few months of his life, I certainly had not appreciated how delicately and deliberately my life and death are interconnected. I assumed a good death was something reserved for firemen, soldiers, or Hollywood myths. What I came to realize, and what has been life changing for me, was that dying heroes already exist all around us. We simply have to redefine our understanding of heroics in order to develop eyes to see and ears to hear their stories, the blessings of which are incalculable.

As a culture, we will continue to miss the invaluable gifts and insights of a good death unless and until we reconsider what it means to live a good life. Otherwise, we will continue to forget not only who our heroes are and the radiant lives they lived, we will also lose touch with the virtues from which our heroes drew meaning for their lives. For me, this is perhaps one of the most significant lessons I learned from witnessing the values and virtues Dallas displayed on the journey toward his own death.

In our culture, the subject of death is almost universally avoided, even in our churches. If, however, we desire to shift our focus away from the foolish assumption that we can live forever, we must be first willing to contemplate the reality of our own death. This need not be a morose or macabre event, nor should it consume our thoughts. But to ignore death completely is to deny its inevitability, which also causes us to miss clarifying the greater purposes for which we live and to which we give our lives.

Most of us avoid death "like the plague," as we say. We are afraid to die. These fears can be broken down into a few primary areas of concern. Perhaps the most common fear is that of suffering a long and painful death. A second fear rests in the potentiality of nonexistence. This kind of fear is not limited to atheistic or nonreligious persons. Even the deeply religious often doubt the accuracy of their professed beliefs about the afterlife.

And the possibility of nonexistence after death causes doubt to surface regarding whether our lives carry any meaning at all, especially if and when one is struggling through a difficult and trying illness.

There are other fears associated with death such as worry over the fate of loved ones who have died previously or even fear of eternal punishment. Yet perhaps the most common fear of death is associated with the idea that there is little if any knowledge we can gain about the afterlife. This not knowing, this feeling of being kept in the dark and unable to control the future of one's life and existence increases our anxiety. Most people perceive death to be the ultimate of unknowable realms and perhaps a subject that might better be left exclusively to speculative fiction. This is also why the bestseller lists often contain books on heaven.

Even so, there is rarely any intentional or significant thought given to the prospect. Instead, we seek to look healthy and happy, and we fight aging with creams, hair dyes, surgeries, exercises, diets, supplements, pills, and all manner of concoctions, in great measure because youthful appearance gives the impression to ourselves and others that we remain far removed from the death knell of old age. Oddly, this attempt to hide from the reality of death doesn't stop at death itself. I never cease to be surprised at the lengths we are willing to go to avoid the realities of death, part of which we witness in the ways we manage or orchestrate our funerals and memorial services. For example, many contemporary funerals include a period of visitation or an open casket where family and friends can view their loved one. Yet at the behest of our cultural sensibilities, morticians hide or "reconstruct" the deceased with makeup and colored lighting in an attempt to create the illusion of lifelikeness.

Our bodies deserve our respect both before and after death. Yet the growing need to protect the modern mind and emotions from the reality and inevitability of death isn't limited to colored lights and makeup. We also tend to place the bodies of the deceased in padded, satin-lined coffins that often appear more comfortable and ornate than any bed frequented while we are alive. This coincides with and supports, perhaps subconsciously, the popular notion that the departed is only asleep. Funeral ceremonies have also been altered. Now it seems to be increasingly more common that when mourners gather at the graveside, the casket is allowed to remain above ground until all have left the area. Perhaps the willingness to witness the finality of the casket being lowered into the ground and covered with the earth has faded, or is fading, away from accepted cultural norms.

Each of these practices may reveal a deeper truth regarding the way we approach and understand the realities of death and dying. We simply don't want to look death in the face, and our society has created acceptable norms that allow us to fool ourselves as to the stark eventuality of our own demise and of those around us. Death has an excellent track record. There is no avoiding it, no matter how hard we try.

Likewise, when sickness and frailty hit our bodies, many choose to be fueled by extraordinary hopes of survivor stories and the optimism of theirs being the one case to beat the odds, if all available means are sought and applied. Such a response to a terminal illness can work out well. Medical research routinely works beneficial and even wondrous effects. Yet it is also true that many terminal illnesses defy treatment and even in the cases of extraordinary survivors, too seldom is the patient's quality of life considered when costly, experimental, or painful treatment plans are sought. In some important ways, death remains imminent. Yet the expense of attempting to avoid death at all costs has become a volatile topic in light of the escalating price of health care, which is a large part of the explosiveness surrounding our national debate on the subject. In 2009 CBS News reported that Medicare paid approximately $50 billion in medical costs during the last two months of patients' lives, which at the time was more than was budgeted for the entire U.S. Department of Education. They further suggested that 20 to 30 percent of these expenditures may have had no meaningful impact.[2] Humanity is scared to death of dying.

Just the End of the Beginning

As I drove past the monastery on my way to the Willard home, I realized more than three years had passed since Dallas prayed that thought-provoking prayer, and it had taken the events of his illness to make me realize I was likely to become an eyewitness to what a good and radiant death looked like. In fact, our last few months together provided me with some of the most powerful, and hopefully, enduring lessons of my life. What Dallas had prayed over his students, over me, was soon to become a reality in his own life, and I too would soon begin understanding and appreciating the necessity of healing the intellectual and emotional schism that separated my idea of a good and radiant life from a good and radiant death.

When I arrived at the Willard home, I learned Dallas was sleeping, and Jane took me aside to discuss his deteriorating condition. Knowing my grandmother had also died of pancreatic cancer and that I had been with my grandmother during her illness, Jane asked if there was anything I could tell them about how the cancer had progressed in my grandmother's situation and the potential challenges that may lie ahead for them. I tried to be gentle and careful in choosing my words, but the medical facts are both troubling and unavoidable. We discussed Dallas's lack of energy and appetite. We talked through the possibility of intravenous nutrition to perhaps infuse strength and energy, and both Jane and Dallas decided to pursue it. Dallas was intent on finishing his writing projects, and he hoped to find a way to remain alert enough to steward his calling until the very end.

When Dallas woke from his nap, he welcomed me as usual, giving me a hug and a smile. He was tired but very alert. Despite his illness, there was never a time when Dallas couldn't summon a thoughtful response or offer his wisdom. His intense focus on matters important to him was readily available. He motioned for me to come closer, and I knelt beside his blue recliner. He thanked me for being willing to stay close at hand. "I really need you," he said with a smile as quiet tears filled his eyes. It was an admission powerful in its humility. He knew he needed help, and he was unashamed to ask for it.

At once, my appreciation for the man grew ever wider and deeper. How much of my life, how much of our world, would be infinitely better if we could allow ourselves the simple mercy of admitting our need for help, especially when we are at our most vulnerable? "I really need you, too," I wanted to say. But I couldn't. The words, and perhaps the humility, were caught deep in my throat, my pride keeping them at bay. Dallas saw my emotions rising at my awkward failure to summon a response to his honesty. He gently patted my hand again and said, "Don't fret. It's all right. This is just the end of the beginning for me."

What a poignant realization to come to at the end of life. How does one attain such a perspective? How do we die well? What is required to face death? What is a good death? What I learned from Dallas is that a good death is directly attributable to a well-lived life. Dallas devoted his life to developing his knowledge of God and growing in his faith and reliance on God's grace. He spoke often of John 17:3, which makes abundantly clear what eternal life is all about. "We Christians talk about eternal life all the time," he would say. "Without a doubt, the Church is in the salvation business. The problem we have is agreeing on what salvation amounts to. That's where we run into trouble." He would then remind his listeners how Jesus plainly explains that eternal life comes from knowing God and his Son, Jesus. Then he would give his stock definition of knowledge: the ability to represent things as they are on an appropriate basis of both thought and experience. That was what Dallas spent his life devoted to: seeking the knowledge of God, reveling in the blessings that knowledge provides, and as a result, helping others to more accurately represent God, as God is, on an appropriate basis through their thoughts, actions, and experience. That's a life devoted to the good. That is a life devoted to loving others and oneself as Christ loved us. And that life also led to a good death.

Death is part of life. We say this often and it is true. Yet few of us truly understand the potent realities and essential qualities intrinsically tied to this statement. The process of dying, and the reality of death itself, presents a crucial opportunity to reveal the nature of how we have lived our lives, what we have discovered, what we have come to know and experience in our lives, and finally, what has become the sum total of our existence thus far.

Extraordinary times shape heroes and heroines. Greatness often emerges from the shadows only when it is desperately needed, much like our fictional superheroes who appear just in time to save the day and then slip back into anonymity. We rightly celebrate greatness born of tragedy, war, and disaster. But we must also come to recognize our own death as a moment ripe for greatness of character and integrity to shine as well. A good death is the ornate capstone that reveals the grandeur inherent in a good life. They go together, for they are inseparable.

The process of death presents an opportunity for a heroic culmination of the wonder and potency of the gift that our lives have been up to the present moment. Viewed this way, death becomes a curtain call, a celebration, a joyful look at what has come from the investment of the time and gifts given us. We can then present our lives as a bountiful harvest to our loved ones, to the world, and to God. In this vein, death's sorrow, grief, and pain are overcome by the valor, beauty, and poignant grandeur discovered at the very pinnacle of a life well lived. The pinnacle, the summit of a life well lived is not at midlife. For one conscious of the purposefulness in every day, every moment of our lives, the idea of being over the hill and on the downhill of life after the age of fifty is ludicrous. The pinnacle is not reached, the finish line not crossed, at midlife, but at the end of life. Such a perspective can only become a reality for us if or when we begin to realize death as just the end of the beginning that leads to eternity, not as an end in itself.

The Hallway

One of the most important lessons I learned about a good death was witnessing how easy it became for Dallas to distinguish between what both Jesus and Paul liked to describe as the mind of the flesh and that of the Spirit, between the Kingdom of God and the kingdoms of our world, some of which are religious kingdoms. The discipleship Dallas had chosen in life had already begun to prepare him for his life reigning with God as a citizen of the heavens (Phil. 3:20). At no time was this more evident than when I was sitting beside Dallas's hospital bed the night before he passed into eternity. He was resting intermittently, napping about an hour at a time. His continual hiccups and abdominal cramping, which periodically caused him to tense with pain, were constant companions. The medication helped, but the combination made it difficult to find anything but a few moments of respite from his ailments. Although fatigued, he remained mentally alert. It took some time for him to form his ideas and words when asked a question. But once he got his breath, he could convey clear thoughts and answers.

It was about 1:30 A.M. when I noticed his breathing becoming very faint. I checked his pulse, and it was slowing. When I touched his arm to feel his pulse, he turned to me and opened his eyes. At times, when he would look at me, it was as if his eyes weren't able to see what he was looking at. Yet on this occasion I could tell he was able to focus on me directly. He said, "I need to tell you what's happening so you can be prepared." I recorded some of this conversation, but before I could use the digital recorder on my phone, there were some things he said that I wrote down shortly after he went back to sleep. He started by saying he was in a hallway—in between this life and the next. And in this hallway, there were people who love us more than we can imagine. He said that for his entire ministry, he really couldn't quite understand what to believe about the Bible's description of the great "cloud of witnesses" (Heb. 12:1). He tried to understand and believe in this reality; he wanted to believe in it. But he didn't know quite what to make of it. "But now," he said, "now I do . . . I really do believe. I know they are here."

He also said his eyes were being opened and that he was seeing things, understanding what Paul was talking about as his mortal and perishable self was being removed and the immortal and imperishable was being "put on" (1 Cor. 15:53). He realized that he was going through a doorway from this earth to glory and that in the "between" space, in "the hallway" that connects this world to the next, there was much for him to learn that was captivating his mind. It was then I remembered to record his thoughts on my phone, so I could recall his exact words.

"What are you seeing?" I asked.

"It isn't a strain," he responded, and after pausing to cough for a moment, he continued, "It isn't an effort . . . or a strain . . . to believe what Jesus said, 'He that keeps my word will never taste death.'"

"So now?" I asked.

"So now I don't like to part . . . from my work and my loved ones. But I believe that will change . . . when I go through, I won't . . . I won't be thinking about that."

"So you're beginning to believe more strongly now than you did before about, about the great cloud of witnesses that somehow that is even . . . more believable now than it has before?" I asked.

"Well, yes," Dallas responded. "And all the things that . . . Paul has in mind when he says in Colossians 3 that since you've been raised up in Christ, seek those things that are above. The things that are above now have become the reality. And so you see how much there is to that. And . . . so that's what occupies my mind."

"So you're just thinking about what is becoming more and more a reality to you?"

"Well . . . and has been there all along," he said.

"That you're now starting to understand better?" I asked.

"Seeing more clearly," he said and smiled.

"Is God speaking to you through all this?"

"Well, I think so. But . . . not as if this is new. It's just that you have a firmer grasp of it."

"So . . . is it almost like you haven't been surprised, but you've been surprised."

"No. I haven't been surprised, but I've been deeply gratified." He smiled deeply, and I saw a sparkle in his eye, one I'd seen many times before when a student understood something new for the first time. "And I'm amazed that I haven't had this before."

"You're amazed that you haven't had this before?"

"That is just part of being caught up . . . in the systems of the world. Which includes most of our religion."

"So you feel something like scales falling from your eyes? Or . . ."

"I wouldn't . . . that's too strong. It's like when you haven't gone to the . . . optometrist for years. And then you go, and you suddenly realize how bad your vision was before that. That is an experience many people have had."

The pain was becoming stronger, and I turned off the recorder and adjusted his covers. We both sensed he might be nearing the end. He began to give me some instructions. He was putting his final affairs in order. He told me how important our work was and to do my best to finish all the projects we had discussed. I promised him I would. His work was very important to him, and even at the very end, he was mindful to steward his calling responsibly. I asked if he wanted me to call the family back to the hospital to say good-bye. He shook his head no. I asked if he was sure. He said, "Yes. I'm sure. Let them rest." I was torn between obeying his wishes and doing for the family what I knew they would want. In the end, I decided to heed Dallas's instructions as I had been in the habit of doing.

I held his hand, leaned in close, and told him I thought he might be close to leaving, and I asked him if I could tell him good-bye. He smiled and said yes. I told him how much I loved him. I thanked him for giving me the great gift of his love and confidence. I thanked him for helping me to become a better man. I told him he was a hero to me. With that, he shook his head gently from side to side and said predictably, "No, Gary. Jesus is our hero." "That's right," I said. "Jesus is our hero." And I kissed him on the forehead, and he closed his eyes to fall asleep.

At about 3:00 A.M., he woke briefly and asked to be adjusted slightly in the bed to try to find a more comfortable position. He was cold. I covered him with a soft blue blanket from home then held his hand for a while. His breathing was shallow, and his heart rate seemed to be slowing. This went on for about an hour. Then, for some reason, his breathing seemed to be more consistent and his pulse became stronger.

As I sat in the chair next to his bed, I began to journal about this interaction. Thoughts and recollections began tumbling into place like a lost combination to a rusty lock. In the months leading up to that recording, Dallas and I had spent the majority of our time together discussing the primary, overarching or underlying assumption that flows through the majority of his work, which centers on the nature and effects surrounding the transformation of human character into an existence where real life, life from above, eternal life can be experienced. As we go through the rest of this work, we will return to these truths again and again. Dallas's primary motivation in his ministry was to encourage others to invest themselves in developing the kind of knowledge and experience of God that would shape their character in ways that would reliably produce both a good life and a good death, and it is the overarching goal of this book. He sought to help others, and to learn for himself, what becoming like Jesus now and forever would require of us. He routinely asked his students questions like the following: What did Jesus know? How did he become the kind of person who could so easily love, befriend, forgive, bless, heal, teach, correct, and guide people in the ways of God's Kingdom? And then how do we become that kind of person?"

Although he was humble, Dallas knew he had become Christlike, and that he was still growing toward Christlikeness. That's why so many wanted to learn from him. Many, like me, sought

Dallas out in order to discover how we might better follow Jesus. And even in his death, he was teaching me how to trust and lean on the sustaining, fear-eradicating, burden-lifting power of God's love and truth. Dallas also passionately believed this learning and transformational growth into Christlikeness would continue after he died. And he looked forward with great anticipation to this opportunity.

We can and must learn the difference between simply being alive and really living life to the full. Jesus has made this opportunity available now so that we may choose to prepare ourselves if we ever hope to move toward Christlikeness when we enter eternity. A significant objective of the work given to Christian teachers, spokespersons, and leaders is to clarify, and bring to light, the amazing possibilities found in an eternal condition—all possibilities which are available before physical death and become increasingly fulfilled after death.

This is not a new teaching. Jonathan Edwards, an early eighteenth-century Christian Reformed preacher, theologian, and philosopher who was instrumental in what is called the First Great Awakening in the United States, also held to the belief that we will continue to grow, learn, and develop in heaven. Arguably, some of Edwards's best writing covers the subject of heaven. One statement in particular is key to our purposes here. Speaking of those in heaven, Edwards believed this:

> That the glorified spirits shall grow in holiness and happiness in eternity, I argue from this foundation, that their number of ideas shall increase to eternity. How great soever the number of their ideas when they are first glorified, it is but limited; and it is evident the time will come when they shall have lived in glory so long that the parts of duration, each equal to a million million ages, that they

have lived, will be more in number than their ideas were at first. . . . It is undoubted that they never will have forgot what passed in their life upon earth, the sins they have been saved from, their regeneration, the circumstances which did heighten their mercies, their good works, which follow them, their death, etc. They will without doubt retain innumerable multitudes of ideas of what passed in the first seventy years; so also they shall retain to eternity their ideas of what was done in the ages of the world, with relation to the church of God, and God's wondrous providence, with respect to the world of men; and can we then think that a whole million million ages of those great and most glorious things that pass in heaven shall ever be erased out of their minds? . . . Therefore their knowledge will increase to eternity: and if their knowledge, their holiness; for as they increase in the knowledge of God, and of the works of God, the more they will see of his excellency, and the more they see of his excellency, caeteris paribus, the more will they love him, and the more they love God, the more delight and happiness will they have in him.[3]

Building on Edwards's teaching, Dallas demonstrated a measured eagerness to learn more about both what was happening and what was going to happen in him as he walked through the hallway between this life and eternity. He knew eternal life provides us with new vistas, new insights, new heights of love to discover, new depths of faith to explore, and new relational intimacies to experience. Yet along with these opportunities, there are also choices to face, corrections to be made, characters to develop, vacancies to fill, lies to correct, capabilities to enhance, and potential to realize. In short, there is work to be done in heaven—good work, eternal work, work hopefully begun on earth and completed in heaven. For God will be faithful to complete in us what he started (Phil. 1:6). Even still, something we know intrinsically is that very little of what God started is actually finished in us on earth. Even in the midst of the sadness of leaving his loved ones and his work, Dallas was looking forward to all of the potentialities that lay ahead.

Three

Why We Exist

At Dallas's memorial service held at USC, I had the privilege of talking with a student who took his introductory class in philosophy. She remembered coming up to him after class one day and asking this very question: "Why do we exist?" Now, many years later, with tears in her eyes, she recalled the moment with fond affection.

It sometimes surprises me how few of us openly ask that important question. Most of us spend a relatively small percentage of our lives seeking who it is that God would have us be, what it is God desires for us to accomplish with the gifts of our lives, and why it is we, along with those around us, have been born in this time and place. Working in a university, I find that as students come to the end of their degrees, a good number enter a very important stage of life when they are solemnly seeking to discover some specific path or destiny for their lives. Once a person has traveled a certain distance down the road of life, however, I find we expect him or her to have settled on a distinct path, for better or worse. To question our direction after a certain age is sometimes considered irresponsible or immature.

Yet as Dallas knew, understanding our purpose on earth, in

this life, is central to both our lives now and into eternity. I can guess how he responded to his philosophy student that day, with something he said often: "We are in training for reigning." Our lives now are lived as both an investment in and preparation for our eternal destiny. So many of us don't know why heaven is important because we don't know how and why our yesterdays and todays are so crucial to our tomorrows. We have a mistaken view of heaven as some kind of final retirement center, a celestial Fort Lauderdale or Sun City, Arizona, for saints. In truth, I believe heaven will be much closer to what we see in Genesis 1 and 2 and Revelation 21 and 22. That is why our todays (and our yesterdays) are so important.

In large measure, our earthly lives are intended to prepare us for eternity. That was Dallas's understanding of the call of God on each person's life, and their potential, first given in the Genesis charter to rule, subdue, or establish "dominion" over the earth. It is also what he believed Revelation 5:9–10 describes as a prophetic reality.[1] Over the years, many have misused this statement to justify imposing a form of Christendom, paternalism, or worse in their attempts to assert some form of authority and power over the world for their own purposes, all in the name of God. That wasn't what Dallas had in mind nor what he believed Jesus demonstrated and taught his disciples.

Instead, Dallas suggested that the goal for us as followers of Jesus is to develop a character so Christlike that God could and would willingly empower us to do what we want to do, because we have become the kinds of people trustworthy to seek and do good. Like Abraham we are blessed to be a blessing. When this occurs, we will reign, with God, and for God, all to his glory and for his sake. That was what Dallas believed Jesus's vision of the Kingdom produced. And the whole earth will be blessed as a result. The first time I heard this message it was revolutionary to my ears. I knew, if Dallas were right, everything would change for me. And it has.[2]

After graduating from college and marrying my wife, I spent nearly twenty years in a professional career in the banking and investment sectors that provided wonderful experiences, the ability to work and learn from expert leaders who possess both integrity and ingenuity, and the opportunity to serve both clients and employees by helping them achieve some valuable and meaningful goals. I will forever cherish those years and the relationships I developed. What I did not investigate during those years, however, was whether my career choices aligned with what I longed to experience deep within the crevasses of my heart. I was too busy, too successful, too enamored, too invested, and too consumed to stop, listen, feel, think, dream, and wonder about what my life and work consisted of and where my choices were taking me.

It wasn't until I failed to achieve the next rung on the ladder of success that I ran into a wall of futility. My response to what should have been a relatively minor career setback, or postponement, revealed to me that my devotion was not to my career as much as it was to the perks attained from my career. The power, financial rewards, and prestige had grown much more attractive to me than the work itself. Thus, when I faced a setback in achieving a personal goal, the job no longer filled my ego's needs, and I was left feeling unsatisfied.

Was it job satisfaction that I lacked? Not really. That was only a symptom. The disease was dissatisfaction with my life, despite my outward "success." Existential discontent is rarely confined to nice, neat compartments. My career was not isolated from the rest of my life. My marriage suffered, along with my parenting, as well as many of my friendships and professional relationships. Even my favorite pastimes no longer offered me the enjoyment they once did. At the time, I was genuinely at a loss for why I could not find authentic peace and sustained gratification from any one area of my life. The desert of despair was costly and trying, but the dawn that followed my dark night of the soul offered warming, directing light. It wasn't until I had stewed long and hard in a period of despair that I began to realize I did not know, nor had I ever seriously contemplated, the answer to the question this chapter asks: Why do we exist? I began to learn the deceptively simple lesson of how hard it is to find the right answers until we are able to risk asking the appropriate questions.

For some, the question of why we exist may seem so plebeian as to be ridiculous. Not for me. Dallas spent a good deal of time talking with his students over the years about this very subject, mainly because it is one of the primary philosophical questions. For others, the question appears so large it can be assumed too monumental to answer. Dallas didn't think so, and neither did many of his favorite philosophers. Dallas's thoughts on the matter came not only from the annals of philosophy but also from the pages of scripture, a fact he didn't consider contradictory at all. This is where theism and theology begin. In fact, a holistic understanding of heaven and the afterlife first requires an understanding of God's intentions for human beings. Human life has a purpose, as do the accounts of God's actions in human history.

It seems that my sense of purpose for my life is most severely challenged when I'm attempting to endure the consequences of suffering. Although there are good reasons to doubt—and Dallas allowed himself and encouraged his students to challenge entrenched ideas and beliefs—I was able to witness how the suffering he endured never overwhelmed his overarching sense of purpose and peace.

On the evening before Dallas entered the hospital for the last time, we chatted for a while about *The Divine Conspiracy Con-*

tinued. But eventually our conversation moved again toward the subject of heaven. Although I can't be sure, I believe Dallas was sensing that his increasing weakness was not likely to abate. We talked about eternity, parenting, fear, the meaning and purpose of our lives, joy, and thankfulness. It may seem as if that's a full slate of topics. And it was. At one point, when discussing the prospect of being apart from Jane, his voice caught, his eyes began to water, and he took a moment, looking down as a wave of sorrow swept over him. But after just a few moments, he took a deep breath and whispered just these words, "When peace like a river . . . attendeth my way." And that was all. He was reciting to himself a favorite hymn, "It Is Well with My Soul," that he had sung a thousand times. And like an old friend, or a warm blanket, he was calling it forward in a time of great need to shield him against the storm billowing in his heart.

Our Purpose and Worth

Quite frankly, there are many instances and circumstances in my life, sometimes too many to count, when "it," whatever "it" may be in the moment, is most definitely *not* well with my soul, nor any other aspect of my life. I often have trouble making sense of the seemingly senseless acts of violence, pain, injustice, and abuse I see around me. There are moments when the level and degree of "un-right-ness," ill will, and tragedy are so sweeping they can top the level of what is endurable. It's then I have to shut down for a while, back away from the news, social media, e-mail, texts, and phone calls because one more bit of bad news feels as if it just might drown my last seed of hope. It's then I tend to feel it almost necessary to be decidedly *unwell* at the soul level of my being in order to avoid being considered callused or obtuse. Sometimes

I can convince myself that frustration, anger, or even fury are necessary emotions required of any sane and healthy person in response to some of the awful circumstances of contemporary life. In such instances, I can become convinced that my "righteous indignation" is not only warranted but also good. What I've come to understand is that such feelings often reveal that I am searching for a sense of meaning and purpose to these events, and at some level, I'm experiencing a bit of my own existential crisis—all of which flies directly in the face of the settled position that declares, "Whatever my lot, thou hast taught me to say, it is well with my soul." Something important is still missing in my soul.

Perhaps that is why I was so moved by Dallas's response to his fatal diagnosis. Despite the many unknowns he faced for himself and his family, his deep convictions about the meaning of human life and the meaning of his own life remained stalwart and unmoved. Facing the uncertain challenges of a terminal illness can cause any of us to waver in our faith or resolve of God's goodness and faithfulness and the overarching purpose behind our lives. Yet Dallas's understanding of who he was and his experience of God's overriding provision in his life, along with maintaining a vision of the all-encompassing purpose for his life, enabled him to stare his destiny square in the eye and sing about the reservoir of peace that flowed like a river over his heart and mind. "It is well, it is well with my soul." Purpose brings peace.

Dallas knew (and lived in the knowledge of) why he existed on this earth and what destiny awaited him. He firmly believed in a purposeful human existence, and he greatly benefited from the reality of his knowledge and experience of the plan God had for his life and for all of creation. A large part of Dallas's peace came from the settled understanding about the quality of life in God's Kingdom that is available now and continues into eternity.

We need a purpose for which to live, and we are meant to

experience purposefulness. But it is also important to note that even some of the writers of the scriptures seem somewhat at a loss regarding the question of purpose. Not every writer engages this question, of course, but some openly express their wonder at God's purposes for human life. For instance, the writer of Psalm 8 asks, "What are human beings that you are mindful of them?" (8:4). That's an honest question of immeasurable importance to both our everyday lives and our eternal destinies. In considering all the good and wondrous works of God's hand, and in light of the excellence of creation, the psalmist wonders, What good is humanity? We need to devote some serious thought to that question in our world today, not only in light of God's creation, but also in light of the stunning level of evil that human beings too often engage in and perpetrate.[3]

One way of capturing the unique purposefulness inherent to human existence is seen in the value we place on each human life. In the Western world, and increasingly around the globe, there is an enduring belief in the value and protection of human life. Human beings are almost universally protected due to an intrinsic awareness of our value. There are certainly some important and contentious battles over what constitutes life, who "deserves" to live, and so on. But once the definition of life is determined, there is general agreement in nearly every Western culture that each human life is to be preserved and appreciated. Undoubtedly, much is to be discussed about how this can be done better, and not just in reference to life but also to the quality of life, especially for those who remain neglected and marginalized in our societies. Still, one of the ways our appreciation of life is demonstrated is in the number of rescue attempts we witness through the news media. Enormous amounts of money, time, and effort go into rescuing those caught in harm's way. These rescues run the gamut of United Nations relief efforts for victims caught in war-torn countries and natural disasters, to those who willingly or recklessly put themselves in danger by engaging in extreme activities such as climbing Mount Everest or diving off ocean cliffs.

We also see an appreciation for human life demonstrated when emergency workers courageously put their own lives at risk to save people who are otherwise strangers to them. Our societies applaud and support risking lives to save lives precisely because we place a high value on human existence. But we seldom ask why this is so. Why are *you* valuable? Why are *you* someone who ought to exist, and therefore, why is it right and good that others should protect and appreciate your existence?

One of the first lectures I heard Dallas give long, long ago targeted the huge question of why human life is valuable in the first place. He started by finding value in the opening story of the scriptures. If we go back to the creation accounts, we can see a series of things God creates that he then declares as good. The first and second chapters of Genesis list a series of good creations, and a careful study of them will give us a fairly detailed structure for understanding why life, especially human life, is *very* good.

The creation story suggests that one of the common attributes each of these creations share is *being*. Being is good. Being is better than nonbeing; existence is better than nonexistence. One of the most depressing thoughts one can have is nothingness. Trying to even imagine nothingness is very difficult; it takes a tremendous amount of training and effort to even get oneself to engage the ideas required for considering the essence of nothingness. The suggestion that it would have been better for there to be nothing rather than for something—anything—to exist at all is evidence of a lack of real consideration of the consequences of nothingness. More often than not, such a fixation on nothingness results from the mind stuck on some very bad thing or event that is driving thoughts in the direction of considering the benefits of nihilism (nothingness). Yet if we were to weigh it all out, including all the evil, pain, and suffering of life, compared with and contrasted against the joy, glory, and meaning that is to be found in existence, all in all, what *is*, even in its dilapidated condition, is still very, very good, especially when we otherwise face the concepts of nonexistence or utter vacuousness and desolation. There remains *a lot* of good in the world.

After creating things that exist, including living things, God spoke, saying, "Let us make man in our own image, according to our likeness" (Gen. 1:26). Thus, humanity is "like" God in the degree to which God's likeness was bestowed upon humanity. While I was attending a weekend seminar with Dallas, I can remember him stopping in the middle of his talk and saying, as if it had just occurred to him, that even though it may seem odd, counterintuitive, or even heretical to some, the scriptures seem to teach here that humanity is intended to be, in some unique and important ways, godlike. He argued that this fact was not often fully appreciated by some more conservative Christians but that it was also taken to extremes by some more liberal-minded Christians attempting to apply a more secular humanist approach to their faith. But it is important to realize that God's likeness is tied to humanity's purpose. Human beings are created "like" God precisely to be and do godlike things. Genesis 1:28 reveals God's instructions to humanity: to be fruitful, to multiply and fill the earth, to subdue the earth, and to have dominion over every living thing on the earth. This is the charge that is still in development today. The assignment is ongoing and heavily laden with purpose, whether one believes in God or not.

If we consider human history from its most rudimentary to its most complex forms, we can see God's creation project being played out on many levels. Despite the fact that much of modern culture has long forgotten about God, and despite periodic and even disastrous setbacks, God's purposes still plug away, progressing in fits and starts, often marvelously and miraculously. Even still, human beings have been designed to be justly fitted to what God has commissioned for the human race to accomplish. God's bestowing of dominion over the earth to humanity was also an act of good. God declared this charge to steward the earth toward its highest and best use as a demonstration of his goodness as well (Gen. 1:31). Therefore, the first factor to consider regarding why humanity is valuable and worthy of preservation is due to the fact that, above all, human existence is very, very, good and has a wholesome purpose.

Today, many of the people who desperately love and protect the things that live in our jungles, grow in our forests, swim in our oceans, or fly in our skies have significant and lingering doubts about the goodness of human beings. Underlying many debates about our environment is the question of whether humans were a beneficial addition to the earth. A friend of mine recently told me of a bumper sticker that read, "Save the World—Raise a Dog Not a Child." This worldview has become a challenge. Are human beings worth the value we have placed on them? Are we overpriced? Was the creation of the animals a better idea than the creation of human beings? Are we really more trouble than we are worth? I think not.

Who We Are Is Found in Who We Were

Human beings were created differently from the rest of God's created works; the most significant difference is the opportunity we have to engage in a unique form of relationship with God. This is the first factor we should consider regarding what is unique and invaluable about human existence. Human beings can know God as no other created being can. Through that divine relationship, human beings reflect and reproduce God's glory in becoming capable—empowered—to do the unique and exclusive work that was assigned or commissioned to the human race. Dallas was fond of saying that God does not stand over our shoulders, then or now, like a cosmic cop waiting for some violation to occur in order to slap our wrists. Instead, we are intended to work with and through a power that is not our own, to accomplish God's tasks for both ourselves and those around us—our neighbors. Primarily, this power-dependent relationship exists due to the immensity of the tasks required to fulfill the vocation of tending to the earth, with all its features, complexities, lifeforms, and necessary relationships.

I recognize that discussing matters as big as reigning over the entire cosmos will push some readers past the point of believing there is anything practical at all in such a set of ideas. This is because so many of us, including me, have a hard enough time governing or managing (having dominion over) our own little gardens, our homes, or even just our work spaces and checkbooks. There are so many moving, ever-changing, and complex features in our contemporary world, with so much to know and learn, it seems impossible for us to even consider exerting dominion over something as large and awe-inspiring as the earth, much less the cosmos. Yet I am arguing this is precisely what the scriptures describe as not only our purpose but also our destiny, and therefore, our future. Again, as Dallas would say, "We are in training for reigning."

Reigning is exactly what occurred for perhaps a very short time when humanity was in perfect submission, union, and communion with God. In the idyllic depiction of a garden, human existence experienced and lived both in and from the source of power that sprang from God alone. The conditions that originally sourced earthly human life are precisely the conditions that now comprise the nature of eternal life. It is, was, and will always be from the sustaining and empowering spirit or essence (in Hebrew, *ruach,* which can be translated "spirit," "wind," or "breath") of God that we human beings receive our power for life and living.

The power or spirit of God is the essence or nature that provides the source of energy, the spark, if you will, that animates human life.[4] The human existence is both spiritual and physical. In virtue of the unique spiritual and physical functionality of human existence, we alone are created with the capacity to participate with God in his governing stewardship of the earth. Dogs can't steward the world. Thus, understanding the spiritual nature of our makeup, and the power available for such a task as magnanimous as stewarding God's creation, is perhaps the first step toward regaining the dignity of God's purposes for humanity.[5]

Will-Fullness

The second step toward better understanding God's plan and purpose for human life involves the human will. Volition, or will, is a divine trait given by God as a gift of human existence. This is another unique feature of human nature that makes us so incalculably valuable. Dallas taught that animals do not have a will. Instead, they live by highly developed and keen instincts. Human beings are the only life-form that demonstrates an independent personhood or will. It is also the very nature of an empowered and independent will that allows human beings to rebel against the giver of their life. Thus, being willful agents carries the dual potential for great good and great evil. Each person can accept and then follow God's good ways or selfishly pursue the illusion and snare of independence. Both choices are available to us. Thus, the potential for greatness or disaster is also unique to humanity. The human race can reach great heights of splendor. We also have moments of individual and collective collapse, resulting in debilitating abasement. We have Mozart and Handel, and we also have Mussolini and Hitler, the Renaissance and the Inquisition, Mother Teresa and terrorists. But the potential on each side of this broad spectrum is unique to the human condition alone. Such depth and breadth of good and evil come from a powerful infusion of will. These are divine gifts, aspects, and features of human existence—gifts of being created in the image, or likeness of God and with the potency of his Spirit.

A shocking fact of human existence is that each individual is the only one who is empowered to willfully choose what to give his or her life to in trade for something else. Each of us has sole command over our destiny. And we take command of our lives every moment of every day with our choices. We might consider Jesus's question in Matthew chapter 16 regarding what our souls are worth. What would you be willing to trade the entirety of your life for? It's a powerful exercise to consider what we routinely give and receive in trade for our lives and souls.

There are plenty of examples we could look at in contemporary life that demonstrate this ageless willingness to trade our lives for something shiny and enticing only to discover we have been baited into a trap of pain and despair. The Bernie Madoff scandal is just one of the latest examples, but unfortunately not the last. Madoff was considered a gregarious, charismatic, elder statesman who walked tall among the power-brokering elite of Wall Street and Washington, DC. He collected all the biggest and newest toys—the penthouse, yacht, and private jet. Perhaps his most valuable asset was his reputation as "the one with the golden touch," the "wonder-worker," the "wise sage."[6] He appears to have been beloved by family, friends, employees, and peers alike. Yet his life was enveloped within an enormous fraud.[7]

In my previous career, I didn't have the occasion to meet Bernie Madoff, but unfortunately, I knew others like him. The financial world is full of many very good, honorable, and dedicated people who work with integrity, who sacrifice personal gain, and who are devoted to achieving, proliferating, and protecting professional excellence. Yet they are not alone. There is a somewhat commonly heard phrase that floats around the after-hours haunts where young, hungry, and morally ambiguous white-collar professionals go to tell their tales of success. If you stay long enough in one of these locales, you'll hear something related to the motto, "You just have to fake it till you make it." It's an old phrase I heard passed down to me very early in my career. It became more famous when a ruthlessly manipulative stock trader played by Ben Affleck in the movie *Boiler Room* delivered it to a room of new recruits.

Fake what? Fake your success. Fake your expertise. Fake your knowledge. Hide your lack of experience. Buy designer clothes, wear expensive jewelry, lease lavish cars, rent extravagant homes—all of which will construct the illusion to others that you have "made it" already. For no one wants to hand over their fortune to an unproven rookie, struggling to pay the rent and manage their student loans. Therefore, if you fake the fruits of achievement, people will assume you have attained the knowledge and experience that precedes success and become more likely to put their confidence (faith) in your "abilities." In other words, it's perfectly okay to live a lie—just don't "tell" a lie. The governmental bodies that police our industries have oversight over the words we speak, and the contracts we make, but not the heart. Only God has the power to regulate and oversee that domain, if we let him.

At some point, Bernie Madoff, and others who worked with him,[8] decided to attempt faking it, to live inside a lie, like so many of us have done. He made a choice to believe that creating a fiction would lead to a better life than living in the honest reality of his true life. He made a single choice that led to many other choices, a trade that led to many other trades. He offered up his life in exchange for the illegitimacy of worldly gain in the hopes the swap would all work out in the end for the good. That's the lie that precedes all the other lies. It never works out for the good. All that glitters certainly isn't genuine gold.

This is the well-worn path that led Madoff, some of his family members, and many others like him toward the cliff of destruction and despair—a path that begins by ignoring who we are created to be and the purposes God intended his creation to inhabit. When we trust our lives to God's direction, we find the essence and substance of the lives we truly yearn for. When we try to make a life on our own, to create an illusion that becomes a reality, our very attempts will, sometimes slowly, but most assuredly, destroy us. The pride of self-idolatry begets ruthless tyrants. Love of God begets divinely empowered servants. The trade is ours to make.

Sacrificial Love

This brings us to the third factor we should consider regarding what is unique and invaluable about human existence. As humans, we have an inexhaustible capacity to give our lives faithfully to God and to the good, even to the point of death. Jesus stated it plainly when he said, "Greater love hath no man than this, that a man lay down his life for his friends" (John 15:13, KJV). The greatness of the human being is manifested through reflecting the identical characteristics God revealed in the life of his Son. Jesus demonstrated God's love and devotion to us in that while we were lost and alone, alienated from God, Christ was willing to devote his life to the point of death for us (Col. 1:23; Rom. 5:8). Therefore, human life is valuable, in part because of our potential to reflect the image of God's spiritual, powerful, and volitional character, and because of the greatness of those who are willing to give themselves up to God, for God, and for the good that God has made. This interplay between bearing the divine image (*imago dei*) and the ability to participate in the divine plan of God (*missio dei*), clarifies part of God's vision for creating humanity and why we as a human race treasure characteristics such as self-sacrifice, faithfulness, loyalty, and heroism.

One of my first encounters with the virtues of self-sacrifice, loyalty, and heroism came one summer as a young boy while visiting my maternal grandparents. While bored one stifling hot Missouri afternoon with nothing to do, I discovered my grandfather's old army footlocker. Inside I found a treasure chest of relics from World War II. There was a red Nazi swastika armband, an old pewter whiskey flask, some tarnished medals, a large black leather picture album full of black-and-white snapshots, and a smattering of opened envelopes with rainbow-colored postal markings indicating they'd traveled halfway around the world. At the bottom of the locker was my grandfather's dark brown service cap. I pulled it out, unfolded it, and tried it on my head. Under the hat was a small black pistol no bigger than the palm of my hand. My heart raced. Just as I reached down to touch it, I was pulled up to my feet by the back of my hair with a not-so-gentle tug. My scream alerted my grandmother who rushed to the bedroom.

"What happened?" she asked.

"The boy's got his nose where it doesn't belong," my grandfather proclaimed.

Looking down at the open locker my grandmother took pity on me.

"Well, let him loose and sit down in the kitchen and go through it together."

With a grunt of protest my grandfather picked up the trunk, and we all moved to the kitchen. It seemed as if he hadn't looked at the contents in a while. I asked question after question about each item. What proceeded was the longest and most intimate and memorable conversation I ever had with my grandfather. Everything was progressing nicely until we turned a page in the photo album, and a picture of four long-lost friends caught his eye. He gasped and put his hand to his unshaven face, covering his mouth, trying to hide the emotions that were starting to overwhelm him. His eyes filled with tears. I was so young I didn't know what was happening. I'd never seen him cry. I looked at my grandmother next to the stove, and she walked over, put her hand on his shoulder, and said, "It's all right. It's all right." I think she was trying to comfort us both. It took a long time before he could talk again.

"Pops, did you know those soldiers?"

"Yes, I did. We were great pals."

"Did they die?"

"Yep. Each of them died very close together too. It was pretty hard on me to lose them all at once like that. Those were the heroes. Yes, sir. They all died trying to save the other, trying to protect each other. Those were the heroes."

It was that conversation with my grandfather that first planted the seed in my heart and mind that would eventually develop into the realization that one of the illimitable glories of the human condition is discovered in the potential we have to give our lives, even to the point of death, in complete devotion to the highest good. There is something awe-inspiring and precious about these qualities when demonstrated within the bonds of human relationships. We laud, mythologize, sing songs, write stories, and build monuments to great sacrificial deeds, and these memorials are but a taste of the realities that can envelop us in our eternal relationship with God. There is no greater or higher good than that found within the glorification of Christ's ultimate benevolence of willingly giving his life for humanity, for love. God's "goodwill to all mankind" (adapted from Luke 2:14, KJV) demonstrates his value of human existence and its unparalleled beauty, meaning, and significance.

Therefore, just as we have an increasingly difficult time conceiving of what God is like, so too, we have a difficult time imagining what we are actually like. We don't know who we are, and we can't and won't come to this understanding even at the most basic level until we know who God is. When the psalmist questions why God is mindful of us, he expresses the mystery and wonder that God, in fact, is very mindful of us. There is a realization in that question that God is so completely devoted to human beings that we must be far greater than we appear at first glance.

In our culture, we encounter those who, we think, maintain too high an opinion of themselves. Perhaps, in fact, some of our problems stem from the truth that we do not think highly enough of ourselves. Ironically, such undervaluing is often the source of the problems related to our arrogance and insecurity. Maybe one of the bits of "fallen wisdom" that has come down to us through the ages is that we do people a favor by keeping them humble through acts of humiliating condemnation. We can be sure that no one ever becomes humble by being demeaned any more than people become more loving by being hated or kinder by experiencing increasing levels of cruelty. Virtue is simply not developed that way. Thus, we fall into a whole nest of problems in how we understand ourselves as spiritually empowered, volitional persons.

Jesus's challenge is to consider that we would never earn a good return on our investment if we traded our souls, our lives, for the whole world (Matt. 16:26). This is a great insight into how valuable our lives truly are.

Again, the scriptures describe that the primary purpose for human life is that each of us can know and experience the unique and creative Spirit and power that pulsate within the life of God by willfully choosing to disciple ourselves to Christ. Jesus said every child and every human destiny is so valuable that to harm a little one is worthy of death (Luke 17:2; Matt. 18:6; Mark 9:43). The reality is that human life intrinsically maintains great value because of the immeasurable worth of the God-given potential in every human life.

Humanity experiences great transitions on a belt of time and space wherein we go through life with one another, engaging opportunity after opportunity to become everything God intended us to be in relationship with him and others. We have the call on us to create something of such immense wonder involving the power and glory of God that the angels are befuddled at its grandeur (1 Pet. 1:10). God will make this come to pass. If we miss our chance, we miss our chance, but God cannot be defeated in his objective goal. He is going to create a community of loving, creative, intelligent, faithful, powerful human beings who will steward the earth on his behalf and through his empowerment. The question is not if; it's who. That's what this life, human life, and experience seek to unveil in purpose and by design. All of human history, including your history and mine, is moving toward the collection and development of an all-inclusive circle of relational harmony where all created beings, including humans, engage with and enjoy God's infinite realm and existence, such that the gates of hell don't stand a chance.

This community is called the Church. Dallas separated the capital C Church from the small c church. The Church is led, built, and stewarded by Jesus alone. It has a quality, vision, and mission that is more robust, grand, and potent than what many of us have yet to fully experience in the local small c church organizations, attempting to do business under the same name, within our communities.[9] The Church consists of heroic, loving, devoted, intelligent, faith-filled people, even unto death if necessary, wherever they are located, who are learning how to live and manage increasing degrees of God's grace and power while placing more and more confidence in their experiences of Jesus's will and way. The result is a mutually beneficial and reciprocal relationship that reflects the Trinity.

It is in this place, the Church, where we come to know and do what God has intended. This is our work, and our vocation, which represents yet another precious aspect of human life. Striving, planning, working toward, and manifesting abundant displays of courage, creativity, faithfulness, devotion, covenant loyalty, love, and joy are all precious expressions of human existence. Only human beings can demonstrate the bounds of these aspects of life, and when we do, we reflect the goodness and greatness of God from whom these qualities are unceasingly generated.

This is the vision cast by the Westminster Shorter Catechism, which describes the chief aim of humanity as glorifying God and enjoying him forever. We have the opportunity to reflect upon, point to, demonstrate, and advocate for God's amazing beneficence and brilliant design for life in all its forms. Human beings carry the potential to bring together every aspect of the created world in a fulfilling harmony. God will make this come to pass, and as he does so, his majesty shines ever brighter throughout eternity.

One Brick at a Time

In answering the question of why we exist, we have seen where purpose and worth are found in human life, and how this purpose is specifically tied to the image of God, embedded in human existence, that is manifested in our power to act, in our will, and in our sacrificial love. Now we turn to the how. How are God's overarching objectives intertwined with human life and action in such a way that we can discover our own unique callings within his Kingdom. In simpler terms, What is God up to?

Many people have had the experience of watching a building being built over a period of time. There was a period of time in my life when I commuted every day past a construction site of what became a high-rise office building. It began as a nondescript empty plot of land. One day I noticed a sign had been erected with a color sketch of the building that was planned. Over time, I watched each stage of construction, starting with the earth-moving equipment, then the foundation, metal girders that framed each floor, and so on. Eventually, the structure grew and matured until finally a corporation started to move in. Yet there were significant periods of time, almost a year or more, when I would pass by the construction site, and it was difficult if not impossible to distinguish exactly what had changed from day to day. For months on end, when the foundation was being laid and much of the work was being engaged below ground level, or when the wiring, plumbing, and heating were being installed, a lot of activity was hidden from sight. My coworkers and I even wondered if the construction was being delayed for some reason. Yet after about a year, a flurry of activity happened all in short order. The first several floors went up very quickly, which was followed by the glass siding. This process proceeded floor by floor in a relatively short period of time. When these stages were complete, it seemed as if all at once the building was taking shape, when in reality, everything was proceeding as planned. Groundwork had to be laid first, then the structure could proceed in a timely fashion.

God, too, is a builder. He is building his Kingdom, one brick at a time. At times, we hear people talk about God like he is someone up in the sky somewhere doing some impossibly high forms of theoretical math or physics. Ancient concepts of the gods had them sitting on a cloud or mountaintop solving deep logic games, contemplating exalted concepts of truth, or simply manipulating the lives of human beings like pawns in an elaborate game of human chess. Conversely, the Hebrew and New Testament scriptures reveal a God who is amazingly active. He's an *act*or, we might say—one who acts, creates, and moves intelligently to create and proliferate good. In that way, he is very much a go-getter, incredibly high functioning, productive, activating, and industrious.

Jesus appears to act as something of the general contractor in charge of making God's vision come to fruition, while using his Spirit to provide the means of power and implementation (John 14:2–3).[10] Jesus has been given authority over the heavens and the earth. He's been tasked to forge a grand home, an estate if you will, for all of us. God's Kingdom necessitates human beings playing a central role in its design and purpose. In God's ecology, human beings are the living stones that act as the structure, while simultaneously benefiting from the very system we participate in forming (1 Pet. 2:4–6). Only human beings have the means to conjoin both manufacturing and manifesting the glorious purposes of God. We are God's workmanship while also being workers with creative wills of our own, working as friends, with God, now and throughout all eternity. We are being shaped by Christ as living stones on which will be placed the responsibility of stewarding creation. This is the work done below the surface, on the inside, often hidden from view, but which one day will be revealed as the rock-solid foundation on which God will form his eternal Kingdom.

If we step back for a moment and contemplate God's design for eternity, it's quite an amazing concept. Even what little we do know and can grasp about eternity is enough to nourish our soul and enlighten our mind. This is what Paul explains in his remarkable first few chapters of Ephesians.

> *You were dead through the trespasses and sins in which you once lived, following the course of this world, following the ruler of the power of the air, the spirit that is now at work among those who are disobedient. All of us once lived among them in the passions of our flesh, following the desires of flesh and senses, and we were by nature children of wrath, like everyone else. But God, who is rich in mercy, out of the great love with which he loved us even when we were dead through our trespasses, made us alive together with Christ—by grace you have been saved— and raised us up with him and seated us with him in the heavenly places in Christ Jesus, so that in the ages to come he might show the immeasurable riches of his grace in kindness toward us in Christ Jesus. For by grace you have been saved through faith, and this is not your own doing; it is the gift of God—not the result of works, so that no*

one may boast. For we are what he has made us, created in Christ Jesus for good works, which God prepared beforehand to be our way of life.

(Eph. 2:1–10)

These familiar verses are often quoted. The most popular, of course, are those about the acts of grace and faith in reference to salvation. Grace and faith are responses to *how* salvation is obtained; they are the means of our deliverance from "trespasses and sins." But what is often lost in cutting the verse out of its longer context is the *why* question, which is answered both above and below the more familiar passages. God, abundant in mercy and love, choosing to exhibit his love in our lives, picked us up and gave us authority and power to demonstrate, for all time, how amazingly abundant and wondrous God actually is. The Church is Christ's workmanship, his canvas, his artistry that illuminates his unbounded love and power to accomplish total good in all things and in every life that is devoted to his ways. Such a vision is overflowing with purpose.

Furthermore, such a vision for humanity is clearly much more involved than simply the forgiveness of sin. Forgiveness is certainly a great and necessary benefit of life with God. But we were created as God's work of art for a purpose beyond being saved in the way we have come to think about it. The saving itself is directed at something much more than the events contained in the rescue. There is a plan prepared before time, a good plan—that we are to execute—only part of which involves our atonement with God. Once relationship is reestablished, then celebrated, it's time to get on with accomplishing the grand purposes for which the gifts of mercy, love, life, grace, and empowerment God bestowed on us can be achieved and shared through us. Only human beings can accomplish these objectives as this is God's call, or vocation, for humanity alone. Only redeemed human beings have the skill set, the potential, the nature, the capacity, and the will to achieve these results. Thus, the Church is perfectly designed to achieve what it has been tasked to do, in partnership with God.

All for Glory

The opening chapter of the book of Job tells the story of a time when the "sons of God," (NASB) including Satan, came before God, and the Lord said directly to Satan, "Have you considered my servant Job?" (Job 1:8, NASB). I want to suggest that God was proud of Job, justly proud of him, and was bringing attention to Job's righteous life even though Job was not a perfect man. There is nothing in all the cosmos of which God is more proud than human beings redeemed by his grace, devoting their lives through the moments and hours of their days to the collective good of humanity and creation—all to the glory of God. That is our privilege. That is a primary reason why human beings were created: to demonstrate to the universe the richness and amazing power God maintains and wields to bring creative goodness out of all things simply as a result of God's being.

When these traits and qualities are present, God is the first to point them out. That is why we are so valuable. No act of rebellion can ruin the majestic potential inherent to God's redemptive plan. Resistance and revolt only heighten and accentuate God's amazing, unconquerable, unstoppable, unquenchable loving power to achieve the highest good. Whatever evil humanity may have intended, or simply falls prey to, God overcomes, vanquishes, and immerses in a sea of unstoppable goodwill. All we must do is choose to know God, as God is, then join his movement (John 17:3; Rom. 1:21).

Much of that faint glow and majesty, which is distinctly bestowed on humans, still shines through our lives and work today. Though many have no understanding of its origin, nor do they grasp its depth and potential, the respect and dignity remain. One fine day, these remnants and echoes of the glory that Adam and Eve once possessed and enjoyed will be fully redeemed and realized in our lives again. This amazing story of human redemption, and the hope of the renewal and reconciliation of all things, have echoed down through the ages of human history and have been woven into the long fabric of nearly every culture and civilization on the planet. Human beings have always longed for this story of peace, of *shalom,* to be realized. We yearn for that enduring, holistic condition of universal flourishing, to dwell in a state of security, provision, freedom, love, and justice. This is why an insatiable yearning for a heavenly state of bliss has remained a part of nearly every culture throughout human history. It's part of the image of God carried within every human soul.

The scriptures paint heaven as the condition in which God's will is achieved and his goodness and blessings flow like a mighty river. The absence of which intuits a longing emptiness and despair, which for most of us tends to simmer quietly just below the level of our conscious thoughts, while we long for all things to be made right. Heaven is as equally a state as it is a place. We long for paradise because we were made in, and for, an existence that proceeds directly and singularly from the Kingdom of Heaven. That is why so much of human existence begins to make sense only in light of this reality.

What we've covered in this chapter are God's overarching intentions for creation, his will, his plan, or *missio dei.* Another way of describing the mission of God is to say that God is bringing out of human history a personal, relational community of immortal beings that will be his primary dwelling place for all eternity. The reason meaning and purpose are integral to our discussion of eternity is due to the fact that much of our purpose in life, and God's purposes for creation, will only come to fruition in eternity. Without an eternal perspective, much of human existence simply will not make any sense at all.

Dallas used to say that if we were to think of all of history in terms of what we commonly understand as time, human history could be understood as a flash of a light bulb in the last second of the last minute of the last hour. That is how long human history is in terms of cosmic history when imagining it as a twelve-hour clock. It's not going to last long. In fact, it could be considered a genuine miracle that human civilization has lasted this long. It is very likely that cockroaches and dinosaurs will have had a lot longer run on earth than humanity. Human history as we have known it on earth will "soon" be over, and the fulfillment of Christ's eternal reign will move forward. So the ultimate significance of human history must lie outside of the temporal, not within it.

Furthermore, human life and its problems have no human solution primarily because human life is not a human project.[11] At the heart, at the start, at the original source of human existence, we find a divine objective and intent. Humanity itself is God's idea and also God's project. Therefore, to live it best, we must be in line with God's purposes as well.

I suggest we have the same opportunity available to us right now to engage the power and plan that Jesus made available to those he encountered on the hillsides of ancient Israel. His Kingdom, his way, his life of endless possibilities, provides us with wide-open vistas where we can run with freedom and grace. It's at hand this very moment. Glory be to God. We can grab God's vision and purpose for our lives with confidence and not let go. This is why we were created. God has great designs for us (Jer. 29:11). We have a purpose and the power to achieve our potential, both individually and collectively. God is building a community, a Kingdom of people, whom he can trust to run the universe on his behalf. What an enormously endless opportunity, what love, what grace to have such a destiny and birthright!

Yet there are hurdles to overcome, some of which are embedded in our religious systems and their beliefs. There is coming a time, and perhaps we are now in this period, or just entering it, when our churches are going to be faced with some very crucial decisions whereby at least two clear choices or alternatives will come to the fore. Primarily, these decisions will directly involve our wills, what we want or don't want, or what Dallas often termed our "wanter." The Bible often describes the will or "wanter" as the heart. Thus, the questions we must face are matters of the heart: Do we want to live in the reality of the truth, or are our traditions, their myths, and our own lies more comforting? Do we want to be free of our bodily lusts, or do we want our bodies to be the primary, if not solitary, driver of our desires, moral compass, and actions? Do we have a sustaining vision of life free from pride and fear? Is our existence devoted to the goodness and omnipotence of God, or are we consumed by chronic, self-centered egotism? Are we known and loved by others just as we long to know and love others? Do we live in the knowledge of God and apply his wisdom to the circumstances of our lives, and do we experience the power of a redeemed, resurrected Kingdom-driven life?

These are some of the key questions that will help us outline the promises and potential available in what Jesus described as eternal life. This is identical to the abundant life, or life to the full (John 10:10). Such a life has no end or limitation in either longevity or quality (John 3:16). The New Testament describes this life as one generated and sustained from above, from the heavens, which can start now and continue forever (Phil. 3:17–21; John 3:31, 8:23; James 1:17).

Of course, we are well aware that there are many different gospel messages proclaimed in, to, and through our churches. And this has been a source of great confusion and even paralysis in many quarters. However, I wonder if we may now be entering a time when these choices are coming out of the fog, being more easily and clearly discernible, which should be a moment of great joy and celebration. Perhaps we are living in a period when the knowledge of the Lord, and his ways, can be spotlighted in the hearts, minds, and lives of those dedicated to his purposes against the darkening backdrop of our culture. Perhaps the struggles and suffering of our age are reaching the point where all of us are better able to discern the key difference between simply being alive and really living.

What is key for us to wrestle with and resolve for ourselves is whether the destiny of eternal living is something we truly desire. If, for whatever reason, God's plan does not seem a worthy vocation wherein one can submit and commit their life toward seeking, heaven will be a most confusing, even discomforting place. Eternity is the dwelling place of God, where those who have chosen God's ways will work with, in, by, through, for, and because of his perfect plan. His will will be our will—willingly. The grand "gain" of death that Paul describes in Philippians 1:21 comes from the release of the entanglements that so easily ensnare us and inhibit us from running the race God has set before us (Heb. 12:1). As Dallas came to realize more and more as he approached his own death, death frees us from our earthly limitations, the web of lies that misrepresent the truth and the systems of the world that create entanglements, some of which are present in our own religions. These are the bonds of sin, but the effects of sin must be confronted as well.

What is left for us to consider more specifically are the kinds of character traits that will be required for us to live and thrive in a state where the good is unavoidable. How do we become the kinds of people that could endure the visceral nature of heaven? Those who can see and hear the lingering murmurs of authenticity, transparency, love, grace, power, community, effectiveness, joy, prayer, honesty, and meaning as we move through the moments of our lives? How do we become the kinds of people who can both dream of and then inhabit God's unveiled presence for all eternity? How do we retune our ears to the call and power of God's wisdom and truth? How is God going to faithfully complete the good work that he started, both in Genesis and in you (Phil. 1:6)? How is God to redeem your life and your suffering to the point where you are able to look upon the purpose of your life and the substance of all your days and honestly report, "It is well with my soul"?

This is where all of human history is headed. God is making all things new (Rev. 21:5). Are you ready? Do you want your life to reflect such an amazing and unbridled sense of meaning and purpose? Let's see.

Four

The Substance of Spirit

For several years, I lived next door to a wonderful neighbor, husband, father, and friend who also happens to be a self-professed atheist. We became neighbors soon after I had left my corporate position and entered seminary. When I first told him I was a seminary student, I was relieved by his laughing reaction. "This is going to be great! I'm an atheist, and you're a theologian. We're going to have some great conversations!" And we did. He was always thoughtful, generous, very intelligent, and very, very curious about me and about what could possibly possess someone in his forties to leave the security of a corporate career to become a theologian.

I learned a tremendous amount from my neighbor, largely due to his willingness to share his questions and concerns about some of the previously unconsidered assumptions of my Christian faith. Perhaps most clarifying was discovering that our primary differences lay not in our understandings of God but in our fundamental perspectives about the nature of the universe. He is what I would call a naturalist and an empirical rationalist. An empirical rationalist is one devoted to science and reason as the primary authorities for determining what we know, or what can be known at

all, about the realities of our world. A simple definition of naturalism is the philosophical belief that everything arises from natural
and/or physical properties and causes, and therefore, any spiritual
or "super" natural arguments tend to be rejected. Thus, the natural world and its laws are all there is to reality.

The way these philosophies tended to play their way out in
our discussions was fascinating. He would only trust a scientific
or empirical point of evidence to act as a valid means on which
to base his understandings of life, and he routinely argued that
the existence or nonexistence of God is neither quantifiable nor
an empirical fact discernible though scientific means. To his way
of thinking, this justifies atheism as a reasonable, rational response to the question of the divine. I, on the other hand, made
arguments for why I was willing to accept both the empirical,
rational, scientific evidences of our world and also the authority
of—and when appropriate, give precedence to—non-empirical,
supernatural facts and phenomena.

It wouldn't take long, whether we were watching the NCAA
basketball tournament, sledding with our kids during a school
snow day, or having pizza at a birthday party, for our conversation to eventually end up retracing our well-plowed debates over
the virtues and vices of my "faith" versus his "facts." For my
neighbor, and perhaps for many atheists, the spiritual, or nonmaterial realities of life, to which religious thought is often devoted, are simply assumed to be self-constructed—perhaps even
well-intended—myths that humans have used for millennia in
attempts to answer the elusive mysteries of life that remain, as
of yet, beyond the reach of science. For him, faith starts where
facts end, and he believed that if and when scientists accumulate
both the time and money to uncover the evidence required for
debunking these myths, the need for God and religious faith will
eventually be erased. For him, enough evidence was already in.

My neighbor's views tended to mirror larger parts of our contemporary, secular culture. Yet I believe these views and the rationale behind them are worth considering for their impact on Christians as well. Living as we do in a world dominated by physical realities, how can we begin to live the sort of life that will prepare us for the spiritual realities of the Kingdom of God?

The effects of our material-focused world are already present in our Christian spirituality, or lack thereof. Dallas drew a connection between the rise of secularism and the decrease of Christian spirituality to the demise of the authority our society is willing to give religious scholars and experts who make knowledge claims regarding nonmaterial, nonempirical, spiritual realities pertaining to human life and living. Likewise, fewer Christians today display the drive necessary for pursuing the actual body of knowledge that undergirds the Christian religion, and therefore, increasingly fewer are capable of developing a faith in anything that they cannot see, feel, or touch. It is precisely this inability to believe anything that cannot be physically verified that has kept my atheist neighbor and me from resolving our differing worldviews as well.

The main issue of our disagreements centered on the differences between two terms: transcendence and immanence. These are two very interesting and powerful ideas that have far-reaching implications that can be hard for some to grasp. But in concept alone, they are really quite simple. These two Latin-based words carry opposite meanings. Transcendence comes from the Latin root that means "to go beyond." In philosophy and theology, we often use the word to convey the idea of a divine reality or experience found "outside," "above," or perhaps "beyond" the realm of the physical, natural world. This is what most religions rest on: some belief in a reality or power beyond the realms of our physical limitations. In contrast, immanence describes the opposite. The Latin root conveys the concept of "inside" or "within" or perhaps even "indwelling." Many Eastern philosophies elevate the idea that the power or truth about life and living exists and can be found only by searching inside, or within ourselves or our world.

It is easy to see then how a person's view of God, or their philosophy of life, is greatly affected by whether they have a primarily transcendent or immanent worldview. The Christian worldview and the gospel Jesus preached require us to uniquely blend the transcendent with the immanent. Yet one of the primary reasons why we have such a difficult time understanding, then living from the power available in the spiritual reality that is both immanent as well as transcendent, stems from what can be thought of as *material blindness.*

Our contemporary Western culture is addicted to materialism's immanence. The physical world often becomes all that we see because it is all that we have eyes to see since we tend to believe and act as if matter, or the material aspects of our world, is what is most important to us. As long as this is the case, we will miss seeing and experiencing all the other wonderful and transcendent, invisible, nonmaterial, spiritual realities and manifestations intended for human beings to enjoy and thrive within.

Dallas was one of very few philosophers who ventured into the widening gap that had developed between materialism/naturalism and the Christian worldview.[1] One of the sets of ideas that Dallas worked with constantly had to do with the pitfalls of modernity, a creation of post-Enlightenment rationalism, which has increasingly focused on empirical research and the physical sciences as the only valid or authoritative means of attaining knowledge of our world. In recent years, the postmodern worldview has called the modern methodological processes of attaining certainty (the scientific method) into question. And for good reason. Science has added much to our lives. Who doesn't like penicillin, air travel, and refrigerators (not necessarily in that order)? But Dallas saw how modernity has also created some very dangerous problems and dilemmas. The questions asked in the postmodern worldview about the limitations of our reliance solely on science and the empirical method are indeed very relevant to the Christian faith. Dallas also understood and taught me how to better see the assumptions behind the methods the sciences apply. And in some circles, such assumptions continue to perpetuate a very troubling phenomenon.[2] As such, we need to consider the degree to which moving from a dominating physical-world perspective to a spiritual perspective will be a radical change to our sense of being when trying to live an eternal quality of life, both now and after our physical death, in full knowledge of the spiritual realities of the Kingdom of Heaven. It is essential that we come to understand the invisible, nonphysical, spiritual world, the spiritual power, and the spiritual foundations that undergird everything around us. This is crucial in order for us to more fully experience the spiritual life now and to be prepared for the realities of our eternal lives after physical death.

The Power of Spirit

Neither Dallas believed, nor do I believe, that all of eternity will be limited to a spiritual, or nonmaterial, nonphysical existence. Rather, Dallas believed we will be resurrected, at some time in the future, into new bodies, that will, in some measurable fashion, be comprised of a distinctly physical and spiritual dimension of life on a new physical earth. He believed that Jesus's resurrected body modeled this for us. Luke 24:39–43 makes note of how Jesus highlights his fleshly characteristics. He spoke with others in a way that seems to indicate he had a physical voice, walked on the ground, wore clothes, handled food, ate food, was touchable and visible. It also appears that Jesus's resurrected body had all five senses, unless we want to assume he couldn't taste or smell the fish he ate with the disciples. At the same time, Jesus's resurrected body was perhaps also able to teleport, to dematerialize and move from one place to another immediately or suddenly (31, 36), walk through walls or doors (John 20:19), and levitate (Luke 24:51; Acts 1:9).

It is certainly possible that the qualities the risen Christ manifested to the early disciples may not be qualities we as humans will have in the future. But we must not forget Peter's ability to walk on water prior to his or Jesus's resurrection, and Jesus's and the disciples' ability to heal the sick, effectively changing the material conditions of physical bodies. The point is Jesus realized and taught his disciples about the nonphysical, nonmaterial powers that lie at the heart of our world and its physical realities. It was not magic, but the power of the Spirit that Jesus utilized, directed, or redirected when he changed the molecular or atomic structure of water into wine, multiplied the physical matter of bread and fish, changed the weather patterns, and eliminated or reordered the energy inside crashing waves. It is this same understanding of the power of the Spirit that Paul also taps into on several occasions during his ministry.

The crucial insight here is that the invisible, or the spiritual, and not the visible or material, is where the abundance of power lies in the world that God created. Likewise, Dallas argued that Einstein's $E = MC^2$ is literally packed with theological significance. In my book explaining Dallas's theology I explain,

> In what Willard terms the theology of $E = MC^2$, he suggests Einstein's theory not only presents an equation that

explains the amount of mass that is in energy, it also
equates the amount of energy required in order to create
the amount of mass one finds in the universe. Energy is
power, the capacity to make change. Thus, thinking about
God as unembodied personal power (energy), one can see
how Willard understands the nature of the physical world
as one inextricably full of or energized by a non-physical,
spiritual power. In fact, one senses he believes them to
be inexorably linked. Thus, Willard argues it is a simple
matter of logic to require a non-physical cause for the cre-
ation of the physical world. In Willard's view, the physical
universe, and human life, requires an alternative explana-
tion and justification from those currently provided by the
physical sciences. Yet, the most pressing issue for his theol-
ogy lies in the existence, presence, and experiences of non-
material reality.[3]

Perhaps it's now easier to see the benefits of learning how
to live under the power and direction of the Spirit of God, for
as Pierre Teilhard de Chardin wrote in *Phenomenon of Man*,
"We are not human beings having a spiritual experience; we
are spiritual beings having a human experience."[4] The spiritual
undergirds the physical, in every respect, for from the invisible
or spiritual, everything in the visible or material world attains
its substance and existence. This is what the opening verses of
John's Gospel attempt to convey.

What if you and I never learn of this reality and we enter into
the intermediate state where everything we have experienced thus
far in our lives is only related to or dependent upon the material
or physical world? What if nothing in our lives was understood
or recognized as transcendent and everything was seen through
the lenses of the physical or immanent? How are we going to

get along in a primarily subphysical intermediate state where everything could be much more transcendent than immanent? If we are only aware of, listen to, or are conscious of the physical aspects of our world and our own lives, what kind of experiences will we be prepared to have in eternity? Let's explore this a little.

As an example, take the issue of experiencing joy, peace, or love. Joy, peace, and love are not bodily realities. We certainly feel and can often see the effects of these attributes on our physical bodies, yet there is no place in our bodies to go to find joy when we experience it. Many will say such an idea is preposterous, that joy is not a transcendent reality but a socially constructed definition that describes a commonly experienced phenomenon that occurs when a certain set of chemicals are released in the brain that cause chain reactions through the central nervous system creating a sensation we label as "joy." The same can be said for peace and love. Yet actually, joy is something that doesn't require a physical body at all. Joy transcends, is outside of, the body. God doesn't have a body, and he experiences joy that is unspeakable and unending. The same is true of peace and love. What we have to learn here on earth, while embodied, is to tap into this transcendent reality in a way that allows us to experience and maintain the qualities and attributes of love, peace, patience, gentleness, kindness, and self-control despite whatever physical conditions or material obstacles we face.

Dallas pointed time and again to John 3 as a wonderful example of how Jesus is helping Nicodemus to understand the transcendent power of the spiritual realities of God's Kingdom. This is also, in large measure, what Jesus is referring to in the Sermon on the Mount when he discusses the lilies of the field and our tendency to worry about material possessions, or our attempts at sustaining our lives (Matt. 6:25–34). If you've ever tried to justify doing something wrong or immoral, such as lying, stealing, cheating, or even killing, by arguing, "How else are we going to survive?" then you know what it is to place priority of the immanence of the material world and its ways and means over the transcendent spiritual reality of God and his Kingdom. And we do this for one simple reason: because we don't believe in the power and effectiveness of the spiritual realities of God and his ways to overcome or supersede the physical material realities of the world we live in. Jesus expressly states, "Do not worry about your life" (Matt. 6:25), and again, "Therefore do not worry, saying, 'What will we eat?' or 'What will we drink?' or 'What will we wear?' For it is the Gentiles who strive for all these things; and indeed your heavenly Father knows that you need all these things. But strive first for the kingdom of God and his righteousness, and all these things will be given to you as well." Then finally, again, "So do not worry about tomorrow, for tomorrow will bring worries of its own" (31–34).

I have to admit that it took me a long time, and I still have a very long ways to go, to actually understand what Dallas was teaching about the invisible, spiritual, transcendent realities of the Kingdom of God. I listened intently to his words and ideas, took notes, asked questions, smiled, nodded my head, and acted like I was tracking with him step by step. And I think that is what most of us do when we come to these kinds of ideas. We listen, and we have a sense that at some level what we are hearing is true, or likely true. And we profess belief in the concepts.

Looking back, it's clear I didn't really believe in these realities because I didn't live as if what I was hearing was true. Dallas had this haunting saying: "We always act up to the level of our true beliefs." Unless we act on what we say we believe in, we never develop knowledge of whether or not what we profess belief in is actually credible and trustworthy. What I began to learn from Dallas's teachings about the reliability and robustness of the invisible substances of God and his Kingdom took me years to actually put into action in my life. And I'm still learning to trust what it is I say I believe in.

All of which means, in some areas of my life, I don't actually know, by experience, what it is I'm talking about. Which makes me something of a hypocrite. An actor. And it is in these areas, where belief has not been replaced by knowledge and experience, that I am desperately lacking confidence, or faith, in my relationship with God. Like 2 Peter 3:18 encourages us, I still need to grow in the grace and knowledge of Christ, which is more than knowledge of Christ as a person. I need to discover what it is that Christ *knows* about everything, which Dallas used to say is a lot because Jesus was the smartest person who ever lived—something we dismiss at our own peril.

One of the most revolutionary lessons I learned from Dallas was how to clearly define and respect the unique differences between my beliefs, my knowledge, and my faith. We often conjoin belief and faith, acting as if they are synonymous. Dallas thought of them differently, especially in the ways belief and faith work their way out in our Christian lives. When we profess belief in something, our profession requires no evidence. Yet *true* belief, contrary to *mere profession* of belief, regardless of the lack of evidence, demands that one act as if what one believes is actually true. This is why Dallas said we always act up to the level of our true beliefs. When true belief is put into action, and our belief is validated based on experiential evidence, then belief immediately becomes knowledge. When this knowledge, even when partial or incomplete, is applied to similar events not yet experienced in the future, faith is the result. Faith is a product of knowledge. Faith without knowledge is relegated to the level of mere belief. Again, belief without action is only profession of belief, not true belief.

Dallas taught that such an understanding is what the writer of James is suggesting regarding the issue of faith and works or action (James 2:14–26). Also, the apostle Paul hints at the unique differences between belief, knowledge, and faith in 2 Timothy 1:12: "For this reason I also suffer these things; nevertheless I am not ashamed, for I know whom I have believed and am persuaded that He is able to keep what I have committed to Him until that Day" (NKJV).

Here is a simple example of the differences between belief, knowledge, and faith. I have a friend who says he believes in the safety of air travel. But he won't get on a plane. The truth is he doesn't believe in the safety of air travel, he only *professes* belief. True belief would require him to actually buy a ticket and make a trip. We could apply the same analogy to something as mundane as a chair. I can say I believe a chair will hold my weight, but until I actually sit in the chair, I'm still just professing belief. When I do place my weight on the chair and experience the fact that it is sturdy enough to hold me up, then belief vanishes in an instant and is replaced by knowledge. I no longer just believe in the chair; I now have knowledge and assurance the chair is worthy of my belief. I still don't know everything about the chair—there is always more to learn—but I do have some limited but important experiential knowledge that is valid and true. Now, the next time I come to that chair or one like it, I take the knowledge of my experience in the past and project it into the future. *That* is faith—the assurance or confidence (*confide* is from the Latin, meaning "with faith") of things hoped for, or the conviction of things not seen, which lie ahead still beyond us in the future (Heb. 11:1). Knowledge and faith are crucially linked.

Let's look at how this works in the Christian religion when actual knowledge is often lacking and profession of belief, not actual faith, is keeping us from living the eternal kind of life Je-

sus describes. Consider for a moment the tremendous number
of promises in the scriptures, promises about what life should or
will be like in God's Kingdom. Promises Jesus makes like "Ask
whatever you wish in my name and it will be given you . . . or . . .
you will have springs of living water gushing out of your heart"
(adapted from John 4:14). Paul says we will know the love of
Christ that surpasses understanding, filled with all the fullness
of God . . . by the power at work within us . . . that is able to
accomplish abundantly more than I can ask or imagine (adapted
from Eph. 3:19–20). First Peter states that those who love Jesus
will "rejoice with an indescribable and glorious joy" (1 Pet. 1:8).
The writer goes on to say those who love Jesus will have a genuine mutual love pouring out from their hearts (1:22). They will
rid themselves of all malice, guile, insincerity, envy, and slander
(2:1). They silence their detractors by simply living right (2:15).
When they have cares, they cast them all on Jesus (5:7). Wow. Big
ideas and big promises.

There are times in my life when I have dared to dream, dared
to profess my belief in such a life. Those times always fill me
with a sense of great expectation and hope. Yet the dimension
and quality of the life Jesus seems to reveal is one my mind can
imagine only in fits and starts. The blaring realities and troubles
of my daily existence jar me away from my imaginings. But nevertheless, the vision, the hope is there—significantly more than
a dream while just as significantly less than my everyday experience, and therefore, my knowledge of these realities remains limited. These statements and promises of a life of joy and peace,
patience, strength, power, and love are the primary colors of the
kind of world God inhabits. Of that I feel sure, and I want to
believe in them. But like my friend, I have to do more than just
profess my belief. I actually must take the risk of acting upon
what I say I believe in and get on the plane, take the trip, experi-

ence the realities of the truth behind these promises, and attain the knowledge of what it is I'm talking about.

Here is one of my problems. I find it hard sometimes, in a cynical, materialistic world, to fully place my trust in these statements when so much of what we are told today is nuanced and spun. Sometimes I feel like the Bible has a tendency to overexaggerate its claims. These promises are just so magnanimous, so revolutionary. I want to believe them. I want to go all in, throw caution away, and jump gleefully into the open air of these hopes. But the risk of disappointment looms heavy. We live in a world where people are always overpromising and underdelivering. It can become easy to suspect that Peter's fishing business and Paul's understanding of Greek culture and debate may have allowed them to learn a little too well how to manipulate their customers and students. Perhaps they are employing some twisted salesmanship to exaggerate their claims. Is that what's going on? Am I being sold a bill of goods?

I think it's much more likely that I do not experience those statements in my life as an ongoing reality often enough, and therefore, in order to protect myself, it's easier to discount the claims than it is to inspect my doubts. Therefore, my fears and pride prevent me from acting on what I say I believe and gaining knowledge of God's faithfulness, and my Christian culture lets me get away with simply professing belief in the truth of these statements without ever experiencing their reality. We've become good at finding ways of rationalizing away the biblical descriptions of Jesus's teachings and vision of the Kingdom of God and its power. Ironically, this also seems to be the primary strategy of the "new" atheist crowd. If they can reduce the New Testament's claims and promises to nothing but overzealous statements of fanatics who pontificate only on the ideal and not the norm, then we're all off the hook. Right? But it's not just atheists that try to wiggle out of these promises. Theologians also tend to categorize many or most of these claims as eschatological expectations that God will accomplish only in eternity.

Yet what if, what if these statements perfectly describe what Jesus really knows and expects of human life when sourced from above? Maybe what he is describing is the potential he has provided for you and me—now. Maybe living water, joy, love, and gifts and abilities that go far beyond what I can ever imagine, are all available for me to experience, come to know, and increasingly learn to place my faith in right now.

And if so, that is very bad news! Because if all of that is available to us now, what a majority of us know for sure is that a majority of the time we don't encounter anything like that in our day-to-day living. So that must mean we're not doing something we should be doing. Or perhaps we need to stop doing something we are currently doing. Or we might just need to change the way we're doing something already. Or, maybe worse, it's a combination of all three. Whatever the case may be, drastic change in some measure needs to happen. And that is really a bummer. That's going to take risk, work, effort, discomfort, trust, and maybe even sacrifice. Usually, we don't want any of that.

So our default position becomes one of two options. First, we can choose to sit back and complain about our lives and the failures of the spiritual endeavors we see around us (often directed at our local churches). Or second, we can give up all hope and learn to lower our expectations to the point where we neither get excited nor depressed about anything of consequence. Then we pray really hard for Jesus to come back and take us out of the entire mess.

But maybe there is another option. My relationship with Dallas provided me with a vision to pursue, and a mentor to watch, which together began to spark a hope in me that maybe I—like so many of the characters described in the New Testament, and like my Israelite brothers and sisters before me, whether they were coming out of Egypt for the first time or coming out of Babylon or coming to the end of their Roman occupation—have forgotten that life, real life, endless life, eternal life is supposed to be much more than food, drink, clothes, work, homes, positions, achievements, and accumulations of material *things* that consume so much of our time and energy.

Dallas helped me to think deeply about and see a vision for what our life could be like without the overt, endless, and extreme focus we place on the outward physical needs and wants of contemporary existence. Can you imagine what it would be like not to make decisions based almost entirely on a nearly endless and unconscious stream of devotion to the material concerns of life? Some of us can't imagine what it would be like to not know where the next meal is coming from. And I'm not talking about whether dinner will be takeout or drive-thru but whether or not a meal is to be had at all. Can we imagine an existence where what we wear is of no significant concern? Or how our hair, our weight, or our abs look? Is it possible to let our minds wander to a way of life that is not always aware of what car we are driving, the social status that is conveyed by our home and neighborhoods, who we are seen in the company of, what kind of job or profession we inhabit, what authors we can quote, or even what church we go to? All of these things are in many ways dependent on a physical reality, aspect, or condition. Certainly, not all of what I have listed here is merely physical. There are many spiritual connections to be made in these instances, but what spiritual aspects there are, in an increasingly secular world, have become primarily mediated and understood only in physical or material terms.

Eternal life, and life after death, is primarily spiritual and secondarily material. In both the intermediate heaven, and during the final state of heaven, the physical world will not be dominant, but subservient. Just as it was when Jesus walked the earth. Since this is the case, it is important to think about what will replace our current overwhelming devotion and concern with our material needs and existence—what will consume our attention in heaven? The answer is love. And remember, love is not a material reality. Nor is joy, peace, patience, gentleness, kindness, or grace, all of which are byproducts, or manifestations, of love. This does not mean that love and peace and the like do not involve some physical act or material representation. They often do. For instance, creation itself is an act of creative good, a gift of love for all humanity, given by God to all of us. As is life itself. But love existed prior to the creation of the world. Love is the motive behind the act of creation.

Thus, if we do not grasp the nature of the nonmaterial spiritual realities and powers of human life and existence on earth, if we don't stop merely professing belief in Christian spirituality and instead come to an abiding knowledge and faith of the power and significance of the spiritual realm, then heaven will likely be a most confusing place. Heaven is a spiritual place from which the primary forces of life and living that preceded the material world are sourced, and from which the material world came into existence. Within the heavenly, spiritual realm, the true force and potential of love, grace, peace (and so on) is discovered and harnessed.

Jesus is our teacher, connecting us to these forces: He brings us into proper relationship with the physical realities of our bodies. He realigns our engagement with others. And he helps us understand the impact of our will on our little kingdoms of home, work, learning, worship, and play. The ancient problem of dualism verses monism is oxymoronic. It isn't the preference or dominance of body over spirit, or vice versa. Rather as Rob Bell has so creatively argued, it is true now and forever that everything is spiritual.[5] The sooner we learn to live and apply this crucial fact, the better unified and integrated our lives will become.

This transformation simply will not, cannot, happen until the primary limitations and shortsightedness of being consumed by reliance on the material world, including our physical bodies and the overindulgence we have learned to give to their incessant needs, is subsumed by an experience of the substantial concreteness of spiritual life. Again, this should not at all be taken as an argument against the body, nor should this in any way be taken as even a nudge toward pitting the spiritual against the physical. God designed both to exist in mutual dependence and harmony, the seen and the unseen, each in its proper and rightful place. God is spirit, which is good, and he created the physical, material world as well, including the human body, which is good too. And again, we will one day be resurrected to physical bodies, albeit perhaps to enhanced or redeemed physical states other than what we now possess. At least we can hope for such.

What we are speaking of here are simply the effects that result from a blind addiction that has become almost unconscious in a secular society since the dawn of scientific rationalism. Scientism, materialism, naturalism, and rationalism have now risen to the state of becoming their own religion by assuming to define their methods as the nearly solitary standards and measurements for any credible claim to knowledge of any reality. And any good religion has its creeds: if it can't be seen, measured, or put in a beaker, it likely does not exist at all, or at minimum should not matter very much. That such a creedal position requires a tremendous amount of nonscientific, nonmethodically validated ignorance, and is as large a statement of blind faith as that carried forward in any of the most nonsensical of religious tomfoolery seems to be lost in the mix.

The Red Pill

Our difficulty in entering this new life, this life from above, this Kingdom of God, may be due entirely to our failure to remember that the "way in" is inexorably connected to our "inner way," or the immanence of spiritual transformation of our soul. This is the way of Jesus. I first captured a vision of this truth from the movie *The Matrix*.[6] The main character and hero of *The Matrix* is Neo (from the Greek *neos,* "new"), who is haunted by the possibility that there is something more to his life than the meager and unsatisfying existence he now endures. One evening, he encounters Morpheus (literally "the changer") and begins to get some clarity on this thing, this idea called The Matrix.

What Morpheus is trying to show Neo is that there is a world, a real world, that lies outside of the realm Neo currently understands, depends on, and lives in. What Neo is about to find out is that there actually is no such thing as virtual reality. It's either the real or the non-real. The word *virtual* is oxymoronic when it comes to discussing reality. Neo is offered an invitation to come face-to-face with a new life, a real life, with Morpheus as his guide. To do this, Neo is faced with a choice. If he swallows a blue pill, his memory of his encounter with Morpheus will be erased, and he will wake with no recollection of all the contrarian notions he has learned thus far. If he takes a red pill, he engages his volition to discover the true nature of what his life, and all life, actually is.

I can't think of a better analogy for our present-day situation than this. Jesus comes to us today, and like Morpheus holds his hands out with a red and a blue pill. He presents us with a choice. This is seen in his discussions of the blessings and the woes in Luke 6:20–26. Jesus lists the conditions in life that can be blessed or made better by life in the Kingdom of God, and those conditions outside the Kingdom of God that result in sorrow and woe. Very much like the beatitudes given in Matthew 5, Jesus is providing almost a one-to-one comparison of life lived in the ethics and ethos of the Kingdom compared to life outside the Kingdom.

The problem many of us face in our lives and in our churches is that we try to live a red-pill life without ever taking the red pill. The red-pill reality of God is the reality of his Kingdom. And that reality stands in stark contrast to the schemes we have constructed over time to survive in our world. We all create elaborate Matrixes wherein we seek to live and escape the fear, shame, or inconvenient truths about our lives or our characters. And many of those Matrixes can allow for church attendance and professions of faith in Christ while remaining distinctly outside of the reality and effect of God and his Kingdom.

This is the primary thesis behind C. S. Lewis's *The Screwtape Letters*.[7] Screwtape recognizes that, if strategically left alone, just like Neo, our senses will become progressively dulled, and we will be easily pulled away from our primary sources of power and vitality. Doesn't life act like that sometimes? Sometimes don't you look at the people around you, at a baseball game or a church service or a movie theater and wonder how conscious we all really are of the things in life that ultimately matter? We can so easily get caught in destructive cycles that feel overpowering and impossible to stop. Habits form, traditions set in, meaning gets lost, and hope starts to fade. Pretty soon, our reality looks nothing like that which we find in the scriptures. Or it looks exactly like those characters in the scriptures set before us as the "bad" examples. Those like Saul, Sampson, Jezebel, or Judas. The life we read about that Jesus demonstrates can become so foreign and high minded that we can't even imagine or dream that such a life could actually become our daily experience. So we settle on getting up every day to bake our bricks in the hot Egyptian sun, and with every drop of sweat, we slowly lose the hope of a promise, an inheritance, a benefactor, and a life.

But I have a bigger problem: Of all that has been written about Jesus, I don't see any evidence that he is one we could accuse of baiting and switching his message. Instead, I think Jesus is trying to bring color, definition, and emotion into the empty black-and-white outlines of our lives. The life he offers us is not a complicated maze of beliefs and duties that only the professorial or übermystical can grasp. Instead, Jesus invites us to leave our doubting burdens and heavy religious labors and step into his training school. His life is easy and light. Yeah. Now I'm starting to remember.

The gospel that Jesus presents us is undeniably connected to the transformation of the invisible, spiritual realities of our existence. Discipleship is the process by which we are re-formed by our understanding of the powers that run the universe God created. These powers are grace, peace, forgiveness, hope, joy, and faith. These are the undergirding realities of the universe, and they are all invisible, nonmaterial, spiritual realities that live and grow in a mutually submissive community of *agape* love. When we slip away from them, we are living in a blue-pill reality.

How do we know the difference? Discipleship to Jesus is the only way. We learn from him what is real and what is false. In this process, we are delivered, saved, from our delusions—saved from ourselves and our self-deification. This is the good news, the *euangelion*, the evangel, the gospel, the knowledge and wisdom of God.

Even still, before I can make any sort of change or have any lingering effect for the good of others, I've got to make the choice to leave the contrived world of The Matrix and go down the rabbit hole of truth that breaks out into the wide, hopeful, authentic vistas of Zion.[8] The way I live, think, love, work, talk, relate, pray, play, feel, consume, give, and receive—all these aspects of my life are transformed and approached as new opportunities to experience the grace, power, life, and hope of God. My life is no longer hardened and calcified. I'm now moldable clay in the hands of a loving triune God. We all need to take the red pill. And with it, we move from mere belief to actual knowledge of God.

Hidden in Plain Sight

The New Testament understanding of the spiritual substances of the Kingdom of God (Matt. 4:23; 9:35; 24:14) demonstrates that the good news of the reign of the "heavens" (the word occurs 32 times in Matthew's Gospel alone) is now working its way through human life. Thus, early Christianity did not understand heaven only as a *place* to go when we die but also as a powerful reality that has come to us. Consequently, heaven was not reduced to psychological terms that point to a *feeling* of euphoria or an altered state of consciousness that took one completely out of the physical realm or into an out-of-body experience. Instead, heaven was understood as able to invade both.

The word *kingdom,* or *basileia* in Greek, conveys a frame of reference, a worldview, a realm and reality wherein God's personhood and character are pervasive. This is exactly what Paul desires to convey to the often confused and disorderly worshippers in Corinth, who are trying to summon "heavenly" experiences through ecstatic worship practices. He reminds them that the *form* of this world (the word he uses is *schema,* which is the characteristic appearance, nature, shape, or model of something) is quickly devolving.[9] The implication is that the reality of heaven is coming to pass, while at the same time, the current earthly realm is "passing away" (1 Cor. 7:31).

Yet there is no need to make an either/or decision about whether one condition is better or more blessed than the other. From the very beginning of scripture (Gen. 1:1; John 1:1–3), we find the nonmaterial Spirit of God creating the material world through the implementation of the power (energy) in the Spirit or Word (divine *Logos*) of God. Thus, we have an example of a nonphysical, spiritual reality in the midst of God's creation, and Christ is now ruling equally over both the nonmaterial heavens and the material earth (Eph. 1:20–21). The Psalms and prophets further declare that God is Lord over and creator of both the physical and nonphysical, the visible and the invisible, aspects of our reality (Isa. 37:16, 42:5, 45:18, 65:17, 66:22; Pss. 32:6, 102:25). These passages tell us that the entirety of creation is not simply the physical creation, that the nonphysical creation is a divine masterpiece as well. This is something we tend to forget, which is to our own detriment.

Paul captures this when describing the nature of Jesus as "the image of the invisible God, the firstborn of all creation; for in him all things in heaven and on earth were created, things visible and invisible, whether thrones or dominions or rulers or powers—all things have been created through him and for him" (Col. 1:15–16). This echoes John 1:14, which states that in Christ the nonmaterial nature of God (*Logos*) assumed the material form of flesh in order to be among us (in Hebrew, *Emmanuel,* meaning "God is with us"). In total, the scriptures present two distinct realms (at minimum) in which human beings are to have both knowledge and competency.

Again, Dallas and I discussed Nicodemus more than any other biblical character, save Jesus, because he was such a good example of where we are choking on the red pill of the gospel, and thus, we fall far short of our intentions and potential. What is very difficult in a culture increasingly dominated by secular empiricism and materialism is that the Kingdom of Heaven functions on a counterintuitive schema. God and his Kingdom ways do not hit people over the head. Jesus is seen often telling those around him to listen, look, and notice that the Kingdom is directly in front of them, while they continue to miss it as if it is hidden in plain sight. That is the point. It is in plain sight, but the development of eyes and ears honed and focused on the spiritual realities and powers of the nonmaterial world is required in order to perceive and heed its features.

All kinds of people missed Jesus in his day, and we still miss him now. The closeness of the Kingdom is different from the ways we have learned to gauge proximity of a physical object. This is why we have to develop a new schema, a new framework of understanding, perceiving, and living. This is what repentance (in Greek, *metanoia*) requires—rethinking our thinking, replanning our plans, and revisioning our visions. If we look for only or primarily material and physical signs of the Kingdom, we will remain blind to the spiritual realities because "flesh and blood" cannot enter the kingdom (blue-pill world) since the Kingdom of the Heavens (red-pill world) is surely not made from things, nor operates from the sources, nor carries the same dynamics of, "this world" (1 Cor. 15:50). Jesus reinforces this twice to those who presided over his trial. "My kingdom is not of this world (blue pill). If my kingdom were of this world, my servants would have been fighting, that I might not be delivered over to the Jews. But my kingdom is not from the world" (adapted from John 18:36). Instead, Jesus's Kingdom is available to all who will follow, study, learn from, and develop the character and power of God (red pill).

When we live in and from the power of God, we become what Paul describes as citizens of heaven (Phil. 3:20). Paul uses an interesting word in "citizen." The word is *politeuma,* from which we derive the English word *politics*. Paul is suggesting that our governing center, our allegiances, priorities, responsibilities, and rights are maintained and stewarded by nonmaterial, spiritual truths and realities. This is not to suggest that we become so heavenly minded that we are no earthly good. In fact, we are to be heavenly minded (red-pill world) in order to do earthly good.

Paul again picks up this analogy of citizenship and power when he suggests to the Ephesians that they have been now, by grace, before death, put in a position of authority (raised), with Christ (Eph. 2:5–6), who currently sits at the right hand of God in heavenly places (1:20–21), and is head over all things and every name, forever. Paul then realizes that the effect of such an awe-inspiring actuality would specifically affect our lives and behaviors in such a way that we may lead lives "worthy of the calling to which you have been called, with all humility and gentleness, with patience, bearing with one another in love, making every effort to maintain the unity of the Spirit in the bond of peace" (4:1–3).

This is not a "then" hope, but rather a "now" potentiality. We are to take advantage of our time to "live" (walk) not as unwise but as wise, because the days of our physical lives are affected by evil. Such evil schemes can be resisted, not only with physical protection, but with spiritual protection as well. The protection for such a battle is suited to the threat, which does not come from "blood and flesh [physical, material] but against the rulers, against the authorities, against the cosmic powers of this present darkness, against the spiritual forces of evil in the heavenly places" (6:12).

Spirit and Matter Working Together

How we live and move in the spiritual realm has always and will always affect the physical realities of our lives. The red- and blue-pill worlds are not so much separate as they are distinct, with their own unique and diverse properties and relations. But we need to leave the analogy of *The Matrix* here in order to state again clearly that the spiritual realities are neither better nor worse than the physical realities. The spiritual and the material are simply two core aspects of a complete universe God rules over. The bread of heaven, the manna in the desert that fed the Israelites for forty years, was real and sustaining; yet it was not a product of human ingenuity or labor. Instead, the manna was a physical representation of the sustaining spiritual force (life) generated from God, which was demonstrated daily as a reminder of who the Israelites must place trust in as their ultimate source of provision—he who "comes down from heaven and gives life to the world" (John 6:33). In a Kingdom ruled by God, spirit and matter are conjoined, working in tandem to effect the good.

Until there is a new heaven and a new earth and we have new bodies from which to better engage these ultimate realities, we will likely be learning more precisely, or perhaps for the first time, to handle what poor Nicodemus, sitting befuddled at the feet of Jesus, was trying to understand about how life really works. In the paradigm of the invisible—that willful energy loosed in the spiritual realm—Nicodemus revealed himself as woefully inadequate. There is a paradigm shift inherent to the Kingdom of the Heavens that was required for Nicodemus to transform his thinking and perspective to develop a conjoined spiritual and physical worldview. It was so radical that Jesus uses the illustration of being born anew. In many ways, Jesus is saying we have to start all over, from where we are now.

So many of us need this reawakening to the spiritual realities of God and life from above. Few realize that the "born again" phrase says nothing about the forgiveness of sin but is instead introducing Nicodemus, and therefore us, to the spiritual nature and essence of our existence. Both natural (water) and supernatural (spirit) awakenings are required for life in the Kingdom of God (John 3:5–6), which, of course, includes forgiveness among many, many other wonderful graces (gifts). We have all been born once. Our physical birth was not of our choosing. Only some are born twice, for that choice is only ours to make.

Unfortunately, the initiation into the spiritual life is one that too few of us have learned very much about. Paul well understood this phenomenon.

> *When I came to you, brothers and sisters, I did not come proclaiming the mystery of God to you in lofty words or wisdom. For I decided to know nothing among you except Jesus Christ, and him crucified. And I came to you in weakness and in fear and in much trembling. My speech and my proclamation were not with plausible words of wisdom, but with a demonstration of the Spirit and of power, so that your faith might rest not on human wisdom but on the power of God. Yet among the mature we do speak wisdom, though it is not a wisdom of this age or of the rulers of this age, who are doomed to perish. But we speak God's wisdom, secret and hidden, which God decreed before the ages for our glory. None of the rulers of this age understood this; for if they had, they would not have crucified the Lord of glory. But, as it is written,*
> *"What no eye has seen, nor ear heard,*
> *nor the human heart conceived,*
> *what God has prepared for those who love him"—*
> *these things God has revealed to us through the Spirit; for the Spirit searches everything, even the depths of God. For what human being knows what is truly human except the human spirit that is within? So also no one comprehends*

what is truly God's except the Spirit of God. Now we have received not the spirit of the world, but the Spirit that is from God, so that we may understand the gifts bestowed on us by God. And we speak of these things in words not taught by human wisdom but taught by the Spirit, interpreting spiritual things to those who are spiritual.

Those who are unspiritual do not receive the gifts of God's Spirit, for they are foolishness to them, and they are unable to understand them because they are spiritually discerned. Those who are spiritual discern all things, and they are themselves subject to no one else's scrutiny.

"For who has known the mind of the Lord
so as to instruct him?"
But we have the mind of Christ.

(1 COR. 2)

The world is catching on to the spiritual life and the benefits of spiritual disciplines to the point that some non-Christian, nonreligious groups are now far ahead of too many of our local churches on these matters. The incredible rise in the group called "spiritual but not religious" is a case in point. Although we can't make too much of this phenomenon yet, it may be that the secular vacuum is starting to implode as people find very little meaning and assistance for their lives in a cold, dead universe. One of Rob Bell's recent books, *What We Talk About When We Talk About God* is hitting a strong chord with those looking for something good and meaningful in their lives. That this "force" or "supreme power" has a name and a plan for their flourishing should be good news. That it too often isn't should give us pause to at least consider why.

Perhaps, in part, it is because we who are supposed to be guides and ambassadors into the life from above (think Nicodemus) are still infants. We crawl instead of run; we speak in babbling sentences of incoherence, still unclear about our developing sense of who and what we are; we are still afraid of every dark shadow and bump in the night. As a result, we simply do not have knowledge enough to instill confidence in others to follow us into what we have not yet seen and do not know by experience or reason. We are but babes in the spiritual world. Eternity may be where we finally grow and mature. Having diminished the physical for a while, perhaps we are enabled to learn of the baser essences and elements of life that have, thus far, largely eluded us.

John the baptizer immersed disciples in physical water. The Spirit of Christ immerses disciples in fire (Luke 3:16). Fire is power let loose. We need to experience, learn of, and master the effects and consequences of this second birth, this baptism into the spiritual energy of God that flows in and through his Kingdom. But first, we must desire, thirst, and hunger for God's power and goodness to flow through our lives. Then we can develop the character to withstand its potential. It's time to stop merely professing belief in the reality of the Kingdom of God. It's time that we develop a faith based on an experiential knowledge that is growing day by day. Dallas helped me to stop trying to just believe in Jesus. Now I know Jesus, and I want to know him better, growing and developing my knowledge, in order to forge a strong and enduring faith that will stand amidst the storms of an unknown future. Like Paul, I am coming to know whom I have believed in, and I am being persuaded that Jesus is able to keep what I have committed to him, my life, my death, and my eternal destiny (2 Tim. 1:12). Eternal life with Jesus is mine for the choosing, but I must choose it.

Five

Choosing Eternal Life

J udgment is an event that declares the reality of the truth of
the matter at hand. Judgment, however, need not wait until
death. We can judge ourselves and allow God to judge our
hearts even now. Long ago, we called this "coming under conviction." To be convicted is to understand, or be brought to the
understanding, that one is wrong or has committed wrong. This
is the psalmist's cry in Psalm 139, asking God to search the heart
and mind to find any offensive way that can be corrected and
changed. This can happen now. But it will certainly happen later.
As recorded in Deuteronomy 30, Moses reminds the children of
Israel they must choose life, love, and blessing over death, evil,
and evil's curse. Again, the choice is ours.

Too often, and for too long, the local church and Christian
teaching have ignored the real substance of the heavenly life.
There is much attention paid to "getting" to heaven. We are good
at telling people what they need to be saved *from*. We are not
as good at helping people discover what they are saved *to*. Or
that choosing heaven is actually a lifelong process of submitting
our hearts, minds, bodies, relationships, and souls to Jesus in
an apprenticing relationship and not merely a one-time decision

(Luke 9:23; 1 Cor. 15:31). Likewise, there is little attention paid to whether heaven is a place one would enjoy. Again, we have to realize this second perspective is only a concern if one does *not* assume that the character or essence of a person, colored by a lifetime of decisions, willful actions, thoughts, beliefs, experiences, reasoning, and positions—all working together to form a worldview—is radically altered and corrected instantaneously at the moment of death by passing through some cosmic car wash. To recap, such a position comes to us from the idea that one's sins, even one's entire worldview, are instantly transformed if certain righteous acts are accumulated or specific doctrines are professed, specifically beliefs about the nature of Jesus as God's Son and his act of atonement accomplished on the cross.[1] In this view, the lone requirement for eternal bliss is the presence of a certain degree of good behavior, or theological astuteness found resident in the mind. Once past the security checkpoint and its doctrinal "scanner," the idea seems to be that we are immediately recreated into the "ideal" version of ourselves, without any effort on our part, and despite a lifetime of willful rebellion to the very existence we somehow have miraculously received. And off we go into eternal bliss, complete, sinless, and seemingly very different than what has thus far been demonstrated in the scriptures as what it means to be human.

Dallas did not believe that faithful Christians enter eternity as anything but completely human and therefore willful and free. He also taught that to assume God would create, much less condone and allow, for such a system as I've described is to either miss or ignore that true Christian faith and beliefs would be manifested in such overt ways that no doctrinal scanner would ever be necessary. Such articles of faith, if truly present in the heart and life of a Christ follower, will be as visible as a glistening city on a hill. The absence of such qualities will also be just as evident. The scriptures describe this as the separating of wheat from chaff and goats from sheep, otherwise called the judgment (Matt. 3:12; 25:32–33).

In fact, there are many people today, whether they call themselves Christian or not, who may very well be uncomfortable in an eternity with God such as the scriptures describe. The realities of eternity are much more stark, unavoidable, and consequential than the fictionalized depictions of angel-like characters sitting on clouds and playing harps that have seeped into our traditions and myths. The fact is many of us feel uncomfortable right now with even the idea, much less the reality, of God's person and presence. So we must take a careful look at what the scriptures depict regarding the nature of human existence, especially within the teachings of Jesus. Only then can we make appropriate decisions about the essence of our lives, how our characters are formed, and the ways these facts impact our eternal destiny.

Free Will

Often lost in the discussion about continuing our personal growth and development in eternity is how we consider the matter of choice regarding our eternal destinies of heaven and hell. For those who believe in predestination (the idea that God has ordained who will enter heaven or who is saved), or double predestination (the idea that God has ordained who is destined for heaven and who is destined for hell), the matter of choice is tricky. Is choice necessary to the nature of human existence? Are human beings created as inherently free and willful beings, now and always? If so, where and how is choice discerned, and where does it start and stop? These questions can lead to endless minefields within the fields of theology and philosophy that can't be fully unearthed here. In summary, Dallas was not an advocate of predestination either now or in eternity. He believed and advocated both theologically and philosophically for human will and a wide range of human freedoms to continue and be increasingly perfected in eternity. How free our free will is now and will be in eternity he was reticent to speculate about. "Free enough," he would say. "Just like we aren't totally depraved now but we're depraved enough."

Dallas also advocated that God was open to adapting his influence and response to a willful humanity, in general or in specific, as a result of being in a developing, dynamic relationship with free human beings. This may perhaps come as a surprise to some, but Dallas always taught and believed in the principles of God's openness to the prayers, goodwill, and creative interest of human beings working in concert with his grace. Therefore, Dallas believed that God was willing for the future to be changed and adapted by human agency, especially when in partnership with his will and power. This openness would naturally affect what God may or may not choose to be aware of about the future and his responses to the future. What is important to understand is that God does retain the ability to know the future, while at the same time God can *choose* not to be aware of the future. It's not the same as stating God doesn't know, has to come to know, or perhaps can't know the future.

Dallas pointed out that the scriptures demonstrate God has changed his course of action as a result of his engagement and empowerment of human agency. Yet God remains omnipotent in his ability to discern what is best and beneficial for God to know or not know about the circumstances and situations of reality, which includes the many facets of human existence.

Some have suggested such a position is a strike against God's omnipotent power. Yet Dallas recognized that to assume God could not choose to ignore something is to project a much more impotent view of God. To suggest God must know and cannot turn away or limit his knowledge is to limit God's willful action and destroy omnipotence. God can choose not to know something if he wishes. He can turn away. He is that powerful. For instance, Dallas suggested that God likely chose not to be aware of where Adam and Eve were hiding in the garden because that independence was for their good. This ability is a display of God's greatness, not God's weakness. Therefore, Dallas understood that God could be trusted to choose to do things he would not otherwise have done, or not do things he otherwise would have done, based upon the prayers and requests of his children. Consequently, Dallas firmly believed God's hand could be moved by his people. To consider anything different, for Dallas, was to render prayer psychologically impossible.

These issues of God's goodness, knowledge, and omnipotence are found right in the middle of this discussion about heaven and hell. Does God sentence people to hell, even before they are born? Does he know who will and won't choose to live their lives in his ways and accept his grace? Is that fixed—destined? Or do we have choice, and has God allowed us to truly choose him?

On these issues of choice, omnipotence, and eternity in both heaven and hell, N. T. Wright argues,

> *When human beings give their heartfelt allegiance to and worship that which is not God, they progressively cease to reflect the image of God. . . . My suggestion is that it is possible for human beings to continue down this road, so to refuse all whispering of good news, all glimmers of the true light, all prompting to turn and go the other way, all signposts to the love of God, that after death they become at last, by their own effective choice, beings that once were*

human but now are not, creatures that have ceased to bear the divine image at all. With the death of that body in which they inhabited God's good world, in which the flickering flame of goodness had not been completely snuffed out, they pass simultaneously not only beyond hope but also beyond pity. There is no concentration camp in the beautiful countryside, no torture chamber in the palace of delight. Those creatures that still exist in an ex-human state, no longer reflecting their maker in any meaningful sense, can no longer excite in themselves or others the natural sympathy some feel even for the hardened criminal.[2]

It seems Wright's position is that somehow, over time, there is a steady devolving away from love and grace to the point where those souls distanced from God become fainter and weaker, to the point that their humanness, or perhaps even the image of God that once resided in them, is eventually extinguished. They are no longer human. What they become at that point, for Wright, remains a mystery.

On the same issue, C. S. Lewis writes,

Finally, it is objected that the ultimate loss of a single soul means the defeat of omnipotence. And so it does. In creating beings with free will, omnipotence from the outset submits to the possibility of such defeat. What you call defeat, I call miracle: for to make things which are not Itself, and thus to become, in a sense, capable of being resisted by its own handiwork, is the most astonishing and unimaginable of all the feats we attribute to the Deity. I willingly believe that the damned are, in one sense, successful, rebels to the end; that the doors of hell are locked on the inside.[3]

The point I want to highlight is the overarching importance and relevance of the will to choose. Lewis seems to say that willfulness continues after death. Wright may be more agnostic about the will, at least for those in the intermediate state and for those who are not citizens of heaven. But both discuss a picture of the reality that now exists and will come to exist even more fully in the life to come. The questions we must continue to ask ourselves are, Am I ready for this? Is life with God what I sincerely desire? Do I now know what that kind of life requires? All questions that, if honestly engaged, would go a long way toward eliminating the suffering and angst of our earthly lives.

Dallas has stated elsewhere that God is the sort of person who would let into heaven anyone who, in God's considered opinion, could possibly stand it.[4] He believed that Lewis was accurate in his wonderfully vivid descriptions of the lost, confused, and stubbornly resistant characters he introduces in *The Great Divorce*. Dallas understood the reality of heaven to be completely and unendingly unfettered and unmediated. In fact, Dallas mused about the possibility of the "fires" of heaven being twice as hot as those encountered in hell.[5] This is a very important reality to consider. Such an idea intends to convey the inescapable presence of God and the immanence of truth as an all-permeating, falsehood-undermining, fear-eradicating and evil-obliterating actuality. There is no room, no potentiality in heaven for the fears that shadow, hide, resist, and obscure God's omnipresent love and power. Darkness then can only be where God is not.

Therefore, a great measure of what God will determine, or judge, is the degree to which any human being is prepared for the intensity of his being, and if, in the end, we would thrive or shrivel in despair and run for cover under such weighty, glorious circumstances. As Jesus's parable of Lazarus and the rich man reveals (Luke 16), being out of God's presence was perhaps the most graceful thing God could have allowed for the rich man, given the choices he made and the person he had become.

Discipleship, apprenticeship, and friendship with Jesus prepare us for being in God's presence. There is no other school of learning that will prepare us for eternal life from the heavens. Jesus makes this point as clearly as any he ever made to Nicodemus when he says, "If I have told you about earthly things and you do not believe, how can you believe if I tell you about heavenly things? No one has ascended into heaven except the one who descended from heaven, the Son of Man. And just as Moses lifted up the serpent in the wilderness, so must the Son of Man be lifted up, that whoever believes in him may have eternal life" (John 3:12–15).

But how many of us are still starving for lack of knowledge and continue to needlessly suffer from the consequences of bad choices? How many of us are alone, afraid, and lost in a web of confusion and despair about how we are to live? Even those of us who claim to be "saved" need to ask ourselves honestly, *Have I been saved?* If so, what—precisely—have I been saved *from*— right now, here on earth, before I die? What do we continue to suffer from because we are unwilling to heed Jesus's words and face the facts about the nature of our lives and characters? And do we dare face the reality of the surgeon's scalpel now, so that we do not suffer then, to cut away the chaff deeply lodged in our hearts and minds? If we are assumed to be perfected in the instant of death, why struggle for sanctification now? Why apply the spiritual disciplines to our lives, our bodies, minds, relationships, and souls? God is going to fix it all up in the end anyway, right? New heaven, new earth, new soul, no struggle, no strain, just hang on until the rapture, or the Second Coming, or even death, and it all works out in the end. Isn't that what we'd really like to hear and believe? Forget about character transformation, forget about stewardship of the earth, forget about justice between nations and love of neighbor and self: Just hang on. Jesus is coming.

Yes, he is. I just don't believe he is whistling that tune. We have to choose now to be Jesus's disciples, to choose engaging on a daily basis with the eternal life that he is offering right now. For Dallas, this was the great omission that demotivated most of modern evangelical Christianity away from the narrow way of discipleship. I also believe it is the primary cause of the pain and frustration in my grandmother's life and untold numbers like her.

"That Makes Sense."

As I was leaving Dallas's hospital room one evening, I noticed one of his physicians standing in the hallway taking notes on a chart. Dallas's friendly demeanor and gentleness to everyone around him—the nurses, the physicians, the technicians and cleaning personnel—was contagious. As a result, the staff reflected his generosity and cooperation. He seemed to bring the best out of everyone around him. Even those he barely knew. There was a magnetism to Dallas that defied conventional wisdom, which drew people to him, even in his severely weakened state.

As I walked past the physician, she politely introduced herself and asked how I was related to Dallas. I told her I was one of his students. She looked at me quizzically. "His student? Really?" I nodded my head. "What does he teach? I see you are working together on something," she asked. I told her Dallas had been a decorated professor of philosophy at USC for several decades, but that he was perhaps best known for his work in Christian theology. I was tempted to add that he was one of the most respected Christian thinkers and writers of his day, and that he was a world-renowned philosopher who was especially recognized for his uncanny ability to harmonize any number of philosophical inquiries with biblical truth. But I didn't, mostly because I knew Dallas wouldn't have wanted me to. Instead I told her we were attempting to finish a few writing projects we had started together. "On what subjects?" she asked. "Well, one of them is on the topic of dying and eternal life," I answered.

I wish I could adequately describe the look on her face when she was finally able to take in what I had just said. It was a curious combination of awe, interest, and hopefulness that was bridled by a long-suffering skepticism. She stared deep into my eyes for a lingering moment. I've long wondered what thoughts were circling in her mind during those few seconds. Was she feeling a latent desire to believe in the eternal rising up within her? Was this a hope that she had long since given up on because of the nature of her work? Or had she unsuspectingly come across a glimmer of hope, a seed of light that she had been looking for all along? I don't know. I regret that I didn't ask. It was a sacred moment, and I missed it.

She turned and looked into the open door of Dallas's darkened room as he slept silently. She stood quietly still for some time pondering her thoughts. Finally, turning her gaze to the floor, she whispered, "That makes sense." As she turned to leave she rested her hand on my shoulder. "He's quite something, isn't he?"

"Yes, he is," I replied.

Turning her gaze back onto Dallas, she said, "I wish I'd had a mentor like him. You are very fortunate. But I'm sure you already know that."

"Yes. Very, very fortunate," I answered.

It was then I realized none of the medical staff had any idea whom they were serving. But they were very aware of being in the presence of someone living from a reality they deeply admired. The life Dallas lived, and his way of being, was touching people, influencing them, moving them, drawing them toward something better, deeper, fuller, and richer, even despite his weakened physical condition.

Unlike his physician, I first met Dallas at the height of his intellectual and ministerial strength. I was just two short years out of college and had been married the same amount of time when Dallas came to lead a weekend retreat at our church in the San Francisco Bay Area. My wife Susie and I were trying to settle into our new life together, and I was attempting to establish a professional career when our church hired Keith Matthews as an associate pastor. Keith, who would become a lifelong friend, introduced me to Dallas's works and eventually invited Dallas to lead that fateful retreat.

To say that retreat was influential in my life doesn't come close to describing the transition that has followed over the past several decades. As was his habit, Dallas used the retreat setting to gather, organize, and present his ideas on what would eventually be published as *The Divine Conspiracy*. I was more than captivated by his vision of the Kingdom of God. However, the most memorable and enticing part of the retreat for me was how inspired I was by Dallas's interpersonal countenance.

I met Dallas during a period in my life when I seriously doubted whether there was any religious leader who genuinely represented the nature of the realities in the gospel they preached. We were in a time in American Christianity when the hypocrisy of "fallen" leaders was mounting at a mind-numbing pace. And Dallas was the exact opposite of such caricatures. For many years after, Dallas was one of the very few Christian teachers or ministers I had met who inspired me. He also helped build my confidence in my faith, confidence that I was not a fool to place my trust in Jesus, and that Jesus could, and would, make a difference in my life: a measurable, noticeable, manifest difference that both I and others could experience. He also allowed me to believe in the idea that I could know Jesus, intimately and rationally, and have confidence in the reality of that relational engagement like I could with any other living person. For that is exactly what Jesus was and is, a living person.

I've reflected many times that when I first heard Dallas speak at that retreat and in many other instances over the years I often sensed that I was with a man who just moments before had been with Jesus. It was such a vivid experience that it wasn't hard for me to sense what it would have been like to spend time with John, Peter, or even James, Jesus's brother, as they reflected on their time and experience of Jesus as well. Dallas maintained an undeniable, even contagious, authenticity that came from a special mixture of the way he spoke and the nature of what he described. The best way I've found to communicate this unique phenomenon is to suggest that Dallas seemed to reminisce about Jesus, like he and Jesus were very close, longtime friends. It wouldn't even be hard to believe that Dallas had just returned from a fishing trip with Jesus and the other disciples on the Sea of Galilee. Sometimes I could almost imagine the smell of fish and the musty fresh Galilean air on his clothes. Something new and alive was in the air when Dallas was in the room.

Yes, I had first met Dallas at the very height of his mental and ministerial prowess. His physician had met Dallas toward the end, seemingly in the most feeble and diminished period of his life. Yet both of our first encounters with Dallas provided almost identical reactions. Such is the undiminished nature and enduring power of a character built on the solid foundation of a spiritual existence. Our spirits can blossom even when faced with the trials of disease that shrivels our bodies and diminishes our physical strength. In times of great difficulty, Dallas had learned through his enduring and intimate relationship with Jesus how to lean his heart into the sustaining power of God's grace. Like a tree that has endured seasons of drought and as a result has grown roots that stretch deep into the earth and drawn life from a subterranean stream of living water that never runs dry (Ps. 1). Dallas chose eternal living by loving the Lord, walking in his ways, and observing his commandments, decrees, and ordinances (Ps. 119). And as a result, he flourished; his life was blessed, and others knew it.

Those of us who claim to experience the grace and love of God can and should do a better job of communicating and embodying the reality of God's goodness, plentitude, and wisdom found and experienced in God's eternal, heavenly form of life. The whole earth groans in waiting for his will to be applied (Rom. 8:19–23). God has already provided the vision and the means. All we must do is provide the willful intent to capture that vision and apply his means. Let's start capturing that vision and applying those means right now. The world is waiting, longing, searching. This is our chance. This is our destiny.

What we all felt around Dallas was the palpable power of his spirit. He was sustained by the spiritual realities of eternal life in the Kingdom of God. His spiritual life was robust and meaningful. But it was more than that. It was an actual sustaining substance, which was discernible and experiential, though, for those like his physician, not always easily definable for everyone he encountered.[6] Those who knew Dallas well, however, knew he lived from, and manifested, a power and an experiential knowledge of God and his ways that was able to bring him great joy and satisfaction despite times of great crisis and suffering. This is the nature of the spiritual life, devoted to the love and grace of God, which we learn to embody in ourselves and manifest to others. That was the spiritual *something* that was alive in the air when Dallas entered a room. And it is to this quality of life, one which all of us, deep in the shadows of our hearts, long to experience and dwell within, where we now turn our attention.

Going forward, we will focus on the kinds of characteristics that will endure the fires of heaven, the refiner's fires (Mal. 3:1–5). What we will discuss in the next several chapters are the elemental aspects of what eternal living is comprised of.

We should expect that life from above is inexhaustibly honest. We live in the light of eternity when we live in the light of truth. We live from eternal resources when we are free of fear. Such a fearless life devoted to and living from the truth is necessarily embedded with power and seeks to work in concert with God and others in seamlessly intertwined beneficial relations. Altogether, boundless joy and purposeful meaning highlight eternal living, such that every moment and every action is directed toward the proliferation and advancement of limitless well-being and harmony. The gospel of Jesus teaches that honesty, fearlessness, power, beneficial relationships, joy, and a meaning-filled destiny are the primary colors on the palette God is using to build his Kingdom of the Heavens. It is to this breathtaking rainbow of God's renewing world that is at hand, within arm's reach, where we will now turn our focus.

II

The Solution

Heaven at Hand

"There have been times when I think we do not desire heaven, but more often I find myself wondering whether, in our heart of hearts, we have desired anything else."
—C. S. Lewis, *Surprised by Joy*

Six

Honesty

I remember the first time I saw my father cry. I was sixteen years old, and we were living in Texas. Every fall, all the schools in the state closed for a day or two so students and teachers could attend the Texas State Fair. As is the case for everything in Texas, the state fair was a "big" deal. Since my mom couldn't get the day off work, my father decided to use a rare vacation day in the middle of the week to take my younger brother and me to the fair. My father was excited, and my brother was beside himself with anticipation. But like many teenagers lost in their own self-centered world, I wanted to go with my friends and couldn't imagine anything worse than a day riding roller coasters and looking at prize-winning llamas with my family. So I hatched a plan. I would play sick. I was rarely able to fool my mother with a feigned illness, but Dad was a relative rookie against my acting abilities, and I was pretty confident I could pull off a "Ferris Bueller–esque" ruse.

When he came into my room to wake me up, I gave him my best worst-stomachache maneuver. He seemed to buy it at first but soon returned with a thermometer. After he placed it in my mouth, he left to call my mom to seek advice. I took the opportunity to tiptoe across the hall to the bathroom and ran warm water over the thermometer. Before he hung up the phone I jumped back in bed with the sickness-proving thermometer in my mouth. When he came to my bedside he asked why the water was still running in the bathroom. A momentary wave of panic surged through me. When he pulled the thermometer out of my mouth I told him I'd thrown up and was washing out my mouth and forgot to turn it off. I groaned for effect. The look of empathy on his face told me I'd narrowly escaped being found out. Until he looked at the thermometer. His eyes narrowed and he looked down at me with equal parts concern and anger.

"Did you run this under hot water?"

"No!" I protested.

"Are you sure?"

"Yes! Dad, that's stupid. I would never do that! Why?"

"That's odd because it says here you should be dead. Your temperature is 112."

Still I pleaded. I couldn't stop the lie. "No," I said. "The thermometer is wrong! No. I'm really that sick. No . . . No . . . No . . . really, Dad! Really!"

He walked out of the room. Now I really was starting to feel sick. Shame and guilt had turned my stomach into knots. After a while I walked downstairs. The kitchen was a mess. I discovered my dad had been up early making breakfast. A rarity. He'd also begun to pack lunches for us. The old green aluminum ice chest was out and open, full of sandwiches, drinks, chips, and cookies. He was trying hard to make this a special day because he loved us. But I wanted none of it.

Of course, this wasn't the only time I'd lied, nor was it the only difficult situation my parents and I faced during my tumultuous high school years. This was just perhaps one of the most painful and unnecessary of slights. In the midst of the mess, my father was standing at the kitchen sink, the thermometer still in his hands, his head bowed and his shoulders shaking as he sobbed. It was then for the first time that I knew that I could really hurt my father. Suddenly, he was mortal, not an unmovable block of granite, but a man whose heart could be broken by someone he loved. By me.

I can't recall exactly, but I believe I did end up going to the fair with my father and brother. I do remember apologizing and admitting how ashamed I was. And I also learned the lesson that lying has a devastatingly long tail. It seemed an eternity to me at the time before I was able earn to my father's trust again. It was a hard lesson.

Before that day, I hadn't figured out how to communicate with my father, and he too was learning how to parent his oldest child, his first teenager. Our relationship was very different from his relationship with my grandfather, and my father was learning, just as I am now learning with my teenage daughters, how to adjust expectations from our own upbringing in order to provide what is best for our children who are living and maturing in a very different context. The day I chose to play sick lay in the middle of what proved to be a long, difficult, confusing period of years during my adjustment from childhood to adulthood. My father was weary of my struggles; he was also hurt and confused. As he would later say, he was near the end of his rope with me. But he didn't give up. And neither did I.

My lie revealed the harsh realities about my character and the nature of our relationship. It was brutal and painful. But in the end, I needed to see how my actions affected my father. That was crucial for me in order to see my responsibility in our relationship so that we could start rebuilding from a mutually agreed upon assessment of the truth of who each of us were to the other. Thankfully, our relationship has steadily progressed for the better ever since.

Can We Handle the *Truth?*

The topics of honesty and truth are so easily passed over in our churches today; they are not even thought to be relevant for our lives. *Of course,* we think, *heaven must be a place of genuine honesty and truth.* But are we honest, truth-filled people? Do we even know what complete honesty means anymore?

Like many people when they first met Dallas, I was initially a bit starstruck. He was larger than life to me. Dallas remains one of only a few heroes of mine. Early on, I probably treated him like more of a celebrity than a friend. Having met him at a young age, and having a limited amount of time with him until I would begin my dissertation research, it took a while for us to become friends. He specifically resisted any notion of celebrity and took the initiative with me to take our relationship to the friendship level. He did that by making sure I didn't maintain any false impressions of him. And what that required was for both of us to be honest with each other, to not allow pretense and our facades to stand between us and prevent real, honest engagement with one another.

I remember clearly our first step in that direction. We were out on a walk in a large open field behind a retreat center where he was teaching. During our walk, I was making some sort of complimentary statement about a certain idea in one of his articles. I don't remember my exact words, or even the specific subject we were discussing, but I do remember him slowing his pace until he finally took my arm, bringing me to a standstill. Then with a tone and volume I had never heard him use with anyone, before or after, he said emphatically, "Stop!" My first thought was that I had been so engrossed in our conversation and not paying attention to where I was walking that I was about to hurt myself by stepping on a snake or into a hole in the ground. I looked around and said, "What, what is it?"

He looked directly at me and said, "You must immediately stop flattering me." He had something of an urgent, frustrated, perhaps even a perturbed look on his face. Rightly so. I was stunned. And at first, I was also offended. The blood rushed to my face. Who is this guy to say something like that to me? I thought. If he thinks he can talk to me like that he's got another think coming! I'm not some naïve. . . . You get the idea. Thankfully the absurdity of these thoughts quickly ran their course, sober thinking returned, and in short order my defensive thoughts moved toward embarrassment. Dallas could see this transition in my reaction. We stood there for a while, and I stared blankly at the ground, brushing the tall field grass with my foot like a child.

"Yeah. You're right," I said. "I'm sorry. I guess I'm trying to get you to think I'm smart."

Then he put his arm around me, and we walked a few steps together, and he said, "You are smart." And he just let that hang in the air for a while, as the great gift it was. Then he said, "But too few people realize smart is not enough. In order for us to do what we need to do together, and do it well, you have to be smart and courageous, and that requires being willing to take apart every one of my ideas, hold it up to the light, scrutinize every word, as if the truth itself hangs in the balance. I need you to promise me you will do that. You owe yourself, and you owe me your honest reflections and critiques. You've got to be hard on me and my ideas. I'll have it no other way. We have to be honest with each other." I took a deep breath, and I agreed. And then he said, "Okay, let's start. Where do you think I'm wrong?"

It wasn't easy at first, but eventually, I became more and more comfortable critiquing his ideas because I realized how much easier and closer my relationship with Dallas was becoming when we "talked tough," as he liked to put it. I actually had already formed many thoughts and ideas that were somewhat different from his views and was very aware of other scholars and theologians whose work contradicted or extended beyond Dallas's formal writing. So we had much to talk about, all of which he enjoyed. He was just as interested in learning as he was teaching. But I learned something perhaps more important that afternoon. I experienced how conflict breeds intimacy if both people are searching for the truth.[1]

Dallas was devoted to the truth. All of it. And we can be too. We have the opportunity to really be set free, for when we abide in the *Logos* of God and remain his students, applying his teachings, we will know, not just profess belief in, but actually know the truth (John 8:31–33). We may not know everything there is to know about the truth, yet what truth we come to always gives birth to freedom. That is what we need to willfully engage our world. This is why it is so important to establish, through the use of scripture, reason, and experience, that the life to come will be, at least for "a time," focused on the spiritual realities of our lives and existence with God. If we seek this, with our whole heart, we will find it (Jer. 29:13). But we have to be honest about the entire process.

Now we can think more closely and intimately about several of the features such a life might hold for us. As I've stated previously, we are trying to fill in many of the colors and features of eternity that have been left undefined by the framework of scripture. Yet we are basing all our ideas on that sturdy (if incomplete, cloudy, or dimly lit) vision the scriptures provide of the life to come. Like Dante, Bunyan, Lewis, Tolkien, and even Augustine—those who offer fleeting insights into many of these areas—I too am only able to summon conditional understandings and educated guesses about some of the puzzles of heaven and the hereafter.[2] So here we need to make a turn and come back to the shallower waters and more familiar shoreline that represent the practical realities of our lives.

The scriptures do provide us with an abundance of wisdom and direction on Christlike character. Therefore, "all" we have left to do then is reimagine how such character traits would manifest themselves as spiritual realities in the absence of sin. These characteristics include honesty, courage, beneficial relationships, empowered living, joyful meaningfulness, and gratitude. There are a significant number of traits we could consider. This list I've presented here is one Dallas and I narrowed down before his death by considering the aspects of Christlikeness that we believe would have the greatest impact on our lives; thus, they are perhaps some of the most difficult but endurable character traits to instill.

An environment of total honesty is much more transparent than a place simply devoid of lies or "half-truths," the latter of which would be considered "whole-lies" in a perfectly honest world. We need to learn how to live honest lives. Perhaps in decades past this hasn't been as difficult as it is today. We now live in an age when we expect to be lied to. This also means that at some level even the most honest of us must wonder if we can survive here while remaining completely devoted to living in and speaking the truth. Yet if we don't learn how to be honest, which is much more than not telling lies, we risk missing one of the greatest gifts of grace God has so mercifully provided us access to: the red-pill world of reality.

Today, endless discussions, sometimes beneficial and sometimes not, take place about "the truth" in the most prestigious institutions of higher learning. Despite the frequent inaccessibility of these lofty discussions, we instinctively know that truth is often, perhaps overwhelmingly, a very simple matter. Children don't need to be taught about the existence of truth. From a very young age, we can discover something is untrue and know it instantly. With sometimes dramatic protest, children fight against untruth. The protest comes because we instinctively understand that we cannot navigate our world with untruths. To survive, much less thrive, we must quickly develop our ability to engage our world and our relationships, not as we hope them to be, or imagine them to be, but as they actually exist. We can wish away gravity, or lie and confuse ourselves and others about its effects, but we do so to our own peril. Learning and relating to the truths about our physical world is absolutely essential to human life. To flourish, we are required to come to an honest appraisal of the facts and circumstances of our world. You don't last long or do well on our planet if you aren't honest about or remain conscious of many essential and unassailable realities.

The truth is important because, whether we admit it or not, we are constantly dealing with it, whether we want to or not. Truth is inescapable. We are making decisions about truth almost every moment of every day, incessantly and often unconsciously. The truth is never in trouble. Only resistance to the truth is troubling.

Dallas liked to say the most widely engraved Bible verse on college campuses was also the most partially quoted verse in the Bible. Nearly always, universities or institutions like hospitals or courthouses tend to cite John 8:32: "And you will know the truth, and the truth will make you free." But this is not Jesus's complete thought on the matter. The entirety of Jesus's statement is necessary in order to understand how one arrives at the truth. This is stated in John 8:31–32:

> Then Jesus said to the Jews who had believed in him, "If you continue [abide] in my word, you are truly my disciples; and you will know the truth, and the truth will make you free."

Jesus would never want to sic the truth on people without conjoining truth with an ability to handle it wisely. The truth lies both in God's Word or God's *Logos* and then our abiding in that reality. This is foundational to our handling the truth astutely. "The unvarnished truth doesn't set one free," Dallas quipped, "but it surely will cause us to flee as fast as we can." Indeed, the truth can be threatening, for it has a way of cornering us the moment we try to resist it. Especially when we are wrong.

To illustrate this point, let's consider the entire field of advertising, which now largely rests on regular attempts to distort reality. We have now been made painfully aware of how fashion magazines and advertisers regularly photoshop away the real features of a model, even when the very premise of these advertisements suggests that the makeup, hair product, or diet drink this "person" is using has achieved for them the preferred "look" they attained. In reality, of course, the "look" being sold doesn't actually exist except in a graphic artist's imagination and computer program. Such false images and ideas are all around us, distorting our perceptions and manipulating our thoughts about what is true, good, and preferable for our lives.

Similarly, lying has moved out of the pit of deplorable behavior and into the arena of a spectator sport. We watch as witnesses are brought before government oversight hearings where hands are raised, oaths are taken, and the lies begin. Many will remember the now infamous Watergate investigations, the Oliver North hearings, the "Tobacco Row" panel that swore smoking tobacco was not addictive, or the lineup of professional baseball players with their testimonies about performance-enhancing drugs (PEDs). These spectacles too often become pathetic representations of truth-seeking endeavors. Politicians routinely use such a platform to demonstrate not a devotion to justice and the truth but instead an undaunted display of manipulative egotism that has now become accepted as routine grist in our political mills. Those testifying under oath also tend to demonstrate how hopelessly lost they have become in their desperate attempts to rationalize themselves into believing their only way forward is to back themselves deeper into the abyss of deception.

Still, lying is not the full story. Honesty also involves accepting truth's transparency to direct our actions, thoughts, feelings, and beliefs. If we seek honesty, we are seeking reality as it is. Yet contained in the phrase famously coined by Jack Nicholson's movie character in *A Few Good Men,* is the idea that we are haunted by the voice inside our own minds that screams, "You can't handle the truth!" Such an idea becomes a rationalization often used by leaders, governments, and even pastors to justify an outwardly benevolent protective scheme of lies to guard the people from themselves. Nevertheless, Nicholson's iconic phrase is truer than we'd like to admit. We regularly do not handle the truth very well. So much of our existence balances on the thinnest threads of deceit, with the hope the connections hold together until our lies are either forgotten or become "true enough" to cover our vulnerability and lack of integrity.

Too frequently, as in the scene between my father and me, we find ourselves caught when out in the open, vulnerable, and afraid of the very truth we seek to avoid. In this way, lying is an attempt to speak fiction into reality, an effort to manufacture, manipulate, transform, or cajole what *is* into what we want it to be (the first lie we tell ourselves), all under the self-perpetuating, self-deifying delusion that we are seeking our own "best interests" (the second lie). This is the basis of our justification for the first lie. In this way, lying can be viewed as a feigned act of a distinctly mortal god seeking the power to speak things into existence. Such fictions are only myths that proceed from the second lie. The second lie justifies continuing the ruse that the first lie can and will forge a situation or circumstance to our liking and benefit and was therefore the best path to choose.

Fortunately, for the liar and the lied to, reality is not so easily manipulated. Dallas used to say reality is that rather immovable object we eventually bump up against when we realize we are wrong. Truth does not yield to what we want or what we feel. We can't hide from ourselves or distort our approach to reality in order to evade the circumstances of our lives forever. Eventually, one way or another, the truth invades and perseveres. Truth is a gift from God for us to be able to engage and know reality (John 8:32). Yet like my foolish attempts to add lies to my lies, when we come face-to-face with the unadulterated truth of our circumstances, we may decide to invent an even bigger story that casts an even deeper spell of deception in order to camouflage the cracks in our webs of deception; or we may come clean and face the certain wrath of those who have relied on our misrepresentations as a truth by which they set the courses of their lives.

Of course, we can spend our time and energy focusing on the more notorious cases of deceit, such as the sad sagas of Lance Armstrong or Richard Nixon, but doing so would be only a diversionary tactic. The more uncomfortable truth is that nearly all of us live in only the half light of truth. Pretense is the mainline drug of choice for most of us. We pretend to be people we aren't, to believe something we don't, to be happy when we are sad, to be secure when we are terrified, to have accomplished something we didn't, to maintain hope for something we know is impossible, to search for something that doesn't exist, or to say we are just fine when in truth we are full of seething anger or hopeless dread.

Few are willing to brave the spotlight that exposes every shadowy hiding place of deception. We live in such a truth-barren world that we have become numb to lies, and strangers to honesty. Dying of thirst, we drink the sand in our sun-scorched mirages, and we lose the ability to taste the difference between spring water and dust because we have forgotten the sweetness of truth. Yet it's not easy to live in this world of lies either. Lies take a lot of effort. They isolate and demand; they require protection, defense, support, and feeding. History has proven it impossible to construct an entire alternative reality with our words, but humanity remains largely undeterred in continuing such efforts.

Finally, we come to the effect of lies on others. We've all been lied to, whether we know it or not, often by those we trust. Finding out that we must be doubtful of those who were to be guides and instructors to us is a breach from which some of us never fully recover. How does this play into the subject of honesty? It goes to the core issue of trusting that those with whom we are closest can be depended upon to keep their word, their vows, promises, and covenants.

Social theorist Anthony Giddens has argued that the issue of trust is directly connected to what he calls "ontological security." Commenting on Giddens's work, Andrew Root noted that in infants and young children, the foundation of ontological security develops in direct relationship to the mother and father.

> *The child possesses a strong ontological security system if there are many strong positive routines in relation to the mother. The trust that evolves between the child and the mother is a kind of vaccine, which prevents the child from being exposed to unnecessary dangers and threats. Trust is thus the protective shield of the self, enabling it to handle the many new situations of choice which constantly appear. Consequently, trust becomes a necessary precondition and foundation for interaction with more abstract systems.[3]*

How can we grow to trust anyone or anything when our primary and most developmentally significant relationships prove to be unreliable?[4] What value can be learned about telling the truth and keeping commitments and obligations if those whom we should trust instead fail us in these very matters? How are we to develop confidence and faith without foundational security in the primary relationships that frame our ability to withstand significant upheaval or change? Giddens suggests, "Trust in the existential anchoring of reality in an emotional—and to some degree in a cognitive—sense rests on confidence in the reliability of persons."[5] The fact is many of our lies and hypocrisies are modeled by what we have experienced with and seen in others. Today, untruth is so prevalent, some rarely, if ever, experience the refuge of truth's essence and reliability in who they are, who others are around them, and what is real.

The Cynic

C. S. Lewis attempts to illustrate the effects of such a vacuous state of ontological security in *The Great Divorce*. In Lewis's vision of heaven, even the seemingly delicate blades of grass are so real, so substantive, they are able to wound the feet of those who have yet to develop the substance of character to endure the unvarnished reality of eternal living. For those spending a lifetime trying to either escape reality, create an alternative reality, or manipulate the reality they are in to fulfill their own "best interests," such immutability is terrifying.

One way to deal with the fear of the indefatigable truth about our lives and our world is to become a cynic. A cynic is very different from a skeptic. A skeptic's challenges to claims of truth and knowledge are an attempt to better grasp their dimensions.

Skeptics ask the question, Is this really true? Galileo was a skeptic and a hero. However, a cynic, or an extreme skeptic, calls into question *if* truth and knowledge exist at all. Such a position may seem liberating from morals, virtues, responsibilities, and so on. Yet one cannot live long without making a decision in which knowledge, experience, tradition, and the like must be employed. This is how we were made to function, and we do so very effectively most of the time. Cynicism—as a philosophical base for approaching all of life in a jaded or scornful manner of distrust of any means afforded to engage the truth about our world—is, quite literally, useless. Even still, cynicism is growing as a popular coping mechanism when approaching our deceit-filled world.

Lewis describes the cynical approach to life in the character of the Hard-Bitten Ghost.[6] The cynic has seen it all; everything is propaganda, advertising stunts. Never can you rely on what you are told, and everything is the same old lie that's been told over and over again. Only the form of the lie is changed, never the substance. As a result, there is not much point to life and living; disappointment looms around every turn. Even a cloudless morning brings an expectation of rain in the afternoon. Hope becomes only a cruel trap waiting to snatch up the next unsuspecting fool willing to accept the world at face value. The cynic is too smart to be fooled twice, the wound of deceit being too painful to risk yet another injury. But as a result, the cynic never enjoys the hopeful expectation of discovering the light of the truth again.

If Lewis is accurate in his assessment that dishonesty is, at its core, a desire to escape from the harsh, unyielding, unpleasant, or merely inconvenient realities of our lives, what might our existence be like when the truth is inescapable? Surely, delusion and distortion would be impossible, and the fogs of manipulation, pretense, and facade would evaporate under the resolute, genuine gaze of God. If we do not want and are not preparing for a time when all we do, say, feel, and think can face the exacting scrutiny of God's perfect and ceaseless truth, present throughout the cosmos, we will eternally search for a hiding place that doesn't exist.

It is very difficult to stop believing what you think is true. It's nearly impossible to do so simply by direct effort. Typically, the first step is the admission that we are wrong. Even then, it can take a time or two or three to really grasp how wrong we've been on so many levels about what we "knew" was "true," but simply wasn't so. Jesus is master of and over truth. Access to the truth, through Christ, is what God, by his grace and love, offers us through walking with him, watching him, listening to him, learning from his yoke, his words, his manner, and his perspective. Collectively, this is what Jesus revealed to us in what he called his truth, his way, and his kind of existence (John 14:6). It is through these revealed means that the reality of our life with God is accessible. We can't get to the truth without him.

Human beings can learn to work with "truths" without acknowledging God. But not all truth is as accessible as the low-hanging fruits of gravity or the laws of mathematics and geography. Truths such as why we exist, where we are going, who we were created to be, what we are capable of, how we develop a loving character, and how we discern between good and evil in the many facets and dilemmas of our lives are often not found and therefore not applied among much of humanity. These truths need to be revealed to us, and God continues to reveal love, grace, wisdom, truth, and knowledge to anyone who seeks them genuinely and with their whole heart (Jer. 29:13). The question we must answer daily is whether we want to live an honest life, seeking the truth in all that we do and say. For in heaven, truth is as fundamental, essential, and beautiful as water, fire, soil, and air are on earth. We simply can't live, and wouldn't want to live, without it.

The Goodness of Truth

If there is one thing Dallas shared with me, and countless others, that would allow us to live honest, truth-seeking lives, it would be his understanding of God's goodness. I first heard Dallas discuss God's goodness from a place in scripture that at the time I thought was very odd. I was expecting him to pull from one of Jesus's parables or perhaps a favorite psalm. But instead he referenced Exodus 20. That's right, Dallas saw a primary manifestation of God's love and goodness to humanity in the Ten Commandments. Dallas often used the example of God's instructions to Israel as testament to his loving parental care of his newborn children of Israel. By extension, Dallas knew that this same Heavenly Father comes to us through Jesus in Matthew 5–7 in the famous Sermon on the Mount, which essentially restates these same truths.

The Holy Trinity reveals to us what we wouldn't otherwise know. God's ways, truth, statutes, way of life, which are both true and best, when applied—treating each other well, not stealing, coveting, murdering, and so on—will allow us to experience the eternal quality of existence that human beings were intended to abide within. We flourish as a result, which is precisely what God wants for us. That is what every good parent wants for his or her children. This is also the type of life 2 Peter describes as one growing under the grace and knowledge of Christ. Holistic flourishing is what everyone really seeks after, in every culture, every tribe, every nation, every family. Everyone is searching for how to not just survive, but to thrive.

I can remember like it was yesterday bringing my daughter Taylor Jane, our first child, into our little rented home for the first time. What a special day that was. All the trauma and danger of the birth was over, and we were really starting our life together for the first time in our own little space in the world. I remember sitting in my favorite chair and weeping with joy as I held this little bundle of life in my arms. And I introduced myself to her. It may sound silly but I did. I said, "Taylor, I'm your daddy." I told her how amazingly her existence had affected me already, that I was so glad she was my daughter, and that one of the greatest joys of my life would be to love her for her entire life. I promised to feed her and clothe her and protect her and I promised that I would always do what I believed was best for her. I also said that I was excited about teaching her everything I knew about life, and that there were so many wonderful things to look forward to, like ice cream, sunsets, sand castles, and afternoon naps, along with experiencing a lot of fun adventures like riding a bike, catching a fish, singing songs, and meeting Jesus. And there were also hard things about life to look forward to as well, like scraped knees, math tests, burned fingers, and broken hearts. But that in all of it, in the bitter and the sweet, I promised I would be there with her. To guide, comfort, teach, and correct as best I could. I was committing myself to her by giving her my word, by passing on the truth, direction, provision, and correction I had been given.

This is what Dallas helped me to see that Father Yahweh is doing with his newly born people of Israel. Just having come out of the trauma and bondage of slavery, they are weak, weary, needy, and vulnerable. They have to learn all over again what it means to be human. They've forgotten who their Father is. And he has to remind them again that he's committing to be their daddy.

I think many of us have, as does our culture at large, a hard time even imagining what it would be like to actually live honest lives devoted to seeking the truth in every corner of our hearts, minds, bodies, and relationships because so few of us can imagine God as God really is: totally, unchangeably, and irreducibly faithful, loving, and good. This is what Jesus comes to tell us, to show us, to prove to us. Jesus reveals what eternal living with God can be like by allowing us to taste and see who our loving Father truly is.

Eventually, I came to realize that if I could think about the Ten Commandments as the ten words of love passed on from a father to a child, it would change everything. God gives the ten words of love, grace, and truth to you and me as he cradles us in his loving arms, telling us we can face the truth, and with courage and confidence begin to live an honest life, to the point where we come out the other side not damned but blessed. Why? Because our Father's arms are not too short to save. They are arms full of omnipotent grace, protection, and provision for whatever harsh realities we may face. They are also arms that were willingly stretched out on a cross and scarred by the sting of sin. Yet they remain arms open wide to accept and forgive all that has come before, and they remain ready to provide all that we need for the future. It's these arms, these hands, these ways, these truths that Jesus has made available to us. When we come to know, not just profess belief in, this eternal reality, life from the heavens starts immediately, and the good life follows in lockstep thereafter. But we can only experience that flourishing if and when we are able to face the truth about our lives. Such courage is birthed in an abiding confidence in God's power, love, and care for our souls. Honesty and true knowledge of God's character go hand in hand.

The Power of a Secret Truth

During a period of solitude between nurses checking IVs and doctors' visits, Dallas and I spoke about my having recently met Trevor Hudson, a longtime friend of his from South Africa. Trevor and I had discussed the impact of Dallas's several visits to South Africa just before the end of apartheid. Neither I nor anyone else I knew had any idea of the nature of his involvement there. I asked Dallas if he thought his work there had made a significant impact on the eventual dissolution of apartheid. He said quietly, "Well . . . yes. I think the pastors there finally were able to convince de Klerk they were behind him." This answer seemed characteristically too deferential, so I pushed him a little, asking if he thought his influence had helped the clergy to pressure F. W. de Klerk into accepting change. Again, after a pause he said, "I think so." He then went on to confess that those trips to South Africa were a ministry he felt God had asked him to pursue. But he quickly added, "De Klerk is a good man, a Christian man, and he wanted to do the right thing. But he needed to feel the support of the Church behind him in order to accomplish what deep down he always wanted to accomplish. It was the clergy that finally helped him get over the hump."

I then asked Dallas why he never told anyone about this. He smiled and looked deeply into my eyes and said, "That is the great gift of the spiritual discipline of secrecy." He went on to say how serving in ways no one will ever know about carries a powerful blessing. The reality of such a revelation was almost too much for me to take in. Again, he patted my hand and smiled, grateful that the truth of his life and the blessing of his secret had now blessed me as well.

It was one of the more eye-opening revelations I had ever learned from Dallas. And I am confident there was no way, short of his death, that he would have ever discussed the nature of his crucial role. But the progression of his death began to lessen the need and the benefit of the blessing he had received in maintaining almost three decades of secrecy on the matter. He realized the blessing now was to pass the lesson of the power and potential of secrecy on to me.

Although I don't want to make a rule or principle from this event, nor would Dallas, I think it is helpful for each of us, especially those facing their own death, to consider what lessons, deeds, and experiences we have had in our lives that we have kept to ourselves for good reason, but which now would benefit others in knowing. Care and delicacy must be employed in these matters. Perhaps some secrets should go with us to our grave, but there may also be some things, some wisdom, some counsel, some experience we've held back that others who are left to live their lives without us would greatly benefit from knowing. Perhaps some of these confessions are best delivered in the confidentiality offered by a counselor, priest, or pastor. But death has a tendency to clarify what is essential and what is temporal. Dallas helped me see that if others can and should hear what we have kept hidden, for good reasons or ill, we can and perhaps should begin to face the prospect of the transparency that is certain to become our reality after death, which has largely eluded so much of our experience in this life.

As Luke 12:2–3 states, our secrets will be revealed, whether we want them to be or not. The question is whether we will be honored or dismayed by what our secrets have attempted to hide. Dallas's secret influence on the demise of apartheid demonstrated and developed the strength of his godly character. He hid his involvement in order to assure himself of his righteous motive. His secret glorified God, and God, who saw what was done in the secret place, rewarded him and us (Matt. 6:6).

Do we hold the kinds of secrets that glorify God, or do we wish to hide our secrets from God? We would do well to think deeply about our secrets, why we hold them, what effect they have on our lives, and if it is good and best to continue maintaining these secrets, and the realities they cloak inside our hearts and minds. Does the truth about us—who we are, what we do in secret—honor God? Or do we try to keep our thoughts and actions secret because we fear the shame that would proceed if we were truly known for who and what we are? We cannot and should not believe we can hide the truth, or hide from the truth. It is for this reason Jesus gives us a way of dealing with the truth that allows us to survive the secrets we seek to bury while also helping us to thrive in the freedom and light of the truth when we are students learning to walk in his ways and word.

As you will see, the rest of these chapters discuss the character traits of fearlessness, joy, and power and how we engage in relationships. We will, however, continually refer back to the many ways the truth of who we are, who we aren't, what we want, and what we desire to be is central to the kinds of people we are now. We will also reflect on the type of existence we will experience in eternity. For without developing a willingness, even a thirst, for the enlivening waters of the truth, we can too easily be fooled into settling for the poison of untruth as an acceptable alternative. Nothing of the sort will be possible in heaven.

Late one evening, after working all day on our chapter on moral knowledge for *The Divine Conspiracy Continued,* Dallas reminded me to look up the full text of Patrick Henry's famous "Give Me Liberty or Give Me Death!" speech. I wrote down the reference, but in the confusion of the details of those final few weeks, I lost track of my notes. It wasn't until after Dallas's death I was able to complete that task. I was stunned by what I found, and how perfectly it fits into the courage required to face the honest realities of our lives.

> *It is natural to man to indulge in the illusions of hope. We are apt to shut our eyes against a painful truth—and listen to the song of that siren, till she transforms us into beasts. Is this the part of wise men, engaged in a great and arduous struggle for liberty? Are we disposed to be of the number of those who, having eyes, see not, and, having ears, hear not, the things which so nearly concern their temporal salvation? For my part, whatever anguish of spirit it may cost, I am willing to know the whole truth; to know the worst, and to provide for it.[7]*

Henry had in mind the specific issues related to political liberty and temporal salvation. Here we are pursuing existential freedom and eternal salvation from the lies of evil. Still, his words, the realities they depict, and the questions he evokes are the same. Are we willing to know the truth, the whole truth, as it is? For heaven will be a place that provides for nothing less.

In light of the truth and reality of God and his Kingdom, the next aspect of eternal living we need to consider is fearlessness. Heavenly existence is a fearless existence because love is perfected in eternity, and perfect love eradicates fear. It literally drives it out. It can't remain; there is no foothold, no reason, and no means by which fear can be justified. Love is the water that drowns the flames of fear. What might such a life be like? Can we experience that now? Do you want to? Let's see.

Seven

Fearlessness

During the late evening of my first night with Dallas at the hospital, a longtime friend came to visit him. Although he was deeply sorrowful about Dallas's condition, his sorrow moved him to action. There is an unwritten rule that we as a society seem to follow in times like these. We don't want to be a bother. We don't want to intrude and are afraid to risk spoiling some tender moment. These instincts and acts of deference are often good and appropriate. But then there is the example in the New Testament of the woman who breaks with convention, overcomes her fears of the scorn of others, and pours out her dowry of perfume onto Jesus's feet, risking the scorn of her society. Yet because she takes such a risk, she also receives an eternal blessing. Such was the case for this man.

He knocked on the door, and we met outside the room. We talked briefly about Dallas's condition. I relayed that Dallas was resting but losing his strength. When awake, however, he was fairly alert and only intermittently in pain. In a trembling voice, the man told me he felt compelled to say his good-byes. I understood.

We walked into the room, the man lightly touched Dallas's

hand, and when he did, Dallas opened his eyes and smiled. Words of appreciation and respect were traded. Dallas took a deep breath and proceeded to bestow a wonderful blessing on his friend. There is an amazing power in the gift of a man on his deathbed extending parting words of encouragement and approval. The scene made me think of Isaac bestowing his blessing on Jacob or Jacob's blessing of Joseph. It was very poignant and moving and required a certain measure of boldness and fearlessness on the part of the man who came and received the blessing.

After the visitor left, I sat in the chair next to Dallas while he slept, and a teaching of his from long ago echoed in my memory. Dallas interpreted Matthew 11:12 differently from most other people: "From the days of John the Baptist until now the kingdom of heaven has suffered violence, and the violent take it by force." Dallas saw the virtues of the Kingdom of God as providing patience (another word for suffering) to those who are able to overcome their fears and risk violating the norms of society and the scorn that often follows.

The kind of violence Jesus was talking about was not physical violence but the violence produced by those who breach social norms, expectations, and political correctness. This is especially true of violations of religious norms that tend to block us from experiencing God's love and truth. And it is just these kinds of violators, motivated by love as much as their own hunger and thirst, who, regardless of the ridicule of others, will not be deterred from fearlessly seeking God's goodness and grace. These kinds of outcasts will and do take the Kingdom by storm, by the throat, and never let go. Even on his deathbed, Dallas was patient and encouraging to courageous seekers of life, such as the visitor who came to see Dallas that night, as they demonstrated the virtues that come from above.

I don't know that I can accurately or completely communicate how fearlessly Dallas faced his own mortality, even with the pain and suffering he experienced, some of which was considerable. It was remarkable to witness. It wasn't that he was putting up a front, or trying to be strong for his family, which many people do when facing hardships and is often an admirable and loving act of grace. But Dallas was different. It wasn't that he was suppressing his fear, or managing his fear well. It was that fear wasn't in him. Therefore, it wasn't a struggle to be brave. He simply and easily faced the facts of his life, and his death, without the presence of fear. I can't imagine an easier yoke to walk with during my final few days than one completely absent of fear. It reminds me of the lyrics to one of my favorite contemporary hymns, "In Christ Alone." The last verse is a prayer we can all hope to experience.

> *No guilt in life, no fear in death—*
> *This is the power of Christ in me;*
> *From life's first cry to final breath,*
> *Jesus commands my destiny.*
> *No power of hell, no scheme of man,*
> *Can ever pluck me from His hand;*
> *Till He returns or calls me home—*
> *Here in the power of Christ I'll stand.*[1]

Dallas came gradually to the knowledge that there is nothing to fear in this life. However, this knowledge just didn't fall on him. Over time, and through trials and failures, he came to willfully and gratefully accept God, as God is, in the core of Dallas's own soul. As a result—and it is a result—he lived in and experienced the truth of God's loving, empowering, grace-filled nature. This allowed him to progressively learn there is nothing, absolutely nothing, to fear.

We once talked about fear, only for a short while. He said that as a young man, much like my grandmother, he suffered under the idea that God was a kind of cosmic sheriff lurking behind a highway billboard, waiting to punish him in order to justify his existence. But over time, Dallas become able, even willing, to accept the fact that God, shown to us in the person of Jesus, is not like that at all. When Dallas let loose of that Zeus-like picture of God, he discovered that he didn't have to fear facing the facts about who and what he was, and what he wasn't. I now see that when we reach this level of peace with God, we don't have to run and hide from our expectations that lightning bolts of divine wrath are on their way to smite us down. Instead, the truth becomes something we can welcome, without manipulating it to fit our fears, needs, or wants.

Dallas knew that as he entered into the end of this life, he was really just at the start of the eternal life to come. That hope, peace, and confidence in the Good Shepherd was the foundation on which not only his death, but also his entire life proceeded. We often pray, and rightly so, for a peace "which surpasses all understanding" (Phil. 4:7). However, I realize now that Dallas actually lived in and from a peace that was perfectly reasonable. His understanding and experience of Christ formed his life and sustained him in facing his death. The hope he knew prior to his illness propelled him through his trials and out the other side. Through this, his hope was not diminished, but instead elevated. Enduring a long and painful death is not the primary reason to place one's confidence in Christ's sufficiency for all our needs, but it is a real and sustaining blessing that many experience as a living benefit.

Dallas avoided the manipulative altar-call strategies used by many evangelizing preachers to induce a fear of hell in order to conjure a "salvific decision for Christ." Recognizing the need for salvation through Christ only as a contractual or judicial means of avoiding hell is a rather anemic basis on which to forge a commitment to the transformative life Jesus offers. But Dallas did firmly believe that when we place our confidence in Jesus, he would reliably provide everything we are in need of, both now and into eternity, whatever our condition. This would necessarily include facing the often-frightful reality of our physical death. Jesus is with us, even through the valley of the deathly shadows, and that hopeful assurance and gratitude of being delivered from evil, both in, through, and beyond physical death, were most evident in Dallas's final days.

When we have met and engaged the endlessly loving God that Jesus knew and described as the Good Shepherd, we can learn to face even the cold, hard facts of our lives, the emptiness, the tendency to run from the consequences of our actions, and our loneliness, addictions, pride, and self-centeredness, all of which are products of our fears. Love is the absence of fear. And God is love.

It's not just the negative things, however, that we hide from in our fear. Many of us hide from or ignore the beautiful and inspiring victories and successes of our lives out of worry we will be thought arrogant, egotistical, or haughty. Some of our fears keep us from revealing to others, not only our sufferings and frailties, but also our victories, accomplishments, and blessings. Not celebrating our successes can become another way of not living in the realities of our lives as they actually unfold.

To know and interact with God is to live a life without fear of any kind. Fearlessness enables us to stop managing and manipulating ourselves, our engagement with the truth, our expectations of ourselves and others, and our lack of control over the present or the future. We can also overcome our greatest fears, which tend to lie in waiting beneath the mysterious and threatening unknowns of our lives. Thus, fear and dishonesty are siblings. We change or adapt the truth because we are afraid of what the truth might mean. We concoct elaborate plans to manipulate threatening facts that fester at the center of our most menacing difficulties and trials. Fear prevents us from accepting what is true about us, and thus, we remain insulated from actually living in the concrete existence God has given to us. God did not intend, nor is it good, for us to live our lives in padded rooms constructed by fantasy or fear.

Our culture certainly doesn't help. Inciting fear has grown into an industry today. The majority of our industrial media complex—print, Internet, television, movies, radio, and social media—is nearly always preying on our fears. The strategy seems to be to create stories and news reports that form a huge, dark cloud of despair, and then in a final segment, we are given some glimmer of hope in a feel-good piece to show the silver lining behind the gloomy storm of uncertainty.

I clearly remember a time in my early high school years, while living near Dallas, Texas, when my brother and I were left at home while my parents went to dinner with friends. As we were watching TV, we heard the tornado sirens blare, and the emergency broadcast system began to squeal across the TV. Not long after, my parents called, instructing us to get under the stairwell and wait until the storm had passed. It was one of the few commands my parents gave me in high school that I didn't argue with. My brother and I were pretty scared. The sky was an eerie blackish-orange, and there wasn't so much as a cricket chirp outside. So we huddled together under the stairs with a couple bottles of RC Cola and a box of Oreo cookies to wait out the storm.

As we consumed more and more sugar, we peeked outside the stairwell door at the TV just around the corner. The storm was affecting the antenna reception, but we could still see and hear the weatherman telling us where he thought the storm was progressing, thanks to the newly created Doppler radar system. I distinctly recall the feeling I had when I heard the weatherman announce the tornado had touched down east of town and was headed north toward Allen, Texas. I knew, then, we were safe. My brother and I looked at each other. I was relieved, but he was still somewhat worried. So we stayed in the closet under the stairs and finished off our stash of Oreos, trying to act like the tornado hadn't scared both of us out of our knickers. I remember the instant my parents' key hit the lock on the front door. My brother bolted out of the closet and jumped into the arms of my father, tears of relief flowing down his cheeks.

I tell this story to illustrate a point. The information and knowledge of the weatherman's technology and expertise carried the power to eliminate my fear. The information gatherers and providers in the media industry know well the benefit of keeping their audiences in a general state of fear. When we are afraid, we continue to watch, look, gather, read, and search for more information in order to assuage our fear. That is why bad news continues to outpace good news on television.[2] My brother, however, didn't have confidence in me or the Doppler radar system. His fears were assuaged by the security of being held in my father's strong embrace. Only a bond far deeper than information could erase my brother's fear. His doubts and mine were housed in different forms of insecurity, and therefore, we experienced the same event through a different set of eyes.

Some situations require the right information to serve as a tool to calm our nerves, while other circumstances necessitate a relationship that provides the ontological security that extends deeper than our minds alone can access. It might be helpful to ask ourselves which of these better deserves our attention and concern. There are times when certain information or certain relationships might be leading us toward fear rather than assuaging our fears. For example, the media has not proven a good judge of what we should and shouldn't fear. Perhaps there was a time in the "golden age" of television and journalism when responsible professionals could be trusted to discern "all the news that's fit to print."[3] Today, we must seriously discern for ourselves what is sensationalism, opinion, or entertainment, and what is newsworthy information that we need in order to be responsible citizens in our world.

You may recall when the terrible Beltway sniper assassinations were occurring in and around the Washington, DC, metro area in the fall of 2002. I happened to be talking to my widowed paternal grandmother on the phone during this time. She lived in Missouri, and in passing, she told me she needed to get out to buy some candy for the kids in the neighborhood for Halloween. Yet I could sense some hesitancy in her voice. I asked what was wrong. She told me her car was low on gas and that the store that was closest to her was adjacent to a big parking lot. She said she was fearful that if she stopped to get gas, and parked beside a large supermarket parking lot, she might become a target for a sniper. I reminded her the sniper was in Maryland, not Missouri, and that she would be fine, to which she said, "Well, I don't know."

I'm not sure if the children in her neighborhood ever got their Halloween candy that year, but my grandmother was certainly spooked. After my grandfather's death, she wasn't as mobile as she once was, as years of back pain restricted her mobility. What she did do, a lot, was read her Bible and watch the news. I've never been sure which consumed more of her time, but it became clear to me over the years that the fears of a world gone bad increasingly fell on her shoulders. And it wouldn't take long for any visit or phone conversation to eventually turn toward esoteric and dramatic events in the news that stoked her worrying heart. She seemed to feel a responsibility to maintain a low-level dread about the happenings around the world. I think she believed someone had to.

Perhaps her problem was something Dallas often spoke about: that we are not called to love the entire world, only our neighbor. He wasn't suggesting we turn a blind eye to the issues of our world but that there is no good that comes from obsessing over the world's problems to the degree that we become paralyzed from ever acting on any one issue in particular, from serving where we are able. As Dallas put it, we often use the excuse of loving the whole world in order to get out of loving any one person in particular. This is in part what Jesus is uncovering in the parable of the good Samaritan.

What could have changed my grandmother's outlook are the ideas that lie behind that simple yet true Christian folk song: "He's Got the Whole World in His Hands." Something so profound, yet simple, can stem the tide of fear that can so easily cause our hearts and minds to race endlessly in anxiety and dread. Paul's words to Timothy continue to resonate in my mind when I tend to worry or become fatalistic or pessimistic about life's challenges. "I know whom I have believed in and therefore I am persuaded that God is able to keep that which I've committed to him, against that day" (adapted from 2 Tim. 1:12).

Naming Our Fears

Dishonesty and fear are twins primarily due to the routine harshness of the truth. Truth can be bitter at times, and thus, very hard to choke down. In fact, it is often so difficult that we are afraid to face it, which causes us to try and change it, deny it, or ignore it with lies and distortions. But even if we do try to face the truth head-on, we can become paralyzed by fear of what may lie ahead.

An often quoted, yet unsubstantiated, phrase attributed to Plato suggests, "We can easily forgive a child who is afraid of the dark. The real tragedy of life is when men are afraid of the light." Fear of what might happen, fear of what won't happen, fear of consequences we know of and those we don't know of, these are the doubts and worries that lurk as ominously in the darkness of ignorance and denial as they do in the wide open light of admission. For some, being made aware of exactly what is coming—a terminal diagnosis, a foreclosure, a job loss—is just as terrifying, even more terrifying, than being kept in the dark. Knowledge is something we often have to choose. There are many things in our lives we don't have to know if we don't want to know. Denial is a powerful device of a fearful heart.

Life with God allows us to recognize, perhaps for the first time, that there is nothing to fear, nothing we have to hide from, nothing that cannot be overcome with and through God and his empowering ability to overwhelm fear and eradicate untruth simply with his presence. Ambrose Redmoon is quoted as stating, "Courage is not the absence of fear, but rather the judgment that something else is more important than fear."[4] Something *is* more important. The deeper question becomes, What is it that is more important?

I believe love is more important. Love is stronger, and more robust and enduring, than fear. The courage Redmoon describes must be based on the foundation that love overcomes everything: every trial, every evil, every fear, every doubt, every unknown, every diagnosis, every untruth, every failure, and every loss. Otherwise, courage becomes cheapened by whatever we can convince ourselves is worthy of our lives or whatever fear is allowed to overwhelm our sense of what is good and best.

Did the terrorists on 9/11 display courage or an insane commitment to something they felt was more important than their fear of death? The answer to that question is based on their understanding of and beliefs about the character of the deity they worshipped and served. That is why heaven must be an environment from which an effluence of love is so insatiable as to eradicate and overwhelm fear and falsehood. Dallas understood that the *agape* form of love and a divine level of joy are nonmaterial substances that wield immeasurable degrees of spiritual power. They can literally lift us, sustain us, guide us, and cover us.

Both Paul and the writer of Hebrews make this point over and over again.

> *Therefore, since we are surrounded by so great a cloud of witnesses, let us also lay aside every weight and sin that clings so closely, and let us run with perseverance the race that is set before us, looking to Jesus, the pioneer and perfecter of our faith, who for the sake of the joy that was set before him endured the cross, disregarding [scorning] its shame, and has taken his seat at the right hand of the throne of God.*

(HEB. 12:1–2)

It may be easy to miss that second phrase, "who for the sake of the joy that was set before him endured the cross, [scorning] its shame" and its manner of torture and death. Scholar William Lane argues that in

> *the death of Jesus of Nazareth, God identified himself with an extreme expression of human wretchedness, which Jesus endured as the representative of fallen humanity. As a matter of fact, the attitude denoted by [the Greek word]*

καταϕϱονεῖν, "to scorn," acquires in this context a positive nuance: "to brave" or "to be unafraid" of an experience in spite of its painful character.[5]

Lane is suggesting that because Jesus was living in the reality and awareness of the power of God's love and joy that proceeds from personal experience with these powers, even in the moments as excruciating as his own execution, Jesus was empowered, encouraged, "embravened," to accept and endure his trial. He walked through the valley of the shadow of death and feared no evil (Ps. 23:4).

If Redmoon is accurate, there will be no need for courage in heaven like that which we have known on earth simply due to the fact that there will be no fear. Perfect love casts out fear—perfectly. Paul, too, writes about the overcoming aspect of this way of life free from fear and mistrust.

We know that the whole creation has been groaning in labor pains until now; and not only the creation, but we ourselves, who have the first fruits of the Spirit, groan inwardly while we wait for adoption, the redemption of our bodies. For in hope we were saved. Now hope that is seen is not hope. For who hopes for what is seen? But if we hope for what we do not see, we wait for it with patience.

Likewise the Spirit helps us in our weakness; for we do not know how to pray as we ought, but that very Spirit intercedes with sighs too deep for words. And God, who searches the heart, knows what is the mind of the Spirit, because the Spirit intercedes for the saints according to the will of God.

We know that all things work together for good for those who love God, who are called according to his pur-

pose. For those whom he foreknew he also predestined to be conformed to the image of his Son, in order that he might be the firstborn within a large family. And those whom he predestined he also called; and those whom he called he also justified; and those whom he justified he also glorified.

What then are we to say about these things? If God is for us, who is against us? He who did not withhold his own Son, but gave him up for all of us, will he not with him also give us everything else? Who will bring any charge against God's elect? It is God who justifies. Who is to condemn? It is Christ Jesus, who died, yes, who was raised, who is at the right hand of God, who indeed intercedes for us. Who will separate us from the love of Christ? Will hardship, or distress, or persecution, or famine, or nakedness, or peril, or sword? As it is written,

"For your sake we are being killed all day long;
we are accounted as sheep to be slaughtered."

No, in all these things we are more than conquerors through him who loved us. For I am convinced that neither death, nor life, nor angels, nor rulers, nor things present, nor things to come, nor powers, nor height, nor depth, nor anything else in all creation, will be able to separate us from the love of God in Christ Jesus our Lord.

(ROM. 8:22–39)

Paul describes more of the kind of foundational character that is required to meet the tests of an eternal reality, a character that will not bend to the will of the flesh or conform to lies and distortions of fear.

According to the grace of God given to me, like a skilled master builder I laid a foundation, and someone else is building on it. Each builder must choose with care how to build on it. For no one can lay any foundation other than the one that has been laid; that foundation is Jesus Christ. Now if anyone builds on the foundation with gold, silver, precious stones, wood, hay, straw—the work of each builder will become visible, for the Day will disclose it, because it will be revealed with fire, and the fire will test what sort of work each has done. If what has been built on the foundation survives, the builder will receive a reward. If the work is burned up, the builder will suffer loss; the builder will be saved, but only as through fire.

Do you not know that you are God's temple and that God's Spirit dwells in you? If anyone destroys God's temple, God will destroy that person. For God's temple is holy, and you are that temple.

Do not deceive yourselves. If you think that you are wise in this age, you should become fools so that you may become wise. For the wisdom of this world is foolishness with God. For it is written,

"He catches the wise in their craftiness,"
and again,

"The Lord knows the thoughts of the wise,
that they are futile."

So let no one boast about human leaders. For all things are yours, whether Paul or Apollos or Cephas or the world or life or death or the present or the future—all belong to you, and you belong to Christ, and Christ belongs to God.

(1 COR. 3:10–23)

Paul argues, "All things are yours." What things? All truth, all wisdom, all courage, all eternity—all of it is ours in God through Christ. If the Lord is my Shepherd, he will not withhold any good thing. If I lack wisdom, I ask. If I don't know how to pray, if I am weak, if my hope begins to flail, I ask God's Spirit to intercede, step in, come to my aid, to work all these difficulties, ambiguities, and sufferings together for the good purposes of conforming me, and my whole world, ever closer to the perfectly loving, power-filled, enabling, and durable reality of God's abiding presence. No lies, no deceptions, no fear, no denial, no facade, and no counterfeit scheme would ever be willfully chosen by those who have tasted and seen the authentic goodness of God. No one would ever drink from a toilet bowl after tasting the realities of an artesian spring. It's all ours when we are Christ's. We have nothing to fear.

In light of the glorious fact that there will be no deception, falsehood, pretense, or fear in heaven, ask yourself these questions: How much of my life, myself, my character is fearlessly genuine enough to actually endure "coming clean" before the presence of God? How much of the "hay" in my life will be burned? How many beliefs about myself, my purposes, and accomplishments will actually endure the exposing, unveiling nature of heaven? How much of my life is affected by the unforgiveness that fuels a fear of being hurt again by those whose lies have twisted and contorted my ontological security? How much of what I say I believe do I actually believe, or am I afraid to admit what I actually know and don't know? And how much do I fear that what I actually know or believe won't be substantial enough if my pretending is actually found out?

Are we ready to be seen, found, discovered, and met? Because if we haven't seen, discovered, or met God, nor have we inhabited the truth about who we are and the nature of our life, God is not to blame. Again, he is looking for us (2 Chron. 16:9). If we haven't been found, it's often because we are hiding from some key truth, or sometimes we are afraid that what we believe is actually true. Perhaps you have very good reasons to deny and hide, but no reason is enough to stay hidden forever. God will make sure of that. If we do seek him, or desire to be found, he will find us if we really want him to (Deut. 4:29; Jer. 29:13).

We have to wonder, out loud if we must, exactly what in us would need to change, and how that change would occur, either now or after physical death, to such a degree that we could begin to want what we now do not want, or to be, know, and see that which we choose now not to want, or to be, know, see, and experience. That is the issue that literally lies at the heart of our destinies.

What do you believe God is holding back until you die that would make such a meaningful difference to your life now? Jesus doesn't say anything about God keeping the best for last. In fact, the opposite is true. God holds back no good thing from those who want to live in right, true, and blameless ways (Ps. 84:11). God is abundantly generous. To meet God is to discover the nature, the essential truths, about ourselves and about him, and to realize the foundations of the cosmos rest on a blanket of fearless love. Dying isn't required for us to start that discovery. Jesus fixed that. If we desire him, we find him, and fear-eradicating peace is available. But we have to want it. We have to want the truth, and all the circumstances and connections that soon follow in lockstep accordance with the nature of God and his ways. It's a package deal.

God's grace, mercy, and patience will help us develop or build up the level of ontological security and courage Giddens describes that we need in order to handle and thrive under the glory of the fearlessness we will experience engulfing our souls, our characters, our neighbors, and our world. We can't build with the straw of fear and lies; we must build with precious stones of eternal qualities such as peace and truth. We can be-

come comfortable, at ease, even welcoming, of the peacefulness
and joy of the truth in all its forms. Even when it hurts. Faithful
are the wounds of a friend. Profuse are the kisses of an enemy
(Ps. 27:6). Such strength to face the bitterness of deceit and es-
chew the tickling empty words of falsehood comes only from
a knowledge, an experiential understanding, a working realization, that God is as equally loving, powerful, good, and sufficient
in character as he is in action.

This is what the Psalms claim over and over. David asks rhetorically, "If God is my light and deliverer, who or what shall
I fear? If Yahweh is the stronghold of my life, what is there to
be afraid of?" (adapted from Ps. 23:1). David then goes through
a number of difficult and trying realities that he faced, experienced, and suffered through. He did not need to deny these realities, but rather, he stood through the demands and suffering by
dwelling "in the house" of a loving, powerful, and sufficient God
in the midst of his trials. That was enough. Love is the natural
result of experiencing God's sufficiency that wipes away fear. It
is in and from this expression that human existence was meant to
thrive. Life is harsh without God's goodness and power. Without
God, we must somehow manage our fears on our own, which is
an exhausting and futile attempt to "save our souls" from the
insecurities of a world mired in deception. Sooner or later, we
must rid ourselves of this addiction, and reverse the vicious de-
scending spiral of fear and dread.

Coming Clean: The Power of
Confession to Move Past Fear

A few years ago, a friend of mine who has struggled with sex
addiction asked me to attend one of his Sex Addicts Anony-

mous meetings. I'd attended other addiction meetings with other friends in the past, but this meeting, for some reason, was without a doubt one of the most sacred and holy experiences of my life.[6]

In one sense, the meeting was no different than any other twelve-step group I'd attended. There was a fixed schedule, a reading of a set of rules and guidelines and expectations and intentions. As the meeting started, the room was less than half full. Folding chairs were set up against the wall in something of a square circle. The leader called the meeting to order, and with slow and methodical words, he read a simple yet profound statement. It was just a few lines, perhaps no more than a paragraph. Yet the entire room shifted palpably. The statement described the nature of the sexual addiction and the compulsive disorder that elicits the behavior, which had in one way or another devastated everyone in the room.

The words hung in the air as if coming from a judge pronouncing a death sentence. Some of the men lowered their heads, some looked blankly into an empty distance, some grimaced, and others took off their glasses to rub tired and weary eyes. The cancer of their lives was now firmly established as present and accounted for in the room. There was no denial, no justification or rationalizations given. Every addict intimately knew and admitted to the nature and character of the beast that had just been exposed and named in their presence. It was the cause and creator of the many plagues of loneliness, despair, depression, ostracism, rejection, shame, and insanity that at one time or another had and could even again reclaim total dominance over their souls.

Then the fight against the beast began with a fearless courage that was almost unbelievably inspiring and beautiful. The fight was both individual and collective. As the sharing time began, a reminder was given that last names and locating information were forbidden. As with all twelve-step groups, anonymity is essential. No titles, no power, no authority, no ego, no reputations, no accomplishments matter. Just your name. "Hi, I'm . . . , and I'm a sex addict." Then the room replies in unison. "Hi, ..."

This group was significantly diverse in nationality, race, and economic status. There were men who looked like corporate business leaders sitting next to blue-collar laborers with two weeks' growth on their cheeks and still covered in the dust of their trades. Yet there was one common trait that bound them closer than brothers. One of the men sharing said of the room, "We're all perverts, you know?" And nearly every head nodded in agreement.

Their confessions were stark; each one felt to me like a slap in the face. Sometimes the confession came out fast. Just to get it over with. A few were so fast as to be almost incomprehensible. Other confessions came out so soft they were unintelligible. Sex addiction is a blatant, harsh admission in our culture. Alcoholism, drug addiction, gambling—these are all becoming increasingly socially accepted vices. We've had so many well-known and respected drunks, junkies, and risk takers that the wider culture doesn't seem to take notice that much. It's almost become in vogue, a sign you've tasted and experienced a wild side of life and come back even better because of the adventure; at least, that's often the rationale.

But a sex addict is different. We don't really want to talk about the closed-door activities of our lives. And men especially want to define themselves by both their sexual ability and desirability. Sexuality and sexual desire is a core drive instilled in every human being, yet these men must admit that for some reason, something inside of them has twisted and contorted that which the rest of humanity takes largely for granted and actually desires more of in life.

Now I realize the time of confession was a call to battle, the unsheathing of the sword of truth. No beast of addiction can avoid its sting. The sharing time was where the beast was wrestled to the ground and exposed. There was no cross talk, no advice giving, no referencing another person's share specifically. No asking questions. This was not group therapy. Each person who shared had three minutes, timed by a watchman. The battle was engaged one person at a time.

One man shared the circumstances of a recent temptation involving a next-door neighbor's girlfriend. Another man shared that a friend of his had a terminal illness and how he cried at learning his friend had such a short time to live. He revealed how he was both ashamed but grateful that he was able to allow himself to feel his sadness without acting out. Another shared he may lose his marriage due to another addiction issue. Still, he expressed his gratitude for the group because, knowing the amount of grief and sadness he was currently experiencing, if he had not begun to face his sexual addiction together with his group, he couldn't imagine how much worse his life would be.

Another man described how mystified he was by the way some people's spiritual journeys seemed so glamorous when his journey was really about admitting the harsh ugliness of his faults and despair. He struggled to conceive why so many others seemed focused on how "good" they are or how much better they are becoming, when he couldn't even imagine forgetting how very bad his life had become as a result of his addiction.

The last man to share said he was new to this group, only having attended a few times. But the day before he had "acted out" and lost his sobriety. He was devastated. His significant other had found out, and he was afraid he would lose that relationship. After years of sobriety he had let down his defenses. Now he had one day under his belt. He was ashamed, scared, and humiliated.

But he knew, he was sure, that the only thing that did make sense was to go to this meeting and confess it, to name it, to accept the reality of his new reality in public and take the wind out of the beast's sails for at least a little while.

The room knew where he was. They had all slipped. They had all been at day one. They remembered, understood, and acknowledged his reality as their shared experience. The group absorbed his pain and greatly diffused much of its power. All of a sudden, the beast in the middle of the room didn't look so ominous anymore. It got a little smaller and weaker. It looked vulnerable. Like gladiators in the ring, these men faced and overwhelmed the enemy of their souls with courage, honesty, and mutual devotion.

To my surprise when the timekeeper notified the group it was time to wrap up, the leader of the group looked right at me and asked if I would read the closing. He handed me a laminated five-by-seven card with these words printed on it:

This is how recovery has been for us. Each of us has taken steps of courage and leaps of faith. Each of us has contributed, not only to our own recovery, but to the recovery of other suffering sex addicts as well. We have contributed by showing up at meetings and by sharing our experience, strength, and hope. We have listened to our fellow addicts and supported them in their recovery journey. Like the first members of our fellowship, we continue to remain sexually sober by helping our fellow addict stay sober. Our prayer is that every sex addict who seeks recovery will have the opportunity to find it. And keep coming back. Let's close with Prayer.

As I read it aloud to the group, I struggled to finish it. The intensity of the ideas overwhelmed me. I knew that the words

I was speaking carried with them a meaning much deeper than the words on the page. The words were powerful and necessary, essential for someone in that room. I fought hard not to break down, my speech coming in stops and starts, sometimes as a whisper, choked and blocked by emotion.

I knew the words in both the closing and the prayer that were read that evening should be true for our churches, for every Christian disciple of Jesus, for me, and they weren't. I wondered then if I would ever experience something as transformative and honest connected to my experience of the church. But there, in that room of addicts, of sinners, those words were absolutely true every week. Those were the words that created that sacred place. The confident trust and devotion those men put in those words gave them life and power and transformative glory. Those words are sacred, holy, and as I read them, I was clearly aware that I was a man of unclean lips, unworthy of their sanctity. By being forced to speak these words I was humbled by their power over me. Those were the words of life. Jesus was in those words and in that place. And like what the scriptures speak of in Genesis and John, the *Logos* of God creates new universes, new possibilities, new worlds, and new hope with these words.

I realized that those words from the *Logos* are exactly what I believe so many of our churches as a whole are missing. Not just the words I read but all the words that were spoken that night. I believe that until and unless this kind of awareness, honesty, transparency, and abandon is achieved, our congregations have little chance of experiencing the level of transformation we long for and profess is possible.

It is this sort of transparency and confession that is exemplified in Jesus's conversation with the woman at the well, in which he told her of all her sins and gave her the great gift of being seen, warts and all. It is not in the idle controversies of religious ideologies and traditions where worship is to be defined. It is in blatant, courageous recognition and confession of the extreme vitality within genuine states of affairs where the Spirit and truth reside. Thus, confession, the willingness and ability to acknowledge and agree with the authentic and genuine facts regarding the experience of our own lives, both starts and sustains the transformative process. Confession is the antidote to the poison of fear.

After I dropped off my friend and was alone for a moment in the car, I realized the reason I had struggled so hard to read the closing was due to the fact that I came to that meeting as his guest, and I accepted his invitation out of a desire to show him a degree of politeness and support. And as I walked in, I assumed what to me was obvious. I was healthy, and these men, God bless them, were unhealthy. I didn't feel so much above them or superior in any substantive way. I just didn't feel as if I had a lacking in the area where they were addicted.

What I now realize is that in many ways these men are far, far ahead of me in very substantial ways. They are facing the reality of their existence with a ruthless, unyielding understanding that their lives depend on uncovering and remaining fearlessly devoted to the truth. I needed and still need that kind of realization to hit my heart. I need to know, not just profess, but really know, that without living in the realm of God's love and truth, and remaining obediently disciplined and devoted to his ways, I'll die. It may be slow, painful, and even invisible to those around me. It may take a long time. I might be able to hide it for a while and fool a lot of people. But eventually, my soul will shrivel, my heart will implode, and I'll die. The consequence of sin is death. It's really that simple.

That night I realized I too am an addict, and I'm too often afraid to admit it.

Hi, my name is Gary, and I'm addicted to myself.

Today, I think it just as important as I did after I walked out of that meeting that our churches and small groups should consider how to better follow the example of our brothers and sisters who have long led the way to recovery from addiction and substance abuse. Perhaps the places where disciples of Jesus gather can become sanctuaries where our addictions to falsehood and fearfulness are just as freely and authentically confessed as they are in SAA meetings. Perhaps the twelve steps of sobriety can be used to effectively help us admit who we are—and who we aren't—so that we become sober minded about the opportunities for change that litter our lives.

Can you imagine a place of worship where the truth of our lives is as ruthlessly pursued as sobriety? Can we envision a small-group ministry that acts like a network of SAA meetings?

Hi, my name is Adam, and I'm a liar. And it's been four hours since I lied to my wife.

Hi, my name is Eve, and I'm a fraud. No one knows who I really am, not even me.

Hi, my name is Pete, I'm a pastor, and I'm a cynic. I struggle to believe anything I'm supposed to believe.

Hi, I'm Martha. I'm a workaholic because I hide from who I really am and I don't believe I'm a good person.

Many church leaders today are looking for a new ecclesiology, a new way of doing and being the Church. How about considering this ecclesiology? The SAA ecclesiology? It's been hiding in plain sight for decades. Perhaps it is another one of those "ways" of Jesus that has gone largely untried, not because it doesn't work, but because it's hard, and therefore overly critiqued or ignored altogether. Can we imagine a church where we pray the Sex Addicts Anonymous prayer at the end of every service?

I put my hand in yours and together we can do what we could never do alone. No longer is there a sense of hopelessness. No longer must we each depend upon our own unsteady willpower. We are all together now, reaching out our hands for a power and strength greater than ours; and as we join hands, we find love and understanding beyond our wildest dreams. Amen.

Heaven will be a place where we come clean from these not-so-secret secrets. Can we imagine a place where we could come clean now, without fear and shame? Where statements like these and many others more profound and poignant could be safely confessed? And instead of doling out condemnation and rejection, which fuels more lies, fear, and hiding, we offer love and forgiveness, so that hope, mercy, and grace can shine their light on a new way of living, thinking, acting, and being. If you can imagine such a place, you're getting a lot closer to heaven already and farther and farther away from death. The Kingdom of God suffers those who ruthlessly, fearlessly seek after it. And they take it by storm. Bring on the storm.

Hopefully, we are now ready to discuss what living in the truth, with ruthless honesty, will produce in our lives: power. This is the power that hit my heart and mind like a sledgehammer while visiting the twelve-step group with my friend. It is the power of God to change lives; to create new worlds, new realities, new hope; and to overcome all obstacles. This power is expressed in the scriptures as the mighty hand of God, which makes all things possible, which is never too short, never lacking, to achieve what is good, loving, and just (Deut. 26:8; Pss. 89:13, 136:12; 1 Pet. 5:6). This is the identical power God desires to display and share with us. The question we must now face is, What would it take to abide in such potency and potential?

Eight

Power

S ometime later in the evening of that first night in the hospital, a nurse entered the room with a note from someone I did not know. The note conveyed that the person was in the chapel, interceding in prayer on behalf of Dallas and the family. It took me a moment to find him. As we chatted for a while, I discovered he was a relatively new pastor, the son of a longtime Willard-family friend who credited Dallas's works and words with shaping and molding him into a more Christlike disciple. He was concerned, seeking God's will and healing power in the midst of the possibility of Dallas's death, and he just wanted to be close. Like most of us, he didn't know exactly how he could help. So all he could think to do was come to the hospital, watch, and pray. I asked if he would like to see Dallas for a moment. Somehow, I knew this would be a lifelong gift to this young man. He humbly accepted the invitation.

Dallas was asleep when we walked into the room. So he simply touched Dallas's hand, closed his eyes, and prayed. Almost immediately, I sensed something come over him, envelop him, and I watched as he began to weep silently. There was a power, a glory, a substantial weightiness to this moment that we both felt and realized. The best I can describe the event is to suggest it was something of an otherworldly epiphany, a short opening of a window into the eternal realm that penetrated me to the core of my being with the knowledge of God's immanent presence. With it came a supernatural force that blanketed the young pastor and engulfed the room with a semivisible, nonmaterial clarity that opened up around us and seemed to brighten the room slightly as it spread over the area around Dallas's bed. The significance, or substance, of this moment pressed in on both of us. It took my breath away. The intensity was such that he only stayed in prayer for a short time before he looked over to me, whispered his thanks, and turned to leave. And with him the moment slowly dispersed until all was quiet and still again.

The moment reminded me of that prayer Dallas prayed over his students that first day of his seminar: "I pray that you would have a rich life of joy and power, abundant in supernatural results, with a constant, clear vision of never-ending life in God's world before you, and the everlasting significance of your work day by day. A radiant life and a radiant death."

As I've thought back on that moment at Dallas's bedside, I've realized that eternal living, evidenced by supernatural results, is resourced or empowered by an altogether different energy source than what we have become used to. Working our will through the power of our flesh (Gal. 4:29) or as demonstrated by the principalities and powers using worldly powers around us (2 Cor. 10:2–5; Eph. 6:12) is an altogether different prospect than working through the power of the Spirit of God. Today, we have become almost blindingly dependent and singularly focused on physical, material sources of power and therefore almost incompetent to wield, much less understand, the nature of spiritual power.

The Wide Range of Power

This is not a new problem. It's as age-old as Abraham and Sarah. Where and how we achieve the power we need to accomplish what we can imagine lies at the heart of many of our historical conflicts between individuals, families, villages, states, and nations. The conundrum of power is also one that each individual faces early in life. As children, we want to pick something up, but it's too heavy. Or we can't open a door, or climb up onto the counter to get the cookies that can be seen but remain just beyond our reach. If we don't have the power, then we don't have the potential. Whether the issue is as simple as reaching for a cookie jar or as complicated as providing electricity for a city that flaunts its use of power as lavishly as the Las Vegas strip, power is an enduring conundrum. Especially after the Industrial Revolution and into the electronic and now digital age, the need to develop and maintain cheap, efficient, and "clean" sources of energy is a primary focus for those who are charged with maintaining and developing our communities.

Of course, it is easy to stay at the macro level of these discussions. We can and should engage in dialogue about how to best develop our abilities to use clean, renewable sources of energy. We can discuss how a nation's energy policy (think power policy) affects national-security concerns. We have witnessed an unlimited number of discussions about the conflicts in the Middle East and their ties to oil, one of our major sources of energy (power). Yet oil, water, coal, natural gas, wind, and solar are not the only providers of power that have caused political conflicts. We forget that slavery was, and still is, primarily an issue related to a cheap, consistent labor force. The human body carries a tremendous amount of power inside its physical structure. It doesn't have as much power as a horse or mule, but as the Egyptians discovered, with enough slaves, one could eventually duplicate the power output of an elephant or team of horses. The pyramids remain a testament to this ominous fact.

Another demonstration of power that remains today as it has throughout the ages is military power. The accumulation of manpower in armies has changed the face of the world several times over and could do so again. Perhaps the greatest accumulation of power today is stockpiled in nuclear weaponry, which exists to maintain the prevalence of certain ideas regarding how to best live life to the fullest. Any nation-state's way of life is opposed by and oppositional to whomever that nation has its missiles pointed at, and vice versa. The idea of scaring one's opposition into submission is older than the story of David and Goliath, the logic having far preceded even that event. Naturally, therefore, other nations seek to attain the same fear-inducing power. To not possess the threat of overpowering one's enemies, real or perceived, is to not avail oneself of a seat at the geopolitical poker table.

The energy needs required to build empires are not the end of the issues related to power. Power is also intrinsically connected to security, money, and even sex. The power to protect oneself and one's property and loved ones is often trotted out as a major rationale for gun ownership. Of course, the instrumental power of a gun, for instance, contains equal potential for abuse and destruction as well as for justice or protection.

The earliest known reference to the saying, "Money is power" is given to Russell H. Conwell, the founder and president of Temple University, in his stump speech later published as *Acres of Diamonds*.[1] The complete quote is, "Money is power, and you ought to be reasonably ambitious to have it." The key to such a proposition is found in how one will define and understand the word *reasonably*.

Sex, too, is power filled. Sex is a multifaceted subject with various and complex influences. Such multiplicity is, in part, the crux of the power sex holds over our lives. Sex is not a simple matter, primarily because our cultural conversations related to sex are rarely about the act of sex itself. The ideas and images connected to sex and sexuality, which in turn have an ability to influence the mind and direct the will, are where sex and sexism tend to exude their greatest influence.[2] Some have suggested, perhaps erroneously, that famous narcissist Oscar Wilde once quipped, "Everything in the world is about sex, except sex. Sex is about power."[3] Again, one wonders what kind of power and what kind of lens are being used in such a statement to view "everything in the world." Yet there seems to be a ring of truth inside the statement. Sex is often used in our culture to leverage ulterior motives. Sex is offered up as bait to sell chainsaws as routinely as it is used to advertise "enhancement" products and services. The thirst of our oversexed society is only matched by our hunger for power. They go hand in hand.

The Will to Power

Over the years Dallas and I spent a good deal of time talking through some of the key ideas offered by nineteenth-century philosopher Friedrich Nietzsche. Dallas believed Nietzsche had become the uncrowned prince of our contemporary universities, and as a result, in due course, his influence would spread like an unobstructed cancer throughout Western societies. There were many concerns Dallas held regarding Nietzsche's ideas, but one of the key issues he had was with what Nietzsche termed the "Will to Power."[4] In simple terms, Dallas understood Nietzsche's arguments surrounding the concept of "Will to Power" as something that was even baser, more deeply ingrained, in the life force of all creation than the evolutionary drive for animal survival. Dallas believed Nietzsche was offering an alternative motive that lay behind Charles Darwin's description of human, animal, and plant evolution. Nietzsche argued it wasn't survival of the species that animals in the wild fought and struggled against predators and the elements to protect. Rather, animals, including humans, are willing to die in order to pursue their unending desire to dominate and express their power. Nietzsche writes,

> Here one must think profoundly to the very bases and resist all sentimental weakness: life itself is essentially appropriation, injury, conquest of the strange and weak, suppression, severity, obtrusion of its own forms, incorporations, and at the least, putting it mildest, exploitation. But why should one forever use precisely these words on which for ages a disparaging purpose has been stamped? Even the [society] within which, as was previously supposed, the individuals treat each other as equal—it takes place in every healthy aristocracy—must itself, if it be a living and not a dying organization, do all that towards other bodies, which the individuals within it refrain from doing to each other; it will have to be the incarnated Will to Power, it will endeavor to grow, to gain ground, attract to itself and acquire ascendancy not owing to any morality or immorality, but because it lives, and because life is precisely Will to Power. . . . "Exploitation" does not belong to a depraved, or imperfect and primitive society. It belongs to the nature of the living being as a primary organic function, it is a consequence of the intrinsic Will to Power, which is precisely the Will to Life—granting that as a theory this is a novelty—as a reality it is the fundamental fact of all history let us be so far honest towards ourselves![5]

Although the language is a bit cumbersome, the point is explicit. Exploitation is no longer to be thought the act of the "depraved," but as a necessary—and beneficial, it would seem—function of living. "Will to Power" is will to life, and for Nietzsche, they are inseparable.

Our societies are not balanced in terms of their power. When power becomes too imbalanced, then injustice often results. Yet there is no guarantee that transfers of power from the "strong" to the "weak" will fix our power problems. We watch this routinely in our political process. Every few years, there is a wholesale change in political power, and half the people, if not more, are dissatisfied with the result.

Another issue we have to come to a sobering realization about is how much power lies at the heart of crime, especially violent crime. Today, the seemingly rampant increase in, or perhaps only our awareness of, long-standing, domestic abuse, is one of the most chilling and destructive realities in contemporary society. Much of it can be directly tied in some form or another to an issue related to power. Whether we are seeking money, possessions, drugs, or even attention and respect, the innate desire and pursuit of power is one of humanity's deepest longings. In great measure, the sin of the garden is tied to a search for power and control over one's own life. In short order, we see Cain's willingness to seek power and satisfaction by any means necessary. Thus, it should come as no surprise that an unreserved desire for power lies at the root of some of our most deadly and traumatic human catastrophes. War, genocide, rape, holocaust, infanticide, terrorism, racism, sexism, and many other similar atrocities, some of which grow in scope to the level of world conflict while others remain closeted in the sanctity of a child's bedroom, still find their ignominious beginnings in the move to grab, maintain, or extend some form or base of illegitimate power.

We have, all of us, a power problem, and I've only touched on a few of the different forms power problems can take. Still, one of the common factors found in many of our issues with power may stem from the reality that we may have evolved to the point where our technologically advanced societies simply assume that the power to do what we want to do is an inalienable right, both individually and politically. Recently I was teaching in a classroom when the power was interrupted, and we lost the use of the digital projector for my PowerPoint slides. My students immediately assumed our class would need to be canceled. It didn't occur to anyone, including me, that we could simply walk outside, sit together in the shade of the campus courtyard, and continue our discussions. Which is exactly what someone eventually suggested, and we did just that. It ended up being a wonderful afternoon. But I think our initial, knee-jerk reaction revealed something of an unconscious dependence on material/physical power to accomplish everything we desire to achieve in our lives. We're losing our imagination of how things can be accomplished in our world and in our lives. Heaven has an altogether different power plant and distribution system, and we would greatly benefit from learning how to plug into its grid as soon as possible.

In such a power-driven world, can we imagine what it would be like not to fight for power, position, or privilege? Can we imagine a place or an existence where there is never a shortage of anything good, especially power? Where power is as easy to order, direct, and distribute as speaking words? No need for power lines, power storage, power generators, power distributors, power ties, power games, power plays, power words, power tools, brainpower, war power, or superpowers? All of these terms relate in some form to the manipulation or use of certain kinds of power in a limited, or measurable, sense. In contrast, we face an eternal future that is unlimited in its potential to empower human achievement to maintain and further the good. At times an academic or theoretical discussion about power can lead us away from the primary power problems in which we engage in our own lives. Dallas helped me to see that it is in the crevasses and shadows of the human heart and mind where the real power plays are developed, strategies hatched, and insecurities fed.

Divine Power

Unlike the power systems inherent within the kingdoms of earth, there is something indescribably transcendent and mighty that happens when weakness is used as the means through which God's glorious truth and love are expressed. This was never more poignant and profound than when God's power was demonstrated through the crucifixion and resurrection. Similarly, *agape*'s unmistakable and overwhelming awe-inspiring potency is routinely put on display through innumerable circumstances and events that highlight our human frailty. The surgeon-storyteller Richard Selzer describes a moment after a surgery when he visits a young married couple to deliver the news of her prognosis.[6]

I stand by the bed where a young woman lies, her face postoperative, her mouth twisted in palsy, clownish. A tiny twig of the facial nerve, the one to the muscles of the mouth, has been severed. She will be thus from now on. The surgeon had followed with religious fervor the curve of her flesh; I promise you that. Nevertheless, to remove the tumor in her cheek, I had to cut that little nerve. Her young husband is in the room. He stands on the opposite side of the bed, and together they seem to dwell in the evening lamplight, isolated from me. Who are they, I ask my-

self, he and this wry-mouth that I have made, who gaze at and touch each other so generously, greedily? The young woman speaks. "Will my mouth always be like this?" she asks. "Yes," I say, "it will. It is because the nerve was cut." She nods, and is silent. But the young man smiles. "I like it," he says. "It is kind of cute." All at once, I know who he is. I understand, and I lower my gaze. One is not bold in an encounter with a god. Unmindful, he bends to kiss her crooked mouth, and I, so close I can see how he twists his own lips to accommodate to hers, to show her that their kiss still works. Isn't that what the Christian God is about? God was in Christ, reaching out to us in love, accommodating himself to our condition, to save us.[7]

This event perfectly reveals the transcendent nature of divine power inside *agape* love. *Agape* is a substance, with a power that can and does touch and arrange the heart and soul at a level, and in a manner, that will endure for all eternity. When we discover such power and its effects, like Selzer, we simply stand in awe. None can fathom the limitlessness of such benevolence, nor how such beauty is created, then expertly directed, to so completely dismiss the sorrows from the ashes of our lives. This is the power that creates cathedral pines out of sheer joy, galaxies with only gleeful thought, hummingbirds to simply slack the human jaw, and sunsets that clear the mind with a lightning bolt of wonder.

Then there is the indefatigable depth of love shared between human beings, like that of the husband and wife Selzer described, a parent and a child, or two devoted, lifelong friends. These are the canvases where God manifests *agape*'s most magnificent powers. God shares this power of love with us because he loves us and wants us to experience the wonder and majesty the Trinity experiences so intimately and completely. And the

Trinity uses this power to manifest their love and strength every moment of every day.

Such power was on display during some of the events surrounding the creation and implementation of the Truth and Reconciliation Commission in South Africa, which sought reparation and reconciliation after the demise of apartheid. Similar testimonies of hope rising even amidst paralyzing despair are found in the aftermath of the terrible Rwandan genocide. Laura Waters Hinson's documentary *As We Forgive* tracks the power of forgiveness to guide a nation through the wreckage of complete moral failures at every institutional, religious, governmental, and social level.[8] What could not be accomplished by the might of governments or armies can and is being accomplished by the power of love, grace, mercy, forgiveness, truth, and hope. Gregory of Nyssa mused that "God's transcendent power is not so much displayed in the vastness of the heavens, or the luster of the stars, or the orderly arrangement of the universe or his perpetual oversight of it, as in his condescension to our weak nature."[9] Amen to that. *Emmanuel,* God is with us and for us.

Although I don't want to diminish the accessibility we have to an inextinguishable abundance of power available in the Kingdom of God, I am not suggesting, nor did Dallas believe, that human beings will be omnipotent. He did believe, however, that human beings were created and destined, in partnership with Christ, to achieve their full potential, whatever that potential may be, to wield the power of God for his glory to a degree that has, thus far, not come close to being imagined, much less utilized. The reasons for our current levels of impotency are simple. Just like we can't handle the truth, neither can we handle the power available to us as coheirs sitting at the right hand of the Father with Christ. Scripture clearly describes this position as a power-sharing opportunity, albeit not one of equality (Eph. 2:6;

Col. 3:1–4). For all authority, even that which is delegated or shared, ultimately belongs to Christ.

Hence, Dallas sensed that honesty, competency, and trust were often, but not always, mutually reinforcing prerequisites for divine empowerment in eternal living. We don't allow ten-year-olds to drive semi trucks, nor should we place a chainsaw in the hands of a four-year-old, not because we are jealous or stingy, but because we are wise and loving. The power available in a chainsaw and a tractor trailer has the ability to do great good or harm, based upon the competency and character of the individual wielding, directing, managing, or stewarding such life-altering power.

So, we must ask ourselves, Can I be trusted with divine power? If you were given the power to turn water into wine, multiply bread and fish for the multitudes, or heal the sick, could you be trusted to competently steward such power responsibly? Do you want such a responsibility? I suggest that the answer to these questions is almost always "no." Most of us do not manifest such power, not because it is not available, nor because God has decided to pull back the reins on power for a while, nor because, as a result of the creation of the scriptures, we have entered into some sort of age void of miracles. Rather, we don't have the power we seek because we can't handle it or because of the tragic consequences it would bring to our lives and others— or both. Therefore, God, in his mercy and wisdom, tends to lock up the heavy equipment and is mindful of the keys to the power of the Kingdom for our protection.

The result, for most of us, is a sense of futility in our work. We can see or imagine what we want to do, what we think or believe is good and beneficial for us and others, but we seldom can get it all done, which causes many of us to feel impotent in our lives. Such powerlessness can lead to feelings of depression and hostility. We can become so desperate, even reckless, and sometimes violent in seeking any means possible to attain the power we think we need to survive. Power is only the issue at the surface. The deeper issue is *how* power is used—for what purposes and to what effect—both of which relate directly back to the development of a moral character devoted to *agape*.

Partnering with God's Power in Our Work

I'm suggesting that our lack of potency is not a problem of religious doctrine or tradition, though this may play a part. More importantly, we lack a vision for how to fill our day-to-day actions and motives with the means by which we can succeed in partnering with God's empowering love to accomplish the good and beautiful creative ends he desires. Such is the kind of meaningful work each of us hopes to find in our vocational calling or career. To deny or ignore this simple divine destiny is to dash our hopes of a meaningful existence on the rocks of futility. Our hearts long to devote our lives and our work to matters of consequence. To lose the promise of such a life is to unwittingly court trouble, sorrow, confusion, and greater levels of vanity.

Human labor and work have been given a bad name. To be clear, work is not a result of the fall of humanity and the curse that followed. God is seen at work in the opening pages of scripture. The result of sin is not that humanity was forced into some kind of labor camp, but that we become restricted from free access to God's unlimited sources of wisdom and power. The scriptures' description of Adam's living by the sweat of his brow (Gen. 3:19) was a result or consequence of choosing independence from God. God could no longer trust humanity to do good, and seek *agape*, with the power available to them.

Thus, a rationing of power was initiated as an act of mercy. Nor could God allow free access to the unlimited physical sustenance gained from the Tree of Life. Again, an act of mercy.

Ever since, humanity has struggled to access the power we need to do our work of managing (stewarding) our world. It was never meant to be like this. The power source we need to live our lives as we were intended to live them has been removed from free access out of love and protection. God has limited our ability to achieve our potential, our potency, outside of living in a dependent, submissive relationship with him. The human will, in its self-centered, myopic state, simply can't be trusted or let loose with the power of God onto the universe. At least not yet.

None of these factors should lead us to believe our work is a curse. If we do not work, or do no good through our work, much of our life is wasted. The divine work ascribed and destined for humanity comes in a multitude of forms and includes much more than earning a paycheck. Our work includes activities such as having and raising children, the development of good human relationships, artistic creativity, and volunteering time to charitable or nonprofit organizations. Work is not specifically limited to earning a living. It could include a salary of some sort, but for many of us, for instance the disabled, the retired, the homemaker, the philanthropist, and others, there is no opportunity to "earn a living" from the good work they engage. For others, such as artists, authors, and actors, to name only a few, there is often a need to attain a job, such as waiting tables or various odd jobs, that allows them to trade their labor for a wage. Yet these jobs are often not directly connected to what we understand as our life's work.

I've held many such jobs over the years, where I learned a tremendous amount about myself and developed my character, which allowed me to be salt and light in the workforce while also tasting and seeing what the "real" world is like. And I also was able to earn a living while I grew and matured. But these jobs did not allow for me to develop the unique gifts of writing, thinking, and teaching about Christian theology that I utilize in my work now.

The scriptures teach that in all that we do, in word or deed, we should do it all for the sake of the Kingdom of God and to bring glory to Christ (Col. 3:17). Even still, our job and work can be, but are not necessarily, connected. We usually hope they are, but not everyone is able to find such opportunity. Dallas knew that it's a sad truth that the expectation that our job and the ministry of our work should be conjoined is a needless burden many of us carry, often causing undue levels of frustration and feelings of enduring meaninglessness in our lives. Instead, Dallas taught that our jobs often differ from the work that God calls us to accomplish, and it is perfectly appropriate that our life's work and ministry may never produce a paycheck while remaining fully purposeful and worthy of our devotion. Yet we also need to do all we can to be productive members of our world, contributing and adding value, and caring for others and ourselves to the fullness of our potential.

Although our work in eternity may drastically change in terms of which specific tasks we may engage in, the essence of work and its objectives will not radically change in heaven. Work now and into eternity remains a primary means of defining and understanding human purposes in God's universe.

As a professor teaching in doctoral programs for ministers, I have been privileged to work with veteran pastors and priests, men and women deeply devoted to the work of God in their churches, with decades of ministerial experience. Yet roughly half of these student ministers I meet complain of experiencing significant levels of exhaustion, overexertion, and compassion fatigue in their vocations. Dallas also taught in a ministerial doctoral program, and I watched him counsel many pastors whose exhaustion stemmed mostly from a lack of confidence in their ability to achieve their ministry goals. Dallas would spend a great deal of time and attention helping ministers come to trust God's empowering action with them, utilizing the strong arm of God's "muscle" in concert with their participation and giftedness, to do what they could not do relying on their own efforts (Pss. 118:16; 89:13). He often described this partnership as one that "tapped into" the power and grace of God, letting it flow through them to others.

To illustrate, Dallas often told the story of a period early in his ministry when God spoke to him just as he was about to preach before a large crowd. As he rose to stand before the podium, Dallas heard God say, "Remember, it's what I do with the Word between your lips and their hearts that matters." Dallas then went on to describe the great joy and sense of relief he experienced upon realizing that God alone was accountable to produce the result, and he was only responsible for his preparation. It is God's power, in concert with our efforts and energies, that enables us to accomplish a much greater purpose and outcome than we could achieve otherwise. This is grace.

Humanity was designed to always remain in a power-sharing, power-enabling, results-achieving ambassadorial relationship with God and others. This is a tremendously crucial lesson for each of us to learn, in every vocation and career we engage. If we do not trust God's power to act with us, or if we have never experienced such empowerment, or if we cannot be trusted to become empowered, then we are left to pursue what we alone can manufacture, often with little overarching, eternal significance. Yet, once we can turn loose the results and recognize we are always inadequate but that our inadequacy is not the issue, we can begin to lay down the burden of seeking power. Then the satisfaction we experience in Christ spills over into everything we do.

Henri Nouwen made the point that the main obstacle to love for God is service for God.[10] Service must come out of God's power and love, flowing through us into the lives of others. The minister, banker, parent, carpenter, or teacher who does not engage work from that primary source and sufficiency will eventually teeter close to the dangerous grounds of futility, simply because earning God's love and approval is impossible. For God has always loved and will always love us, and he desires to empower us for meaningful purposes. This is a part of the very essence and character of God's person.

Dallas was keen to state in more than one way that, in his experience, those who fall prey to significant moral failures, usually dealing with the "power tools" of sex and money, are typically those who have failed to live deeply satisfied lives from the sustaining energy that comes from Christ. Temptations arise when we become increasingly dissatisfied and discontent with our impotency to make things happen, despite all our sacrifices and concerted efforts, which we have come to believe are essential to giving us meaning and purpose. When our expenditures produce seemingly little return, such futility fuels temptations, which suggests that a power imbalance lies at the heart of our unfavorable and dissatisfying condition. All of this builds into a complete lack of trust in the powerful goodness of God. Thus, Dallas believed the most efficient guarantee against moral failure is to be at peace and satisfied with the sustaining love and power of God so that the power available to do evil, or wrongdoing, isn't even interesting.

What Power Looks Like in the Kingdom of God

The challenge for most of us is not to find the means of glorifying God in the big tasks of our work, but in the smallest and seemingly most insignificant of tasks. We can and must develop the ability to do everything well to the glory of God, giving thanks by accepting what is put into our lives as his work materials by which we fulfill our callings both on earth and in eternity. Nothing is lost of the good that we do. Ever. Good is stored up in our own selves and in the lives of others, all of which lasts for eternity.

Jesus's parable of the minas in Luke 19:11–16 is, in part, an attempt to prepare disciples for wielding God's power in the age to come. During our lives on earth we are given gifts with which we are to invest in those things that last for eternity. Such things are goodness, peace, joy, love, grace, justice, and the like. When we learn to invest these things and manage our lives well, Jesus, as the master, is able to employ more responsibility, more opportunity. As a result, more blessing flows through our lives— not out of a privileged status—but as a consequence of combining our willful efforts and intentions with God's empowering ability. Those who responsibly stewarded the gift of ten minas were in turn given not more material wealth (minas), but cities to manage as the return on their investment.[11] Dallas would often ask his students, "Can you imagine being given authority to manage a city? Ten cities? Would that be a good thing or not for you and those living in that city?" The room would often fall silent. Then he would ask a follow-up question, "Are our cities better managed by Christians than non-Christians?" No one wanted to answer. To which he would reply, "I suspect some are, and some aren't."

All of this leads us back to the issue of power. Can we be trusted with the power and authority that is to come to those who are ready, willing, and thus enabled to put into effect God's loving will and way in the world? One of the more stunning conversations I had with Dallas was while we were on a walk together one afternoon. It wasn't long after the Tohoku tsunami hit the nuclear power plant, and we talked of the tragedy and the bravery of those who were attempting to avoid a potentially global catastrophe by exposing themselves to deadly levels of radiation poisoning. I turned to him and said, "It's too bad Jesus wasn't there to calm the waters before the wave hit." It was something of a throwaway comment, but it got us talking about whether or not anyone today could, in fact, be trusted with such supernatural powers. We then began to try to imagine what life would be like today for a character such as Moses or Elijah if they lived in our contemporary world, while wielding such extraordinary power for good.

What would your life or mine be like if word got out that we walked out into the Pacific Ocean and, with news helicopters hovering overhead, held up our arms and with a prayer of command, harmlessly dissipated a tsunami filled with untold megatons of energized sea water roaring toward the coastline? We might be thought a god, the son or daughter of a god, perhaps worthy of worship likened to what we see offered to contemporary pop icons or television personalities. We might want to consider the ways celebrity tempts the hearts and minds of so many in our culture and how easily we deify those who seem to speak to our deepest longings and fears. Then we might look at how our innate need to worship *something* can turn idolatrously inward to self-indulgence. Is there anyone today who could survive such overt displays of divine power? Perhaps, Dallas mused, such people, if they exist at all, are kept secret and hidden for our own good and theirs. Or perhaps, he wondered, there simply aren't those alive today of the measure and character of a Moses, Elijah, and Paul whom God can entrust with such power. As that thought crossed his mind, he said. "And the whole earth groans waiting for the sons and daughters of God to be revealed" (adapted from Rom. 8:19–22). Yes, we all groan from our impotence. In light of God's loving omnipotence, we surely have a long way to progress. Heaven is a place where power is readily accessible. Heaven is a place where power flows and where God's will is done, and done well.

Using God's Power in Our Lives

Perhaps the longest and most meaningful conversation Dallas and I ever had was during one visit where we were working together on my Ph.D. dissertation. We met alone early one morning at his USC office and spent the entire day together. During those long hours we very nearly touched on every major subject in his life's work. As evening approached, we moved to a local restaurant for an early dinner, where we continued our discussion on his philosophical work. It was incredibly heady conversation, but Dallas had a wonderful way of breaking things down into bite-size pieces for me. During our discussion, he jogged my memory of something he had written about in an article several years prior. Although I couldn't quite remember the exact title, I fortunately had brought my backpack with me, and I reached down to pull out a large accordion-box file that had a bibliography of every publication, article, interview, book chapter, and published lecture I could find. The list was several pages long. When I finally found the title and recited the name of the article in question, I looked up and saw a very surprised look on Dallas's face. He was surprised, shocked almost, and perhaps a little embarrassed.

"Is that what I think it is?" he asked shyly.

"Well . . . I think so. It's a list of all your work . . . I think it's all your work. It's all I've been able to find so far."

"Would you mind if I took a quick look at it?" he asked sheepishly.

At first, I assumed that he wanted to check to see what I had missed, and whether or not my research was as complete and thorough as it should have been. But it didn't take long for me to realize that my worries were silly. As he perused the pages, there was a softness in his eyes and expression. I realized having the entirety of his corpus laid out before him had become something of a "This Is Your Life" moment. I asked if he had never before seen his list of publications, and he said, "No. Not really. Not like this."

I was dumbstruck as well. I couldn't imagine accumulating such a repertoire of scholarship and not knowing its length and breadth. The list of titles acted as something of a scrapbook of fond memories and ideas long since forgotten, now suddenly brought back to life. And with them all the joy and thankfulness that came with their initial writing and discovery was flooding his heart once again. But the list was more than that. The list represented solid evidence of what God and Dallas had done together over the length of his career and ministry. The list was evidence of the length and breadth of God's power and grace in his life.

As I sat there with him, tears of thankfulness slowly running down his face, I remembered Dallas's description of divine grace. Arguably one of his most brilliant insights was his awareness of evangelical Christianity's need to redefine grace. Grace is often misunderstood as a synonym for forgiveness and mercy. Not for Dallas. Instead, grace encompasses God's ability to give us the means to do what we could otherwise never do on our own. Nowhere does he state this better or more memorably than in a talk he gave that is replicated in *The Great Omission*:

May I just give you this word? Grace is not opposed to effort, it is opposed to earning. Earning is an attitude. Effort is an action. Grace, you know, does not just have to do with forgiveness of sins alone. Many people don't *know this, and that is one major result of the cutting down of the gospel to a theory of justification, which has happened in our time. I have heard leading evangelical spokespeople say that grace has only to do with guilt. Many people today understand justification as the only essential result of the gospel, and the gospel they preach is—and you will hear this said over and over by the leading presenters of evangelical faith—that your sins can be forgiven. That's it!*

In contrast, I make bold to say, the gospel of the entire New Testament is that you can have new life now in the Kingdom of God if you will trust Jesus Christ. Not just something he did, or something he said, but trust the whole person of Christ in everything he touches—which is everything. "There is one God; there is also one mediator between God and humankind, Christ Jesus, himself human" (1 Timothy 2:5). If you would really like to be into consuming grace, just lead a holy life. The true saint burns grace like a 747 burns fuel on takeoff. Become the kind of person who routinely does what Jesus did and said. You will consume much more grace by leading a holy life than you will by sinning, because every holy act you do will have to be upheld by the grace of God. And that upholding is totally the unmerited favor of God in action.[12]

That evening Dallas was holding a piece of paper in his hands that was undeniable proof of the power of God's grace in his life to accomplish what Dallas could never have done on his own, but what they had decidedly been able to accomplish together.

"That's quite something," he said finally. "It is hard to believe what God has accomplished through me. Especially me. This poor old Missouri boy. It's quite something." Yes, God will be with us, even us, especially us, just as he was with Mary and Peter and James and Moses and Ruth and David, empowering us, as we go about Kingdom work.

This is what we often pray happens in our lives and in our world—that God's will is done in our lives as it is done in heaven (Matt. 6:10). But stop a moment and ask yourself if this is actually true. Do you really desire the power required to make that a reality? Do you actually want the ability and the responsibility that necessarily accompanies, such influence? Typically, most of us don't want it, and therefore, we don't have it. Others who do want such power are often those least capable of responsibly stewarding it for the good. Discipleship to Christ is the only means through which we can learn how to want what is best and how to effectively tap into the power sources of God in effective and beneficial ways to accomplish what we want, which is precisely what God wants. *Agape* is the result.

The ethos of heaven will be a power-sharing existence where human potential is fully explored, achieved, and on display for all to see, while we remain in awe of God's glorious abilities and creative genius. In such demonstrations of mutually collaborative efforts, the awesome displays of the aurora borealis or the Eagle Nebula or the flight of a hummingbird will pale in comparison to God's handiwork in and through the hearts of those who are fully devoted and abiding in his power.

The Powerful Knowledge of God

Part of what keeps us impotent regarding the power of God is simply our lack of interest and investigation, and therefore our ignorance, of the knowledge of God and his ways. The power of God is directly tied to the knowledge of God. The knowledge of God is not limited to knowing who God is or knowing God exists. That is certainly a very good start, but the knowledge of God includes knowing what God knows or gaining God's knowledge, and learning how God works, and why, through attaining God's wisdom.

I've recently seen a rather stunning documentary movie entitled *Tim's Vermeer*.[13] It demonstrates the power of devotion, care, curiosity, and excellence in the pursuit of knowledge that we humans have at our disposal, which when harnessed, can accomplish what seems absolutely impossible.

The documentary follows Tim Jenison in his eight-year quest to understand, solve, and then duplicate the techniques first revealed in the masterpieces of seventeenth-century Dutch artist Johannes Vermeer. The interesting part of this story is that before Jenison started this project, he had never painted anything. He was not an artist. Instead, he was an inventor, the founder of a technology company, NewTek, and later a leader in developing some highly successful computer products. The documentary tracks Jenison's attempts to discover what seventeenth-century techniques Vermeer may have used that separated him from all other artists of his time.

For centuries, Vermeer has been widely recognized by scholars and critics alike for displaying a unique, magical, lifelike quality in his work that has remained far ahead of his peers. His skills were so sophisticated and extraordinarily detailed that artists' works developed long after Vermeer's death seemed opaque in comparison. Jenison thought he knew how Vermeer was able to convey such detail in his works but needed to test this theory. So, through many trials and errors, and building on his knowledge of video imagery, Jenison began to play with possible innovative tools that Vermeer could have used to produce his vivid portraits.

The movie ends with Jenison actually producing a replica of a Vermeer, using the same means, paints, canvases, brushes, and optical tools he believed Vermeer used on the originals. What he proved was that Vermeer's brilliance may have been found in his technological innovation, not necessarily in his skill with a brush. What *Tim's Vermeer* helped me to better grasp is the degree of power that knowledge itself carries to produce goodness and beauty, and to what lengths Jenison was willing to go to attain what he believed was the invaluable nature of the knowledge he sought.

There has been a long and tragic historic connection with American evangelical religion and anti-intellectualism or a lack of appreciation of intellectual development in pursuing the knowledge of God.[14] There are many causes for the growth and proliferation of anti-intellectualism, and we can only touch on a few here. Simply put, at its worst, anti-intellectualism assumes or allows for the lazy hope that God will impute knowledge and erase ignorance when needed despite any effort, or lack thereof, to attain or even value such knowledge. Often such a presumption stems from some unfortunate misinterpretations of Jesus's teaching in the Gospels regarding not worrying about how one might respond to the accusations of opponents or persecutors (Luke 12:11; Matt. 10:19; Mark 13:11).

Secondly, resistance to intellectual life has also been based on the inaccurate assumption that the early disciples, and even Jesus himself, were unlearned, uneducated, and thus unintelligent men. Therefore, valuing or pursuing formal education is considered something unnecessary or worldly, perhaps even unholy, and therefore, potentially detrimental to faithful Christian life. In other circles, particularly more charismatic or Pentecostal-leaning groups, there has been a lingering assumption that the best course of action regarding spiritual matters is to empty the mind or avoid reason in order to become better sensitized to the leading of the heart in the direction of the Holy Spirit.

Such ideas, while not entirely without some helpful insight, in application, tend to assume that the Spirit of God works only or primarily through emotions and feelings, and therefore pits emotion against reason as the preferred method for guidance and direction. As a result, reason and emotion become opponents rather than partners. Of course, the same could be said of those who attempt to divorce all emotion and feeling from their lives in order to rely strictly on a reasoned or "objective" approach to life and living. The point is we are integrated beings, with both emotional and intellectual capacities and resources, both of which God has used and does use as effective means to achieve wonderful ends.

Jenison's story works well as a parable for those of us who seek to emulate the character of Christ. The power to do the good demonstrated in Jesus's life and work is gained through seeking both the knowledge of God's person while also pursuing God's knowledge of our world and individual circumstances. Jenison becomes a perfect parallel to Jesus's parable of the man who discovers a precious pearl in a field and sells all he has to attain what he knows is worth the sacrifice (Matt. 13:45–46). Jenison wanted to paint like Vermeer, and he devoted himself to attaining the knowledge required to do just that. If we, like Jenison and the man in Jesus's parable, were willing to go to whatever length is required to seek with our whole heart (Jer. 29:13) and to devote our lives, our whole lives, heart, soul, mind, and strength (Luke 10:27) to live in the power and majesty of Christ's knowledge, wisdom, character, and love, then I argue we could and would achieve our hearts' desires.

Do you and I want to live like Jesus, to know what he knows, to attain his wisdom and discernment about life and living? Are we willing to do what is required to fulfill that desire? Jesus assures us he will be with us in this endeavor, that if we lack wisdom in any area of life, we are to ask him for what we lack, and he will meet us where we are at, empower us, guide us, and shine his wisdom and knowledge on our efforts to magnify his name (James 1:5). The choice is ours.

We see glimpses of this symbiotic relationship between knowledge, devotion, discipline, and empowerment in the lives of Moses, Elijah, Esther, Naomi, Mary, Paul, and many others. Yet the eye has yet to see, and the ear hear, and the mind of a human being imagine, what God has prepared for those who love him (1 Cor. 2:9). But Paul goes on to write, in the very next verse, "These things God has revealed to us through the Spirit" (2:10). Everything is possible that is possible with God. We have not because we ask not. And we don't ask often because we can't handle what it is we know we need. Therefore, too often we do not receive what we seek after because God will not give us a snake if a fish is really best for us (Luke 11:11). Both our hearts and minds have to be in sync with God's will. When they are, we are able to ask whatever it is we desire, and it will be done for us. Many of our prayers go unanswered simply because we don't understand the complexity of what we ask for. Therefore, God has to be trusted to do for us what we should intend to ask but don't. This is so helpful in Jesus's statement, "Not my will, but yours" (Luke 22:42). His way is to defer power and submit his will to the ultimate author of good.

Can we imagine that kind of life? Do we trust ourselves to live in such a potent reality where power is in infinite supply? Where we have the knowledge and are able to think and move in such a way that what we wish and want is absolutely what we are enabled to do, which simultaneously and completely pleases God in facilitating exactly what it is we seek to accomplish? This is life without end, without limit, without boundaries, where goodness and glory flow like a mighty river (Amos 5:24), giving life that is strong and sturdy, bringing forth predictable fruits of blessing, despite whatever conditions prevail (Jer. 17:8; Ps. 1:3). This is power from on high. This is the Spirit-filled, Spirit-empowered existence God intended for us at the dawn of creation. It is also the kind of life demonstrated in several key characters in the scriptures, who accomplish otherworldly feats in the name of God. Can you withstand such power and potential? Do you want to?

We have to begin to ask ourselves if we in fact do want to live such an empowered life. We can start now. If we haven't sought or lived a life of reliance and faith on the power of God we may want to consider why, and what may need to change in us to begin seeking such a life. For without the power of God working in and through us to achieve good ends, we are simply left alone to struggle and manage life as it comes.

The power of God to effect the good is not something we seek for its own sake. Instead, we invoke the power and knowledge of God to effect the highest good for God's glory, and out of our love of others as well as ourselves. It is these key personal relationships, and the formidable dynamics in play between ourselves, God, and others, that outline the primary field wherein we learn and manifest to the entire world the power and durability of God's benevolent will and way. How we prepare ourselves to genuinely love and be present to ourselves and others under the guidance of God is an ever-renewing blessing of life from above. Therefore, relational wholeness is the next key aspect of heavenly life we will now engage.

Nine

Beneficial Relationships

I will forever cherish the last few weeks I spent with Jane and Dallas in their home before he passed. We worked when we could, we watched a little TV, and Jane and I tried to entice him to eat some nutrients and stay hydrated. I asked a few questions here and there, and he would convey a few key thoughts now and again, but he was growing very tired, and Jane made me promise not to tax him with too much conversation. She knew better than anyone that Dallas gave everything he had to his work. Doing so, he could, and often did, exhaust himself unwittingly. Even then, during Dallas's final weeks, she knew he would continue to try and serve me and our books if he was called upon. So Jane appropriately monitored most of Dallas's interactions.

Dallas's relationships with Jane, his family, and his close friends were a major source of comfort and blessing in his final days. There was a consistent stream of acquaintances and colleagues who were making contact, seeking to be helpful, extending prayers of concern and support, bringing meals, cleaning the house, taking care of errands, and offering counsel on the many decisions that begin to mount in these kinds of situations. Yet these services and care were a product of relationships, friendships, bonds, and covenants matured over decades. In some measure, Dallas and Jane were reaping the fruit of a harvest of investing decades of their time and talents into the lives of others. And that thankfulness and appreciation developed in others a desire to give abundantly out of what they had received. Such genuine outpouring of love and care was the product of a life lovingly devoted to the good of others. Countless others. And Dallas was moved by the acts of kindness now being shown to him.

Each interaction helped him to better experience how wide, broad, and deep the love is that we share in Christ, how the bread he had cast out was coming back to him and his family in measures that were overflowing and, at times, overwhelming. The investment of his life was paying benefits far greater than he could have imagined. And as a result, there was a glory, a weightiness, a significant poignancy and potency to his last several months on earth, and he was bearing testimony to that fact. "Gary, don't ever let anyone convince you that giving your life to the way of Christ and his Church isn't worth it. It's hard at times and can be lonely for some spells. But I can assure you, it's worth it."

What I was most struck by during our time together was the depth and strength of the love Dallas and Jane displayed for one another. Jane was close by for every need. Watching his blood sugar levels, keeping track of medications, writing down how many ounces of nutrition he ate, and even reminding him of the time for favorite news programs. She went about her housework in such a way as to muffle any noises that might disturb his rest. Dallas, too, showed great love and care for Jane. He thanked her for every act of service—from a drink of water to a fluffing of a pillow—even when she asked him to chew a bitter-tasting medication. In all the time I spent with Dallas, from the shorter periods earlier in his last three months to the longer days and nights toward the end, I never heard him complain. There was always a thank-you after even the smallest act of kindness, even when he endured the more painful acts of moving from place to place. He remained kind and grateful, never projecting his pain and frustration onto others. Despite his discomfort and the length of his disease, and even in light of his unrealized hopes, Dallas never showed any sign of anger or depression. There were moments of sadness, but not misery. He simply endured his pain and suffered quietly with great dignity and peace. It was quite stunning to witness.

But there was more than dignity in Dallas's demeanor. He knew his illness was very difficult for those around him to witness and endure as well. And he was especially aware that his illness was most trying on Jane. To the very end of his life, Jane never stopped seeking advice and counsel for how to better help Dallas. She was thoughtful and expectant for his every need. And he basked in her care. He would smile the smile of a love-struck teenager when Jane would remind him, for the third time, to drink more water or eat more soup. He would often say, "Thank you, honey," or "Whatever you think is best, dear."

Dallas and Jane's mutual reliance on and enjoyment of each other made me think of Dallas's teaching on the Trinity: a loving circle of mutual submission and sufficiency. For some couples, a spouse's nursing can feel at times like nagging. Not for Dallas. Instead, Jane's attention seemed only to reinstill a sense of gratitude, security, and comfort. It was beautifully obvious that these two souls had been sewn together long ago and had developed a bond not to be broken. It was a wonderful blessing for me to see their marriage in action as I had not witnessed it before. What kept playing through my mind were the vows they had spoken to each other many decades prior:

> *I, Jane . . . I, Dallas . . . take thee to be my lawfully wed-*
> *ded spouse. To have and to hold from this day forward,*
> *for better or worse, for richer or poorer, in sickness and in*
> *health, to love and to cherish, till death do us part, accord-*
> *ing to God's holy ordinance. And therefore I pledge thee*
> *my troth.*

I was witnessing, and they were experiencing, the fulfillment and the sanctity of that faithful, relational covenant to God and each other. Even in the shadow of death, they were not afraid. The bulwark of their love, experience of God, and one another had created a safe haven amidst the coming storm.

As I observed in Dallas and Jane's loving relationship, the beauty of human beings in loving relations with one another is one of the primary examples of heavenly existence on display now for all to see. The model for our relational devotion is the interdependent, mutually reinforcing, mutually submissive, empowering, and deferential loving existence manifested in Trinitarian covenantal faithfulness. Our task and opportunity, both now and into eternity, is to develop, enrich, and become proficient in displaying to the world the holistic flourishing available to those submitted to one another. Therefore, our personal relationships are one of the primary ways we demonstrate our created purpose: to glorify God's goodness in our mutually sufficing and loving relationships. And many of our relationships do that very thing to wonderful effect. So much of our lives is given wondrous meaning and fulfillment as a direct result of the relational bonding we are able to achieve with others.

Dallas and I discussed how our relationships are to work like "factories" of goodness and love. He loved giving etymology lessons about the root meaning of words. He used to say the word *beneficial* comes from an interesting combination of two Latin words, *bene,* which in English is translated "good" (as in benefit or benevolent), and *ficium,* which is an interesting suffix that can mean "factory" or "a place where a particular item is made." Our relationships are to be "factories of goodness" where we create and are sustained by one another in living, supportive community.

We often struggle, however, in our thinking and discussions about relationships because our relationships are a primary area of human failure. Therefore, here we will try to peel away some of the struggles we face in our key personal relationships. We will also seek to discover God's intention for our relational lives and to discover the necessity of developing mutually beneficial relationships now that will continue to grow and blossom throughout eternity.

Enmity in the Garden

The creation narrative of Genesis places God's adversary (Satan) as a tempter who crafts a temptation that, in one sweeping yet subtle blow, causes a rupture in the relational trust necessary between both humanity and God, and between men and women. Once this rupture occurred, it was not long before the relationship between siblings also digressed to the point where contempt and jealousy led to murder. It's a sad story to tell, and one that foreshadowed all humanity yet to be born.

The adversary's temptation sowed the seed of suspicion and fear with a single, yet multifaceted and well-crafted, lie. The story depicts a serpent, a crafty animal, questioning the nature of reality. "Has God indeed said . . . ?" (Gen. 3:1, NKJV). In other words, "Do you really know what you think you know?" Eve then replies to the serpent that she was not to eat of the fruit from the tree of the knowledge of good and evil, and added, incorrectly, that God commanded they were not to even touch the fruit. So the serpent moved to another strategy, claiming to possess God's knowledge and lying about God's true intentions. "You will not surely die. For God knows that in the day you eat of it your eyes will be opened, and you will be like God, knowing good and evil" (3:4–5, NKJV). The serpent assumed to know God's mind and used that to deceive Eve about the goodness and trustworthiness of God's character. This created mistrust, which led to actions that were contrary to God's intent for his glory and power to remain as the solitary means of provision for human life and action.

After their sin, when God returned to the garden seeking their company once again, the first thing we see in the Genesis story is the desire, perhaps even the need, to hide from God. Adam states that he hides because he heard God coming through the garden, and he was afraid, and therefore hid himself because he was naked. It is important here to suggest that nakedness is not so much about clothing. Although this could be part of the issue, perhaps nakedness has to do with humanity's overwhelming sense of vulnerability. Prior to sin, Dallas thought it likely Adam and Eve did not see themselves as naked and did not understand or realize any degree of vulnerability because they were surrounded, robed, engulfed, or covered in a glow of light, or energy, which is a common occurrence with those who display the glory of God.[1] It's possible this display or effect of the spiritual force God had given human beings, which both clothed and empowered them with life, may have in some measure "limited" their ability, or even the need, to understand fully where their dependence upon—and mutual existence with—God either began or ended. This existential dependence is perhaps what Jesus refers to in John 17:20–23:

I ask not only on behalf of these, but also on behalf of those who will believe in me through their word, that they may all be one. As you, Father, are in me and I am in you, may they also be in us, so that the world may believe that you have sent me. The glory that you have given me I have given them, so that they may be one, as we are one, I in them and you in me, that they may become completely one, so that the world may know that you have sent me and have loved them even as you have loved me.

The effect of accepting and acting on a false misrepresentation of God's character was the tragedy of humanity's relational disorientation from God and from one another, along with a disempowered state and the need to hide in shame and fear.

As a result of their rebellion, it is painfully clear that separation from God becomes more obvious as relational discord begins to grow. Adam attempts to blame both Eve and God for his own actions. This is as incredible as it is ludicrous, but it reveals the blindingly quick progression of arrogance and the need for self-preservation that has taken hold. Still today, the idea that God is ultimately responsible for evil, and for our sinful actions, has maintained a long and ominous track record. Interestingly, the only actor in this tragedy who doesn't try to pass the buck is the serpent.[2]

The point to consider here is the display of distrust that marks the entire event. Such distrust also provoked the conflict between Cain and Abel. The cycle of mistrust, anger, and separation marks nearly every human relationship, especially in families, at one point or another and to differing degrees. The effect of sin on our relationships has the power to escalate fear, mistrust, anger, and disappointment to a level where today assault or withdrawal is often the standard measurement of human interaction.[3]

This is true even for those who have experienced the grace of God. It is rare to find a marriage, familial relationship, or friendship that is fully trusting, confident, and satisfying at every level. Instead, it is more common to find some degree of constant testing, the need for ongoing assurance, or an insatiable jealousy and insecurity at work just beneath the surface of even our most secure relations. Uncertainties and doubts about all the delicate relational intricacies, devotions, and commitments between couples or friends, to one degree or another, cause many of our relationships to remain in some state of constant flux and in need of ever-evolving assessment. The insecurity and mistrust implicit in never-ending questions such as, "Is my relationship giving me what I need?" prevent us from ever becoming permanently settled in our most crucial relationships.

Such dysfunction is especially lethal to the development of a mutually dependent and trusting marriage relationship. It is rare to find two people who are completely at home with, confident in, and never in doubt of their own or their spouse's devotion, and who are full of love and concern for one another. Today, the threat of insecurity predominates; therefore, we seek to protect and preserve our being through an elaborate system of assigning blame. This is a tried-and-true way to extinguish love. Finally, the violation of trust in any relationship can allow the spread of insecurity, doubt, and mistrust to continue unchecked throughout the rest of our social relations.

My primary purpose for discussing the absence of God's grace in our relationships is to demonstrate how essential our relationships are in accomplishing God's plan for the world. The lack of trust in our relationships makes it virtually impossible to confidently step forward in the power of God, which would help us to realize the goodness God intended for us to experience in relationship with him and others. For God is just as deeply in love with others as he is with us. Part of the glory of God is revealed in his ability to bring together insecure and prideful individuals who willingly submit themselves to God and one another in harmonious communal devotion. This is an aspect of the power of God that is simply as magnificent as his creative ability to form endlessly awe-inspiring galaxies and nebulae. A godly family or friendship should equally inspire just as much wonder and thanksgiving, for it is no less a work of God's majesty for all the world to see, now and forever more.

Hesed-Covenantal Loyalty

One of the most difficult periods of my life lasted approximately eighteen months. There are moments during that year and a half I wish I could completely erase from my memory, but I can't. Which is in some ways very fortunate because it was also during that period of time that my wife demonstrated the most enduring, courageous, and faithful witness of the Hebrew concept of *hesed* (covenantal love and loyalty) I have ever experienced from another human being.

By her own admission, my wife would agree that our relationship had gotten to the point where we were both considering other "options." We never had "the talk," but our mutual misery was obvious. I was working continuously, traveling nearly nonstop, leaving her to fend for herself with two toddlers. When we were together, we either fought or sat in silence, which made staying away even more appealing. I was trying desperately not to admit to my blinding ambition mixed with my secret disappointment over the trajectory of my career. Susie was trying to get to the bottom of our troubles, and I was terrified of such a prospect. So I deflected, dodged, denied, and used every one of my well-defended rationalizations to remain isolated. I made our life together a tinderbox that could erupt at any point over even the slightest grievance. I was impossible to live with—for myself, but especially for her.

Susie tells of praying one morning after a particularly painful argument. She told God she didn't know if she could stay with me, to which God impressed upon her that he was going to rescue me, that I was going to come through this difficult time. He then presented her with a choice, asking the question whether or not it would be she at my side when I came to my senses, or whether I would be married to someone else. She then saw a vision of me standing with another woman, arm in arm, very sorrowful, offering Susie a sincere apology for our failed marriage, and seeking her forgiveness.

The vision had two effects. First, God's promise gave Susie hope. Secondly, it made her mad, to think of such an injustice. In response, she began to diligently fight for our marriage and for me. She made the decision to pray and intercede with everything she had. God's prompting changed Susie's focus and fervency in prayer. From that day forward, for more than a year, I awoke to an empty bed. Susie would rise before dawn, go into the den off our bedroom, get down on her knees, and pray until the kids and I awoke for work and school. Nearly every morning, I would see her seeking God's strength, wisdom, and grace for us. It took a few months—my pride was ironclad, and change was slow—but eventually something began to soften in me. I began to see my wife giving every ounce of her heart, doing everything she could for us, for our children, for our family, and for me. Her actions of love, devotion, sacrifice, and commitment resonated deep within my spirit.

Eventually, I began to change. God began to use Susie and a good counselor to speak truth, hope, and light back into my heart and mind. God was right. He did save me, again, and I am and will forever be grateful to my wife for her courageous stand to ruthlessly pursue the good for our lives. Most important, I'm glad my wife made herself available to hear God's direction for our family. That willingness to seek God first, and heed God's wisdom for our situation, made all the difference.

This is the picture I think Paul attempts to illustrate in Ephesians 5. He argues that the grace of God that came to us through Jesus Christ was sufficient to heal the relationship between men and women. In loving, Christ-abiding relationships, there is an expectation and characteristic identification of mutual submission, equal responsibility, and equal benefit. When Paul describes a husband's call to love his wife as Christ loved the Church, we can hear the echo of the call of Christ to give oneself, one's entire life, even to the point of death if necessary, to the good God has already given: Christ Jesus (5:25–27).

It may be dangerous to ask how many spouses would testify that such a love has been demonstrated to them by their wives or husbands. Further, we could ask if a spouse expresses such a love, would the other discern its presence, or would doubt of ulterior motives distort even the most sincere demonstration of true love? The acids of pessimism and pain can so easily erode even the most adamant of realities.

One of the awful games played in many relationships is trying to get someone to prove their love. This nearly always emanates from a sense of one's own lack of self-worth. Paul's inspiring description of the marriage relationship as a means through which each partner presents the other as a wondrous benefactor of the marriage covenant can serve as a hopeful testament to the overwhelming potential available to Christian relationships today.

First Peter 3 connects the quality of relationship between a husband and wife to the practice of prayer. The effective communion between a husband and wife is a precursor to an effective relationship with God. If a relationship is in right standing, then it is more likely our relationship to God is right as well. We must not be legalistic, however. Relationships are multidimensional. Too many people have been inappropriately condemned and marginalized because a relationship has failed. Yet this is not to demean the point 1 Peter is making in relationship to prayer. It is difficult to pray with anyone, including those in our families, if there is trouble in our relationships. This is because prayer connects us with the power and truthfulness of God. Prayer seeks the truth about God and his ways in order to apply that truth to our lives. To authentically honor another and come to God in prayer necessitates dropping our assumptions and predetermined conclusions about the circumstances of our lives in order to seek God's perspective and direction.

When our heart is in this condition, God leans in to us to hear and hopefully honor such requests. Thus, it is likely true, although yet unproven, that fewer couples divorce who routinely remain in a prayerful relationship with each other and God.[4] It is more likely the case that many couples who do separate did not pray together. This would be an excellent subject for an empirical study. The simple point is that our relationships, whether with God or with others, cannot be turned off and on like a water spigot. If one chooses to be isolated and alone now, why would we assume such a desire will be overwhelmed by the great cloud of witnesses when entering eternity?

The same principle applies to the issue of forgiveness. Forgiveness is a special kind of relationship that, if not fully inhabited, becomes difficult to understand or benefit from. If one does not receive forgiveness, then the ability to offer forgiveness is hampered because of a deficit in understanding the compassion and generosity of the heart of God. It's the same with prayer. If in our relationships we are at odds with our spouses and loved ones, it is not a far reach to suspect we are caught in a twisted understanding of our position with God as well. Thus, marriage, family, and interpersonal relationships are often a barometer for one's relationship to God. It's very difficult to pray with a mate, sibling, parent, child, or friend unless we truly love them and our relational dynamics are generally in sync.

Our families, marriages, and friendships were never intended to survive outside an abundance of grace from God. If our friends, spouses, and family members are unable to seek God's counsel in pursuit of peace and harmony with us for our communal life, then individually we must do whatever is necessary to seek healing, counseling, or guidance. It is simply a secularized myth to assume that dysfunctional relationships, especially our marriages, do not cause collateral relational damage.

Relationships in the Afterlife

But marriage is certainly not the only relationship to consider. The discussion of marriage is used here only to describe one reason why human beings and our relationships are so valuable. People exist to realize the God-embedded potential within each of us, which includes our relationships with and to each other as well as our relationships with God. We can be sure that much of what is true of marital relations is also true of our relations to other family members, siblings, parents, and friends. For those single or unmarried, these relationships become the central means of God's engagement with our sense of community and belonging. Friendships, working relationships, and neighbor relationships all work under the same primary dynamics. What God will have to "show off" for his glory in all eternity is the fruit of the society of the redeemed.

Primarily, the redeemed relationships of mutually committed and submitted persons is understood to be the Church, defined as those set apart who have set their wills on God's purposes. This community is what Jesus is building as he engages us both individually and then corporately in relational community. There is no other creation in all the world that can demonstrate God's wondrously good works in these arenas other than human beings gathered under the call, guidance, unity, and empowerment of God. Such a thing is unspeakably precious, essential, vital, and therefore, of inestimable value. The Church of Jesus Christ is not a social club or a community-volunteer organization. It is a work God is doing in history and in people.

Ephesians 3:1–12 finds Paul expounding on the mystery of the Gentiles being included in the plan of God.

This is the reason that I Paul am a prisoner for Christ Jesus for the sake of you Gentiles—for surely you have already heard of the commission of God's grace that was given me for you, and how the mystery was made known to me by revelation, as I wrote above in a few words, a reading of which will enable you to perceive my understanding of the mystery of Christ. In former generations this mystery was not made known to humankind, as it has now been revealed to his holy apostles and prophets by the Spirit: that is, the Gentiles have become fellow heirs, members of the same body, and sharers in the promise in Christ Jesus through the gospel.

Of this gospel I have become a servant according to the gift of God's grace that was given me by the working of his power. Although I am the very least of all the saints, this grace was given to me to bring to the Gentiles the news of the boundless riches of Christ, and to make

*everyone see what is the plan of the mystery hidden for
ages in God who created all things; so that through the
church the wisdom of God in its rich variety might now
be made known to the rulers and authorities in the heavenly places. This was in accordance with the eternal purpose that he has carried out in Christ Jesus our Lord, in
whom we have access to God in boldness and confidence
through faith in him.*

In verse 8, Paul states that he understood his calling as one
tasked with preaching the "boundless riches of Christ." And in
this, he would assist in helping the world to see a "mystery hidden for ages in God" (v. 9). What could this be? The mystery
is the eternal purposes and wisdom of God revealed in his redeemed people through Jesus Christ. This has confounded and
will continue to confound the rulers and authorities in heavenly
places. Humanity redeemed will be the mystical and mysterious
bride of Christ.

We need to realize that in heaven, we will have relationship
with God and with others, always. We will never be alone in the
ways we consider isolation and solitude now. We won't be able to
"lock" or "shut" people out of our lives as is so easily our habit
today. We won't be able to ignore those whom we simply find
annoying or unpleasant. Of course, the assumption is that no
one will be annoying or unpleasant in heaven. There is nothing
in the scriptures, however, to suggest such an assumption is an
absolute.

More likely, Dallas believed heaven would be similar to what
C. S. Lewis describes in *The Great Divorce*. People will have
patience, endurance, grace, deference, and submission for one
another as we grow, develop, learn, and mature. Like good older
siblings watching their younger siblings grow, learn, and discover

who and what he or she is, there will be those in heaven who are far ahead of us in their understandings of God and his ways. They are with us, committed to us, and loving us despite our ignorance. And we are with them, blessed by their graciousness, awed by their wisdom, and thankful for their guidance. Perhaps after a few dozen millennia, we, too, might find those whom we can help, guide, direct, and instruct in what we have learned and understood about the nature of life and existence in our world. But one has to develop these skills and desires. One has to be a lover of people, not as we want them to be, but as they actually are.

I've never met a better man than my paternal grandfather. My brother and I called him Granddad. And he was grand. I could see in his eyes how much he enjoyed me. I recently came across an old picture of me as a young boy sitting on his lap. He never laughed harder than when my brother or I said something outrageous. I loved him deeply, and I know he loved me as well.

But he never kissed me. He never told me he loved me, and I never heard him tell anyone else he loved them. He did love us, of that I am sure. Yet every time I went to hug my grandfather, which was a lot, his Herculean body would tense under my skinny little arms. He didn't know how to hug or be hugged. Sometimes I would hug him extra long, just to see if he'd get the hang of it. He never did. It was as if those who loved him were porcupines whom he greatly enjoyed and would have died for, but with whom he just couldn't get very close. I think I know why my grandfather was this way, none of which need be revealed in detail here. Seeds of fear, self-consciousness, and emotional distance were planted long ago and lingered throughout his life. His emotional wounds weren't bleeding but remained somewhat debilitating, even paralyzing at times.

I'm suggesting that when my grandfather died and entered eternity, the bruises were healed, but he still had to learn how to be hugged and hug back. I can imagine a God grand enough to allow for that depth of healing to become a reality. In fact, I think God's Kingdom would have it no other way. That is the kind of event that I think causes the angels to rejoice and sing, "Hallelujah! Glory to God in the highest, peace on earth, good-will toward men" (adapted from Luke 2:14).

Many of us carry wounds inflicted by unresolved, unfinished, unrequited loves that have grown or festered to the point that they block or impede the flow of love in our hearts. Most of these wounds are centered in the places reserved for family members. Some of the deepest of wounds result from being rejected by those we wanted to be our most beloved, or perhaps those who betrayed our love. Healing must come. God will make sure of it. The question we must ask ourselves is if we want that healing. Can we risk opening ourselves up in the very places and to the very ones who inflicted these wounds in the first place? For many, it would be foolish, even dangerous, to try such reconciliation on earth. Heaven creates the conditions in which these kinds of redemptive reunions are possible, if we desire them.

Not long ago, I attended a lecture of a colleague of mine, Dr. Brian Lugioyo, that included some interesting insights regarding what should be, and he argues eventually will be, the foundational basis of all human relationships in heaven.[5] He argued that over time, both before death and certainly after death, our relationships with family members, specifically between parents and children, can transition from representing power and authority, into a peer or sibling relationship. Brian suggests that in the heavenly family of God there will be one divine "parent" to satisfy the authoritative role. Thus, the members of a nuclear family will develop sibling relationships. Each of us will engage with the other equally as children of God and, therefore, assume the roles of brothers and sisters, not uncles and nieces, grandparents and grandchildren, and so on. This is not to suggest that we will not be aware of what role each of us played in the lives of our family members in our earthy life and what authority or responsibilities we carried while living on earth. This knowledge will continue. My mother will always have been my mother. Still, there will be no division of authority, position, or responsibility based on birth or family status in heaven. In the new order of the new heavens and new earth, we will all be equal siblings and heirs of our single, common progenitor.

Can we imagine such a relationship? Actually, I believe we can. There are many who begin to experience a reversal of roles as parents begin to receive care from their children. It is often the case that as the body fails us, and as our mental faculties begin to slip, the adult children begin to provide care to their aging parents who previously cared for and nurtured them as children. Feeding, cleaning, transferring, decision making, and planning need to be delegated to others during the years of vulnerability at both ends of the life cycle. However, these issues of physical care and concern need not be the only areas for which we begin to drop our "claims" as family members one over the other.

Can we begin the period of transition toward acceptance of one another as peers with different but complementary gifts, talents, abilities, wisdom, and experiences now? Do we want to? Or are we confined to the systems of power and authority that currently define and often restrain our relationships? I'm suggesting that for many of us, the experience of our broken relationships has—like my relationship with my grandfather, and his relationship to his parents—become too tangled in the wounds that are expressly tied to certain role expectations and their histories. Therefore, we must be loosed of these earthly relational dynamics in order to reframe ourselves, and our relations, in response to God's relationship to us, before we can effectively heal our injuries with others. This will require deeply abandoning rela-tional outcomes, which can only come about when we are sure God cares for us. Therefore, we can trust him to protect us and provide for our needs so we may fearlessly interact with others.

We can enjoy such assurances now when we choose to live according to God's Kingdom. If we actually seek authentic com-munity, where love, openness, and trust are the hallmarks of life in the family of God, then honesty, hope, and fearlessness will progressively permeate our beings, and allow us to engage oth-ers, seeking and sacrificing for their highest good. This is *agape* in action.

The bride of Christ is being perfected. Every wrinkle and spot is being removed. It is in our relational dynamics where this cleaning and pressing must be most intensely focused. God will make this come to pass. The question is when, not if. We should ask ourselves if we are willing to be straightened out in regard to our relationships. Am I willing to have my spotted bruises exposed to God's light and love? Am I willing to recognize the damage I have inflicted on others, to come under the conviction of the Holy Spirit's guidance regarding my fears, blaming, and isolation so that I can learn how to live in harmony and unity with those in my life who are most near and dear to me and to God? If I'm not, I must ask why. For heaven will be precisely the place that progressively realizes intimate knowledge and experi-ence of human beings in concert with God's person.

Jesus's prayer in John 17 is amazing, mysterious, and beauti-ful in the depth of relationship it describes. Can I endure such intimacy? Do I long to know and be known by others? Do I want to? My relationships on earth will provide all the evidence I need to determine that answer. It's ironic to consider that our prepa-ration for heaven should be marked by relationships on earth so significant, rich, and fulfilling that we are torn by the unsolvable

dilemma of wanting to stay in the comfort of our loving relations here while longing to rekindle and start new relationships
that lie in waiting. Is that how you live your life now? Are you
excited to move effortlessly yet purposefully from the substance
of one fulfilling and enriching relationship to another?

Relationship Before Religion

Several years ago while I was a seminary student, one of my Old
Testament professors was discussing how Jesus's Sermon on the
Mount could be seen as an overlay on Moses's Ten Commandments. One of the commandments Jesus hits on has to do with
murder.

> *You have heard that it was said to those of ancient times,*
> *"You shall not murder"; and "whoever murders shall be*
> *liable to judgment." But I say to you that if you are angry*
> *with a brother or sister, you will be liable to judgment;*
> *and if you insult a brother or sister, you will be liable to*
> *the council; and if you say, "You fool," you will be liable*
> *to the hell of fire. So when you are offering your gift at*
> *the altar, if you remember that your brother or sister has*
> *something against you, leave your gift there before the al-*
> *tar and go; first be reconciled to your brother or sister, and*
> *then come and offer your gift.*
>
> (MATT. 5:21–24)

What was lost on me at the time, and perhaps remains lost
on many contemporary Christians, that was very significant to
those listening to Jesus in the first century, was his suggestion to
forgo religious sacrifice or offerings in order to reestablish right

relationships with those around us. My professor highlighted what I had missed in the significance of Jewish offerings. Sacrifices were signs or evidences of obedience and right relationship with Yahweh, which to an observant and conscientious Jew was inviolate and sacred. No one with a good heart, attempting to love and obey God with their entire being, would consider missing the opportunity to display their devotion before the ruler of the cosmos. It was unthinkable. Here Jesus is not undermining that invaluable idea; he is revealing that maintaining a pure heart, which the sacrifice is intended to demonstrate, is impossible if there is a conscious unwillingness to live in peace, and to demonstrate the love and mercy of God to others.

The apostle John picks this up later where he comes right out and proclaims that we are liars when we profess a love for God but display or maintain hatred for our neighbors (1 John 4:20). In such a state, the sacrifice or religious ritual works in reverse. Instead of enlivening our appreciation and devotion to God, such acts form a deadening cement that fixes hypocrisy in our religious practices and strangles the heart. My professor then asked the question, "How many of you have ever walked out of the middle of a worship service, or a sermon, or refused Eucharist, because in your heart and mind, or because of a prompting from the Holy Spirit, you were fully aware of living in disharmony with someone near you, while refusing to seek any form of remedy?"

That question cut deeply into my heart. Before that day, I had never considered such a means of action. But that is precisely what Jesus is advocating. Since that day, I have been unable to enter the Eucharist without taking inventory of the actual state of my relationships. It takes both humility and courage. I attend a church from a tradition that celebrates the Eucharist or Lord's Supper on the first Sunday of every month. And there are times when I have not been able to partake. I'm sometimes ashamed to admit there have been months on end when I've not partaken, because I know, and God has made it clear to me, there is more I can and should do with certain relationships in my life, that I have not done, and have stubbornly resisted doing.

This is not to say I have not taken communion when I've been in disputes with others. I have. But this is a conversation with God that I engage in regularly, and I am able to discern with him whether I am free, with a clear conscience, or not, to testify to myself and others, that as far as I am aware, I am doing what I can to live at peace with those around me. This is not a legalistic application of some Pharisaical dictate. It's just a question: "Father, am I living with integrity with those around me? Is there someone you are aware of that I need to make amends to or seek peace with?" Then I wait for an answer. It's that simple. When I sense or hear that I am not free, then mostly, not always, I have a clear picture of who this person is. And I am then left with a decision. Will I seek reconciliation? How do I do that? Will I trust God to be with me in that endeavor of faith?

That's what the heavenly banquet, the party, the wedding feast, the family reunion, is all about. A wedding feast is a celebration of a public covenant of loyal devotion between two individuals, and by extension, a demonstration of a commitment to be honored by an entire community. It is these covenantal promises from which new life is birthed, stewarded, and developed. Such symbolism cannot be lost on us. Our preparation for such a heavenly existence requires nothing less. Are you excited to meet, and be met by, Jesus and his friends, to live together forever under mutual covenantal love and devotion? Does communal life sound good to you? Once again, how we currently live our lives today is as honest a reply as we'll ever need.

Ten

_____

Joy

I t was around 7:00 P.M. on the evening before Dallas died that
Jane explained their plan to transfer Dallas from the hospital to his home the following morning. I noticed the IV had
been removed. The hospice doctor had determined that the previous treatment was not working as hoped and that the best that
could be done was to make him as comfortable as possible. Eyes
were red, faces were stark, earthly hope was fading. Yet there
remained a sense of peace through the disappointment. There
were tremendous displays of mutual love and support among the
family. There was a desire to think through all the possible decisions that would be in Dallas's best interest. Love, grace, and
servanthood abounded.

Again, I greeted Dallas with a hug and asked how he felt. He
smiled slightly and said with a whisper, "Still here." His words
were more difficult to understand. He was taking a turn for the
worse. His voice was coarse. His eyes—often glazed over and
distant. His breathing—more labored. The cramping and hiccups were constant. By early evening, he began coughing up
some fluid. Swallowing was arduous. But his mind was still clear,
and he remained aware of his thoughts and those around him.

A few hours passed. The family began to leave. Good-byes were said. Thanksgiving, honor, and intimacies were shared. The sorrow was deep. Joy, peace, and gratitude were deeper.

By 9:00 P.M. we were alone again. His condition was worsening, the pain becoming more constant, and there were fewer positions that offered him any comfort. The illness was beginning to consume his strength. Still, he never complained about his worsening condition.

Later in the evening, Keith Matthews, a longtime friend to us both, dropped by to visit. Dallas recognized him, they exchanged greetings and loving words, but the interactions were becoming shorter and shorter. Single words and nods of the head. It seemed Dallas's body was fighting, but this fight was weakening him very quickly.

In the early morning hours, the nurses and I realized he was fading quickly. The doctors had authorized the use of morphine if the pain was too intense for him to endure. After several visits to the room, one of the nurses suggested we start the morphine to calm the coughing and better manage the pain. I knew what that meant. He had waited as long as he could, but disease was taking its toll. I remembered when my grandmother started taking morphine; she never regained consciousness. So I asked Dallas if he wanted me to call the family in order to say their final farewells. He nodded his head in agreement. It was near midnight.

Dallas elected to wait to administer the morphine until the family arrived. When a wave of pain arose, I would recite Psalm 23 and the Lord's Prayer—two of his favorite parts of scripture. Hearing the words, he would hum softly and nod his head. All I could do was hold his hand and pray. I asked if there was anything I could do for him. He whispered, "It's okay. We're just waiting. Waiting on the Lord." He looked deep into my eyes and smiled. Joy was his. Victory was his, even in death. There can be no greater juxtaposition in terms. But that is precisely what was occurring.

When Jane and the family arrived, the nurses conveyed the situation, and they began to offer their final good-byes. Short messages of gratitude, hope, and assurance were traded. Dallas spoke briefly to each, clasping hands, his voice very faint but his intentions were clear. He was thankful for his family. He was proud of his children, and he was deeply loved by and in love with his wife. Even though his body was failing there was a great yearning within him to offer each person at his bedside a word or phrase laden with love, comfort, and encouragement.

It was then that I realized, as never before, that the love within us is the most powerful aspect of our human existence. The apostle Paul was right. If we have all the power in the universe but have not love, we have nothing. At Dallas's weakest physical moment, he summoned a reservoir of love that empowered and enabled him to provide his family with exactly what they needed most. Then he closed his eyes and faded off to sleep.

The nurses advised that the family return home since Dallas could remain medicated for hours, if not days or weeks, and they needed to retain their strength for the days ahead. I promised to call if there were any change.

After the family left, I must have fallen asleep again and awoke at 4:30 A.M. when a nurse came in to turn him. When she did, he awoke briefly. I took his hand. He told me to tell his loved ones how much he was blessed by them, how much he appreciated them, and that he would be waiting for them when they arrived. I assured him I would.

Several months before, while working in his office together I had spotted several baseball hats high on a shelf in the library. When I asked what they were, he told me of a time years before, when he used the hats as a teaching device. Embroidered on the front of each hat the name of an influential philosopher, and he would literally "change hats" during a lecture or when he answered a question from that philosopher's perspective. Now, sitting by his bedside, I told him I would try to wear a "Husserl" hat when I got to heaven so he could recognize me among the great "crowd" of witnesses. He actually managed a chuckle and said, "Oh, I'll recognize you. I'll be waiting." There was joy in his eyes, even a youthful expectation. Something had changed. Or something was about to change.

I then told him the nurse was there to administer more pain medication if he needed it to stay comfortable and rest. He nodded his approval. I told him I thought this time he might not wake up. I asked him if that was what he really wanted. He said yes with a slight but distinct little grin. The nurse administered the medication, and I kissed him on the forehead and said good-bye one last time. A few moments later, he closed his eyes and smiled. I sat back in the chair next to his bedside and watched him take maybe ten quiet breaths. There was no sign of pain on his face. Just peaceful rest. Then, in a voice clearer than I had heard in days, he leaned his head back slightly and with his eyes closed said, "Thank you."

I tried to stay awake. I sensed the end was near, but I knew I had misjudged that previously. Sometime after 5:30 A.M., I fell asleep again. About twenty minutes later I woke with a start. I looked to see Dallas was still breathing lightly and peacefully. The early dawn had begun to lighten the room. I was tired, my mind a blur, but I knew I could not go back to sleep. Just as the sunlight began to come through the window, I looked up from Dallas to the ceiling above his bed. It was just for a moment, but when I looked back down, he was gone. I immediately felt the sensation of being alone. I stood up and checked his pulse at his wrist and neck. I put my ear to his chest. Silence. I looked at the clock, just a few minutes before 6:00 A.M.

At that same moment, as if on cue, a nurse entered the room. I told her, "He's dead." Just as the words exited my lips, I regretted them. They were too harsh, too stark, too final. A sadness immediately swept over her eyes. She took out her stethoscope and listened to his chest. Nothing. She took out a penlight and looked into his pupils. Nothing. She wrote something down on a pad of paper. Another nurse came in the room. They straightened him in the bed, laid it flat, and gently straightened the sheets and blankets. One of the nurses gently brushed his cheek with the back of her hand and said sweetly, "Good-bye."

My mind told me Dallas wasn't dead. Only his body was dead. But his lifeless form was too stark a reality for my mind to oppose. The deathly hollowness that possessed his body seemed to me an unrelenting foreign invader that had descended into the room with the power to halt all the potential and hope life possesses. Death opposes life just as fire opposes ice and as darkness opposes light. One must flee the presence of the other, and it is nearly impossible for the mind to behold the full scope of such starkly conflicting realities of life and death in the same instant.

Despite my confusion, the shock of the loss caused my heart to ache. The fact that Dallas was no longer accessible began to bear down on me. There was a physical pain in my chest, and I could somehow feel the distance growing between us. His words, his wisdom, his smile, his love, his guidance, his faith, were all gone. His soul will never die, but for his family—Jane, John, Becky, Bill, Larissa—and countless others just like me, all we have left is his impact, his work, and his legacy. What remains for me are my memories and the use of his invaluable gifts.

I walked over to him and closed his half-open eyes. I tried to straighten his hair with my hands. I took a wet cloth and washed his face and neck. My thoughts and emotions were full of a sweet sorrow. While, in one sense, I was overwhelmed, my emotions seemed stuck or delayed somewhere deep in my heart.

Ten minutes had passed. I needed to make calls. I told the nurses I would contact the family. They nodded silently and left the room. This was going to be difficult. It was difficult. Yet each person I contacted was gentle and grateful. They were trying to make it easy on me. I reported to each that, in the end, he died peacefully and that despite the pain, his last words were a tribute of thanks.

The family arrived and arrangements were made. Hugs were shared. Tears were shed. This was a private moment for them, and I left the room. When Bill Dwyer, the Willards' pastor, arrived, somehow I knew my task was done. Bill is a wonderful shepherd and a trusted friend. I hugged Jane. Told her how great a warrior and wife she had been and how thankful I was for her allowing me to be with Dallas and the family during such a sacred time.

I walked out of the ward, entered the elevator, and left the hospital. As I exited the front door, I passed a man whose smile and a dozen multicolored balloons announced him as the proud new father of a baby boy. Outside, the sun was blindingly bright on a cloudless morning. A maintenance worker drove his roaring lawn mower between the rows of cars, leaves rustled in the breeze overhead, and hospital employees in blue and green medical wear walked to their offices with coffee and bags of breakfast foods in hand, ready to start a new day. The power of life is unstoppable. Yet at the same time, I could not believe—I was almost dumbstruck by the fact—that none of these people, no one around me, was even aware of the tragically sad news I carried inside. Dallas Willard was gone, and I wanted the world to stop and realize it—to feel the impact of that reality, to bow their heads and take hold of just a moment of contemplation. *Halt your day just a little. Just stop for a few seconds and cry with me.* But they couldn't hear my wounded heart, and I have never felt more alone.

It was a long drive home from the hospital, so I stopped at Starbucks to get some coffee. As I ordered and waited for my coffee to be made, I found myself in a moment of still contemplation. I looked down, took a deep breath, and exhaled a long and sorrow-filled breath. My thoughts landed on a scene in the movie *Four Weddings and a Funeral.* The scene that always captured my attention depicted the raw mourning of a man reading "Funeral Blues," a poem of lament by W. H. Auden, at his friend's funeral service. It's a gripping display of sorrow. The words started to pass through my mind. The last two verses deliver the full burden of a broken heart.

> *He was my North, my South, my East and West,*
> *My working week and my Sunday rest*
> *My noon, my midnight, my talk, my song;*
> *I thought that love would last forever, I was wrong.*
>
> *The stars are not wanted now; put out every one,*
> *Pack up the moon and dismantle the sun.*
> *Pour away the ocean and sweep up the wood;*
> *For nothing now can ever come to any good.*

I started to weep. No, honestly, it was a sob. A shoulder-shaking sob. Right there in front of the Starbucks counter during the morning rush. I was embarrassed, but at the same time, I didn't care. What more could I lose? All the stress and strain, worry, doubt, hope, disappointment, love, anger, and gratefulness—jumbled and confused in a mix of sorrowfulness and exhaustion—were shaking out of me all at once.

Just as I was beginning to wonder if I would fall to my knees, a strong arm reached around my shoulders and held me fast. I looked up and through blurry eyes I saw a man, slightly older than me, with short coal-black hair, wraparound sunglasses, and a thick Fu Manchu mustache that reached down below his chin. He was wearing a sleeveless shirt, exposing large, very hairy, and very tattooed arms. He never turned to look at me. He never said a word. He just held me. For a while. Those around us focused all their attention on their smart phones so as to act like nothing was amiss. Eventually, my name was called, I went to the counter, retrieved my coffee, and when I turned around, he was gone. I wanted to thank him; I just didn't have any words. I think he understood.

The drive home was a blur. Memories, recent and distant, raced through my mind as tears rolled down my face. I finally pulled into my driveway, walked upstairs, hugged my wife, got into bed, and wept in her arms. When I had gained some composure, we talked about the past few days until my body began to search for sleep. As the power of my thoughts and feelings slowly began to fade, I was able to offer a prayer. I thanked God for Dallas and the gift he had been to me, my family, and countless others. I thanked God for the gift of the years, months, and days I was given with Dallas. I admitted to my confusion, anger, and even disappointment that Dallas had not been healed. There were so many prayers and hopes left unrealized. I asked God for time and grace to deal with my angst. And I prayed that God would continue to reveal and clarify for me the vision of the Kingdom that I first learned about from Dallas.

As exhaustion overtook me, somehow, a wonderful measure of the same peace, like a river, came attending my way. Despite my lot, my teacher had taught me to say, "It is well, it is well with my soul."

You may have wondered why I am telling this story in a chapter entitled "Joy." Very simply, despite my overwhelming sorrow, there was an undeniable and unshakable joy that undergirded those last few moments with Dallas. There was also a palpable sense of joy found in the comfort of both my mystery "angel's" and my wife's arms that continues to fill my heart even now when I bring those memories to mind. There is an enduring, everlasting quality of joy that is so very different from happiness. It's often suggested that happiness is an emotion that follows feelings that range from contentment to physical pleasure, and even significant periods of satisfaction. Joy, however, is a state of being that often, but not always, is manifested even in the absence of pleasure, contentment, or satisfaction. Joy has the potential to be much more permanent and robust than happiness. Happiness is typically derived from external circumstances, whereas joy emanates from internal, spiritual, and nonmaterial sources.

Joy has both transcendent and immanent capabilities. Happiness is limited to the immanent. Thus, in the ebb and flow of emotional upheaval, whether one is on top of the heap or at the bottom of the barrel, joy remains accessible despite our conditions in the moment. Joy is the result of experiencing a level of goodness that is unmistakable and irreducible in its unmatched ability to transform even our darkest hours. Unlike happiness, which is conditional, joy has the power to rise above and overwhelm any condition.

Why do we talk about joy rather than happiness? Because joy is the air of the Kingdom of God, now and forever. Therefore, we must begin to adjust our lungs and nostrils to its scents and the effects it can have on our hearts and minds. In eternity, settling for happiness will likely not be an option. A moment's pleasure is often a reduction, or only a foreshadowing of something much more substantive that we long to possess and abide in at the soul level of our being.

Dallas liked to consider those who win the lottery as a prime example that illustrates the difference between joy and happiness. Is it the actual money they celebrate? Likely not. Rather, he believed it's the hope of experiencing freedom, security, empowerment, and the perception of limitlessness that they finally sense is theirs "forever," all of which evokes the hope of joy's permanent place in their lives. Sadly, we know that for many winners, this joy is not to become their reality. Ironically, studies have demonstrated that many lottery winners find themselves worse off, at least financially, than they were before attaining their "winnings." There are various speculations about why this is the case. Dallas suggested, and I agree, that soon after lottery winners claim their "booty," it must be traded, continually, for items and experiences that will maintain the feelings of freedom, security, empowerment, and continued prosperity they desire. The trading never stops because the feelings are fleeting. But the money soon runs out. For it is an old, yet true, cliché that money can't buy happiness, no matter how much we are willing to pay for it.

Creative Joy

In contrast, heaven is a place where joy abounds. Joy can't be bought, traded for, earned, stored, borrowed, stolen, or won. Joy is the direct and effortless result and substance that emanates like rays of light from the united, loving, Trinitarian whole. One of the things that we tend to miss in our thoughts and teachings about God is how completely and effortlessly joyful God is. All creation was the result of an unlimited profusion of joyful acts.

Sometimes, the most poignant glimpses of this are witnessed in our children. There is a wonderful picture of my nephew Jackson as a toddler that hangs in my parents', his grandparents', den. His face is glowing. His inviting smile and his innocent brown eyes proclaim a pure joyfulness that permeates his entire being as he holds a fist full of mud up to his mother behind the camera. The picture captures the moment perfectly. "See Mom? Mud is awesome!"

Somewhere in all of us, there is a hand full of mud, a brush full of paint, a sonnet, an aria, a piece of oak furniture, a set of curtains, a sundress, a picture album, a popsicle-stick log cabin, a Crayola drawing taped to the refrigerator, or a plateful of multicolored cupcakes that demonstrate the pure joy we experience from being in the world and working our talents and skills to create something that did not exist ten minutes, ten months, or ten years prior. The joy that proceeds from these creative acts is just a taste of what God pours out from himself every moment from all eternity into all eternity. We mustn't forget that God is the most joyous and creative of all the beings in the universe.

And God hasn't finished creating. Somehow, we stop imagining God's ongoing creativity once we pass Genesis 2. This past year, I revisited the National Air and Space Museum. There, for a not-so-small fee, I watched two IMAX movies called *Hubble* and *Journey to the Stars*. In one of them, they showed a galaxy or a nebula that is essentially a star "nursery" where new stars are continually being created. It was one of the most stunning realities I've ever considered.

Most of us have been taught to think of the stars as millions or billions of light years away. This means by the time we are seeing the light from these distant stars we are actually looking "back in time" millions, if not billions, of years. As a result, if a star at the far corner of our universe imploded today, we may not realize it for quite a while. Therefore, for us, such an event would seem as if it hasn't quite "happened" yet. Realities like these tend to make us forget that new stars, new galaxies, and perhaps new universes and new worlds are still being created. God is still cranking out new toys all the time, which at least offers the possibility that God has other projects in the works, which may or may not include human beings at all. Who knows? Certainly not me. Dallas believed creation is still in process partly because God gains joy, creates joy, and gives joy in and from his creative acts. Such gifts of joy are available to be received and absorbed into our minds and hearts.

Unfortunately, we have settled too much and too long for happiness, to the point that joy is left out of the equation, and, therefore, is slowly fading from our imagination. There are likely two primary, but not exclusive, reasons that our search for happiness has crowded out any room for lasting joy in our individual lives and collective societies. The first reason is the developing sense today that we have a right and a need to be entertained, and therefore the desire for entertainment, which is connected to our endless string of hobbies and pastime events that have largely become a substitute for establishing and maintaining real, substantive joy in our lives.

The second way our Western culture expresses a robust absence of joy in contemporary life is manifested in our unimpeded search for increasing levels of drama and its effect on our minds and emotions. There are several ways this finds expression. The fanatic devotion to melodramatic serial-television programming and movie sequels is one example. Yet perhaps the most infamous overcommitment to the deficit of joy and meaning in life is found in the dedication, even fanaticism, given to sports teams and athletic contests. There are several aspects of our sporting culture that positively shape and form important values and disciplines that should remain a part of our society. What can be harmful is the overdramatization and imputed meaning given to the "games" themselves. Any hotly contested "rivalry," at whatever level of competition, is actually an artificially inflated staging of a conflict that works only when a collective level of fiction and fantasy is accepted.

Instead of staging or manufacturing dramatic circumstances to add meaning to our lives, human beings were made to experience joy, meaning, and significance as a result of *real* events and fulfillments that have *actual* substance deep within the core of our being. We are meant to feel and engage with reality in the totality of our personhood. Our sense of heightened dramatic existence was meant to be substantial, and actual, not fictional or artificially contrived. It was not God's intent that we become relegated to spectating others who "live and move and have their being" (adapted from Acts 17:28) in ways that we wish we could, but can't, and are thus left to live vicariously through their achievement. We were made to be participants experiencing joy and creating meaningful and purposeful lives through sharing our talents and skills interactively with God and others in his community of love.

I don't believe there are any sidelines or benches as we have come to conceive of them in heaven. Rather, in eternity we will be encouraged, perhaps even required, to own our lives and pursue our gifts, talents, interests, and purpose as responsible members fitted into the larger body of Christ, while simultaneously assuming our own potential. We shouldn't (and in heaven likely won't be able to) delegate our sense of purpose and giftedness to others. The gift of our lives is ours to facilitate and develop for God's glory. There is no hiding in heaven; there is just what is. And what is, is unavoidable. Therefore, joy and purposefulness will be unavoidable as well. The inability to hide also means the inability to deny or distract attention away from who and what we are and who and what we can be as joyful, thankful, and empowered members of the bride of Christ.

Joy and Depression

Even though I felt sadness following Dallas's death, my experience of joy was a significant and unforgettable moment in my life. Joyfulness was a crucial attribute that Dallas and I talked about long before he became ill. He encouraged me early on in our relationship about the value of instilling the habit of joyfulness into the way I train my mind to focus on certain kinds of thoughts that would lead to actions and responses motivated out of joy. He also firmly believed that joy comes primarily through finding and inhabiting one's sense of purpose and meaning in one's life and work. Dallas helped me to better understand the nature of the connection between my experience of joyful living and how I think of and perceive myself, as well as my faith, or lack of faith and knowledge about God's overarching mission in the world, God's character, and God's call or intentions for my life.

Dallas knew of my struggles with bouts of depression, times when I've had difficulty finding and maintaining joy in my life. Thankfully, I have been able to find resources that have helped me to manage these episodes that still come upon me at times. With the help of others in loving community, I've learned to recognize them, understand what they are, and even use them to my advantage in some ways. When I am moody or feeling much more like Eeyore than Tigger, I have realized I also experience a tremendous amount of creativity and reflective thinking, and

I am now better able to channel those feelings and moods into outlets such as my writing, photography, and music.[1] I also have noticed some of my most meaningful and transformational conversations with others tend to occur during these periods.

There are still some hard aspects to my periods of depression, however, and Dallas helped me in three key ways to better understand, and cope during these down times. First, he helped me to realize that often the depths of my symptoms were regularly affected by the trajectory or habits in my thinking. Those suffering from the symptoms of depression know how difficult it can be to stop one's thoughts from always falling toward futility and purposelessness. Dallas regularly asked me the question, "Is that [thought, feeling, or opinion] real and true, or is it just what you are feeling right now so strongly that it seems more real or true than it actually is?" Talking through these questions with him helped me to take my thoughts captive, slow my thinking down, redirect the paths my imagination takes me down, and not let myself be governed solely by my emotions in the moment.

The second discipline Dallas encouraged me to engage was to routinely bring the character of God before my mind through meditating and contemplating the descriptions of God in Psalms 23 and 30. He suggested I read these specific psalms three or four times a day, at each meal and at bedtime. Third, in light of these psalms, Dallas asked me to write down, in just a few short sentences, the crux of what I believe God has called me to pursue and achieve with my life over the next six months. After reading the psalms and contemplating the difference between what I feel and what is real, he suggested I think about whether or not I believe God is still willing and capable to provide what I need in order to achieve what he has called me to do.

As a result of these simple disciplines, I began to realize that even though the pessimism and dark moods still come, and I still struggle with the slope of my thoughts, the more I engage in these practices, the less easy it is to stay in a pit of despair. I still have bad days, even bad weeks, but not bad years. Although this simple process has been a useful tool for me, I certainly don't want to suggest it as a fix-all. There are times, and I have experienced them, when pharmaceutical treatment and professional counseling are required to avoid the avalanche of despair that can overwhelm the mind and soul. My point here is to argue that, for many of us, simply taking the time to think about, contemplate, discuss, and then begin to accept the reality of God's goodness, sustenance, and provision for our lives is itself a source of great joy and can reestablish a heart of gratitude, thankfulness, and appreciation for the realities of God's goodness and the intense meaningfulness inherent in our lives.

In sum, this is what the discipline of worship seeks to accomplish. True worship is much, much more than a few dedicated minutes of singing in our Sunday services. True worship places us in a position to put wonderful words, thoughts, images, and practices in our minds and bodies that demonstrate or manifest the truth and goodness of God and his Kingdom. Such realities are, in and of themselves, the most dramatic, awe-inspiring, and jaw-dropping the world has ever known. Either many Western, evangelical forms of Christianity have forgotten these attributes and characteristics of God and his Kingdom, or we have become so familiar and unaffected by God's omnipresence that we have developed a contemptuousness that, ironically, stems from an increasing unfamiliarity with God's overarching desires for all creation. We profess belief, but we lack actual experiential knowledge. Simply put, we don't actually know very much about what it is we say we believe in. Such a condition allows a low-burning level of despair to go unchecked in the hearts and minds of many attending our churches. As a result, our corporate-worship services can tend to reflect what we expect from God: not much. It seems increasingly difficult to discern the difference between a worship service that seeks authentic communal engagement with the unlimited greatness of God, and an entertainment venue that tries to impute dramatic flourishes toward the goal of emotional manipulation.

Conversely, when the scriptures discuss the subject of worship, it flows from a response to the joy exploding from creatures realizing God's redemption, empowerment, and freedom to achieve the full expanse of the collective destiny for which they were created. Our very existence is to be empowered to achieve a purposeful, meaningful, and joyous presence. Meaningful joyfulness creates an environment upon which we can bestow our worship of God in a worthy manner. How could a football game compare to life in and with the God of the universe? Why would we even think it comparable? Intellectually, most of us don't consider it comparable. Yet if we consider the phenomenon in total, we may worship our sports and play at our church services, not the other way around.

Ask yourself the question, On what basis do I determine if I am worshipping God in spirit and truth? If we say we do worship God in such a way, is this a practice that routinely leads to a sense of joy, thanksgiving, and purpose in our lives? Or has worship become limited to that period of singing, alms giving, and liturgical devices employed once a week, to marginal effect on the entirety of your life? Is worship a joyous expression, full of acknowledged gratitude that originates from full appreciation of the unfettered realities of an awe-inspiring God, or is worship an activity connected to CD sales, unique conferences, and esoteric religious practices? In heaven, worship will be an orchestra of souls uniquely and communally celebrating who they are, and are becoming, all because of God's goodness and love.

This is, in part, what I believe is behind God's commandment to honor our parents. As reflections of our divine parent, we honor and give proper acknowledgment to all our progenitors for what they have done for us throughout our lives, for giving us our lives, for carrying the responsibility for our many needs of provision, protection, development, teaching, and modeling. We honor our parents because in many ways we benefit from the totality of their existence focused to our benefit. Consequently, much of what we become is directly related to the sum of the gifts given by those who raised us.

Unfortunately, for many, this responsibility carries the potential for not only great blessing but great suffering. The opportunity for deep appreciation and thankfulness for our parents is directly tied to the depth of the impact they make on our souls. Of course, there is a dramatic difference with our heavenly parent, for God is perfect in love and provision for our needs. Therefore, we honor God, glorifying him for what he has done in and through our lives as well. We also celebrate what graces he demonstrates in the lives of others.

Thus, eternal life, or life that is sourced from the power within the Kingdom of God, presents us with an opportunity to humbly live in the unvarnished truth of who we are both individually and collectively, in full knowledge of the magnitude of why we have been created as such. We learn that the answer to the question, "What is man that You are mindful of him?" (Ps. 8:4–8, NKJV) has been answered. The result is a celebration of a congregation of hearts and minds united in agreement around the goodness and glorious benevolence of God.

If you have ever attended a Saturday afternoon college football game, you have likely experienced a moment when the home crowd rises to their feet and screams at the top of their lungs in celebration of what their team has accomplished. Such a moment is a very dramatic illustration of the thousands, if not tens of thousands, of people achieving what they deeply desire, what their wills hope for, what they have longed to become a reality, and as a result, they exalt the realization of that moment in unhindered praise. It is in a moment like this when we can imagine how joy and meaning are indelibly linked. What heaven will ensure is that the moments we long for, the conditions we seek, and the dramas we experience will have actual, eternal consequences with unending beauty and significance.

What is left to consider is whether living a life of joyous praise envelops the kind of worldview, or conscious awareness, that we are willing and able to maintain and cultivate in our daily lives. Do we find praiseworthy meaning in the routine activities of our lives? Are we looking for it? This is what Paul suggests is the importance and blessing of praying "without ceasing" (1 Thess. 5:17). Do we desire to live in the light of God's goodness and joy, or do we allow the undisciplined and unfaithful randomness of our thoughts and fears to lead us into believing something completely contrary to the benevolent will of God toward his creation? Where do we put our minds? Paul is right. We can be continually transformed, all of us, in our entirety, by the renewing of our minds. Meditating and feeding the mind and soul with the joy of the Lord is one of the primary disciplines that develops a plentiful harvest of the Spirit's fruit in our lives, for it is God's joy that is to be our strength for life and living (Neh. 8:10).

The Joy of Our Salvation

There was a peace and joy to Dallas's final moments that surpassed understanding. But as I mentioned earlier, in many ways, this peace or *shalom* of God also made perfect sense. Even then,

then most of all, the realities of Psalm 23 were truer than ever. Jesus was shepherding Dallas through the valley of death, leading him to quiet waters, restoring his soul. Even those final moments of struggle held meaning and purpose for him, and Dallas faced them with a calm resolve, and a heart full of joy. His final words were, "Thank you." This is the joy of our salvation. We have nothing to fear. Even on death's doorstep, joy unspeakable has a tendency to bubble up and overwhelm any scheme designed to restrict its flow. Heaven is a state where such joy breaks through continually. "O death, where is thy sting?" (1 Cor. 15:55, KJV).

Dallas experienced a good and radiant death. And I was honored with the ability to witness his passing up close. What I learned at his bedside that morning was how crucial it is for me, for us, to come to a clear and unfettered understanding of the nature of our lives—good, bad, or ugly—and of God's character. This is the means through which our entire lives become acts of worship that can empower us with an amazing amount of freedom and joy to pursue the purposes of God. Many of us wonder what we would do if we were to find out that we had a month or a year to live. I actually was able to walk with Dallas through that reality for a while. I have known many whose lives have been significantly altered, for the better, due to a terminal illness. And what many report is the worshipful, peaceful, purposeful, and intensified ways they begin to engage every moment of their lives.

I suggest that such a state of mind, when aware of the power and glory of God, his character, his provision, and purposes for us, is not a state of fear, but a state of ultimate meaning, even joy. It is a state of being where we can live moment to moment in the realization of the fact that we live and move and have our being simply as a result of the action of God to provide the breath in our lungs and the beat of our hearts. We are totally and utterly dependent on him, a fact that is not suffocating but liberating, if we know who God is and the nature of his love and care.

I believe eternal, heavenly existence is such that we can live on the ragged edge of dependency as if the Rock of Gibraltar were under our feet. For in heaven, as on earth, it is when we are weak that we are strong. It is when we follow that we can lead others to the truth. And it is in the acknowledgment and celebration of the truth about the grandeur of God and his character that we find our own joy and purpose for life. Heaven is an inescapably purpose-driven reality. Finding clarity and submission to God's purposes for our lives now is just as essential to our eternal purposes then.

Are joy, peace, and purpose characteristics you'd like to know and experience in your life? Do you experience them now? Is there a sustainable level and degree of endurable peace that you want to mark your days? What needs to change in your life for that to happen? What are you willing to do differently? What are you willing to risk?

We have to make some choices. Will we continue to settle for entertainment as a replacement for true, authentic, holistic worship in our lives? Are we caught in a cycle where we relegate ourselves to spectators who assume little to no responsibility for our eternal destinies, while we crave the drama that results from encountering the poignant and powerful activities of great significance in our lives? Where are we going to satisfy these desires? God can and will reveal to us his vision and means for developing lives full of the significance, meaning, peace, and joy we long for—if we want him to. Do you?

Final Things

A t the summation of Dallas's earthly life, which, of course, came at the culmination of his death, he was thankful, deeply thankful. He taught me that to maintain a perspective of thankfulness through the pains, fears, and losses that death threatens is perhaps the final blessing of experiencing the grace afforded to a life well lived. I'm beginning to realize that gratitude is a product of willfully experiencing and accepting grace. That is why the two words are conjoined. *Gratis* is the Latin root of "grace." I'm learning how gratitude is the result of recognizing the grace of God, which allows me to better maintain the proper context and keep an accurate perspective on even the most difficult of life's circumstances and situations.

But the realization alone hasn't made it easy to be thankful. Nor is it something that just comes to me or falls on me like gravity. I'm learning to cultivate and consciously embed the habit of gratitude in my heart and mind. I'm also realizing it is a habit deeply threatened in a culture that bombards us with reasons to remain discontented and needy in order that we go about seeking a purchasable cure. To be truly thankful, at peace, and content with the grace of God is to lack for nothing, despite my condition. I'm working on that. And I'm getting better at it, slowly. I'm not what I want to be, but I'm better than I was.

Perhaps a good goal is to think about what my final words will be. Words that come from my heart. Dallas's last words were "Thank you," words that proceeded from a heart full of thanks. What I sensed in the moment and believe still today is that he was verbalizing his gratitude to God for his entire life and everything in it: the struggles, triumphs, failures, lessons, insights, and experiences of joy, pain, loss, and sorrow, which for all of us are strung together and joined as the chain of our lives. In his last moments on earth, he was thankful for it all. What perspective, what release, what an experience of satisfaction, must be his to consider his entire life and be grateful. What greater gift and experience of grace can we attain than to have the entirety of our existence present itself as its own offering, as a living sacrifice, holy and pleasing to God, in a sacred moment of wondrous thanksgiving? This is what it means to love oneself. To be in love with one's own life. That's a goal worth pursuing, a lifelong goal.

I believe Dallas was grateful for the very essence and totality of his life. Perhaps such a perspective is more easily attained when facing and contemplating the inescapability or inevitability of death. If so, Dallas grabbed that opportunity. May we all live a life in which such realities bring our hearts and minds to praise and adoration of God's grandeur and majesty so that our final words to God in this life, as we enter the next, are of gratitude, thanksgiving, and overwhelming appreciation for all that God has done for us.

The Great Eternal Hope

All the implications of what I learned and witnessed, and am still learning, from Dallas's final few months could perhaps fill many volumes. Yet the most lasting impressions center on the interrelatedness between truth, goodness, joy—and the good life and a good death—that I witnessed at work in Dallas's life. Dallas knew the truth, he was able to do the good, and despite his circumstances, he was filled with peace and joy. He achieved these through experiencing the love and grace of God gained through apprenticeship to Jesus as he learned to live in the ways of the Kingdom.

Perhaps you are facing a set of dire circumstances, maybe a terminal diagnosis, or a very dangerous assignment, or perhaps you are a friend or family member journeying with someone in such a situation who is beginning to prepare for the end of his or her life on earth, and this is causing you to contemplate eternity in a radically new way. Something Dallas and I talked about quite a bit that may be helpful in trying to best deal with the difficulty of what may lie ahead comes from the introduction to Peter Kreeft's book *Heaven: The Heart's Deepest Longing*. Kreeft proposes three questions of ultimate importance for every human being to consider: What can I know? What should I do? And what may I hope for?[1] Kreeft offers three answers. We can know the truth. We should do the good. And we can hope for joy.

Kreeft also recognizes there are important desires that must accompany these answers. We must *want* to know the truth. We must *want* to do the good. And we must *want* to pursue a joyful life. If we do want such virtues to be realities in our lives, then the paramount question is what will allow us to attain the virtues of truth, goodness, and joy? The rest of Kreeft's book describes how the Kingdom of Heaven is the ultimate culmination or fulfillment of truth, goodness, and joy. All of these are attained through placing one's confidence in Christ and experiencing God's endless love, both of which lead us to a joyful life of peace and purpose in his Kingdom.

In short, Dallas devoted his life to thinking, writing, and teaching about precisely how the gospel of Jesus answers these paramount questions. God has opened the doors to truth, goodness, and joy. Whosoever will may come and enjoy these qualities forever. That is very good news!

In many profound and crucial ways, Dallas was experiencing a heavenly existence long before he died. So can we. I can testify that the peace Dallas found, lived with, and sang of has slowly begun to settle into me as well, albeit in fits and starts. In connection with the interrelatedness between a good life and a good death, I think the heading of this section, "The Great Eternal Hope" really summarizes our purposes well. It is my great eternal hope to experience a radiantly good life and death. I now know Dallas's prayer for me in the monastery years ago is being answered. I have, indeed, witnessed both a radiant life and a radiant death. I now know much, but certainly not all, of what is required and what glory can be experienced and demonstrated through a life devoted to the good that results in a glorious death. And hopefully now, regardless of whatever difficulty you or your loved ones are facing, so do you.

I am now more grateful for my life than ever before, and I am learning to live in the knowledge and reality a state of gratitude offers me. You can as well. This is our eternal hope. Next to love, hope may be one of the strongest forces in the universe. No fatal diagnosis is ever stronger than hope. Hope is the settled expectation of impending good. In the Kingdom of God, under the care of the Good Shepherd, hope is eternal. For "surely goodness and mercy shall follow me all the days of my life; and I shall dwell in the house of the LORD for ever" (Ps. 23:6, RSV). This is hope at work.

Dallas faced physical death as the start of the eternal life to come. His confidence in Jesus remained the rock on which his life, and his death, ensued. Now my prayers tend to tilt more toward developing a level of peace that makes perfect sense, because I won't ever forget how contagious Dallas's faith was for me and others. His discipled relationship to Christ formed him in ways that allowed him to face all of life, including his death, with courage and grace. The honesty, fearlessness, power, relational intimacy, and joy he packed deep within his soul prior to his trials thrust him through the valley of death unbroken. This is the nature of the stingless death and the eternal durability of Christ's sufficiency to meet and supersede all our most pressing needs.

Preparing for Evermore

We end this book where we started, although hopefully more challenged, enlightened, motivated, and encouraged to follow in the ways of Christ. Dallas helped me learn how to pack my life, to prepare my heart, will, mind, body, and relationships to endure the eternal realities of the Kingdom of Heaven. I'm storing these treasures not in a steamer trunk but within myself, my character, my eternal soul. I'm learning how to better discern what is true, honorable, just, pure, pleasing, commendable, excellent, and worthy of praise (Phil. 4:8). These qualities of goodness are good for us because they propel and encourage the attainment of the potential implicit in our position in God's Kingdom. God has designed his Kingdom to facilitate and fully demonstrate the nature of what humans were created to be and could become once again under his benevolent reign.

Our lives continue, in one fashion or another, to slope in one direction or another, for all eternity. Each of our lives, our existence, does not end, ever. Dallas believed human beings are unceasing spiritual beings of inestimable worth whom God has created with a unique meaning and purpose in his inventive, imaginative, resourceful, illimitable, and creative love. Yet all of this, by design, requires a choice or a will free to choose. Which slope, which tendency, or which direction we choose makes all the difference. Our decisions echo throughout eternity.

Death to self, the willful submission and acquiescence of the entire life or soul to God, is not optional. As we take up our own crosses and trust the Kingdom of God with our existence and its flourishing, good is allowed to transform our lives until we are glorified as image bearers, children, heirs of the one true God, sitting at his right hand, responsibly sharing delegated power and authority, and miraculously abiding where he is, in him, with him, and by him (John 17). We have not returned to the garden. The garden has returned to us. In the end, the singularity of a garden is transformed into a magnificent and shining city. Such a transformation reveals how marvelously Jesus has been at work, along with those who preceded us into eternity, in maturing the wilds of a garden into a home for everyone who desires to abide therein.

Unfortunately, not everyone will enjoy such a reality. I am sympathetic to those who find such a possibility difficult if not impossible to accept. Yet despite the amazing rescue attempts, despite the wooing, pleading, convincing, and demonstrative acts of God's love and power to persuade, some minds and hearts simply will not change. Dallas once told me that he didn't have a clear picture on how the "furniture is arranged in hell," but he did believe in hell, albeit somewhat begrudgingly. Evil is real and durable. How long it will last and in what form, he would never speculate. However, as a philosophical and phenomenological realist, he knew better than most how definite and substantial reality is and, therefore, it cannot be simply wished or argued away simply because we encounter its inconvenient or troubling effects.

When I asked Dallas to describe what he felt hell might be like, he again referred me to Matheson's book *What Dreams May Come*. Matheson, like Dante, tried to demonstrate what it may be like for a human being to encounter a sin state as it actually is, without the prevenient blessing of God's presence, or the benefits of and buffering that is allowed by our ignorance, naïveté, misunderstandings, illusions, delusions, lies, defenses, and rationalizations of sin, either in theory or practice. Matheson's interpretation of hell is somewhat similar in many respects to Lewis's view. For both, hell is not centrally concerned with, or created as a place of, punishment. Rather, hell, like heaven, is a condition where reality is unavoidable, unvarnished, and unmitigated. It's not the conditions of the surroundings that represent the difference. Rather, it is the existential condition through which one experiences the surroundings that may determine the difference. Dallas suggested that the difference between heaven and hell may be as simple as the "common horse sense contained in the folk wisdom 'one man's trash is another man's treasure.'"

In describing some thoughts about hell, Dallas wrote,

One should seriously inquire if to live in a world permeated with God and the knowledge of God is something they themselves truly desire. If not, they can be assured that God will excuse them from his presence. They will find their place in the "outer darkness" of which Jesus spoke. But the fundamental fact about them will not be that they are there, but that they have become people so locked into their own self-worship and denial of God that they cannot want God. A well-known minister of other years used to ask rhetorically, "You say you will accept God when you want to?" And then he would add, "How do you know you will be able to want to when you think you will?" The ultimately lost person is the person who cannot want God. *Who cannot want God to be God. Multitudes of such people pass by every day, and pass into eternity. The reason they do not find God is that they do not want him or, at least, do not want him to be God. Wanting God to be God is very different from wanting God to help me.*[2]

For Dallas, there were no second chances in determining whether one wants righteousness or not. There are unlimited chances to grow and change in terms of maturing toward righteousness and holiness on earth. There just aren't unlimited opportunities to choose righteousness forever. For if there were, the garden dilemma would be played out continually, for all of eternity, in some form or another, and thus, evil would never be overcome with good. For Dallas, the degree to which we achieve righteousness was crucial but never as crucial as the wholehearted desire for righteousness itself. He came back over and over to one very clear decree in scripture.

> *He has told you, O mortal, what is good;*
> *and what does the LORD require of you*
> *but to do justice, and to love kindness,*
> *and to walk humbly with your God?*
>
> (MIC. 6:8)

God has predictably and perfectly done his part. Glory be to God. We have been shown, told, given, and provided an example of the good life. We have the opportunity to taste and see that the Lord is good and to experience the joy of safe haven in him and his ways (Ps. 34:8). It's up to us to choose, a choice that is appointed to be made during our lifetime; then we face the consequences of our choices (Heb. 9:27). Thank God, we have such a choice. Thank God, we are able to taste and see the depth of his love, grace, power, and beauty, both now and into eternity.

In my introduction to *The Divine Conspiracy Continued*, I reflected on my first meeting with Dallas by saying:

> *Dallas reminded me of Willie [sic] Wonka in Roald Dahl's* Charlie and the Chocolate Factory. *Not that Dallas was silly or fanciful. In fact, he appeared quite the opposite. But the Wonka analogy came from the similar way that Willard stood at the threshold of the kingdom of God and, with glee and the kind of excitement that comes only from encouraging the hopeful anticipation of children, invited us into the most wonderfully delicious experiences that life could ever offer. And I, like Charlie, was awestruck—not by Willard, but by the tales he told of his experience inside God's amazing castle of wonders. Willard invited us in, all of us, telling us and showing us we have nothing to fear and everything to gain. In the many years since, I've listened to numerous stories similar to mine. People from all walks of life, often deeply steeped in a particular faith tradition, tell of sensing that Dallas was revealing the gospel for the first time as "good news" and not simply the opposite of "bad news."*[3]

Sometimes I argue with my friends and colleagues that even though Dallas was noted as a world-class philosopher, theologian, professor, spiritual director, and writer, more than anything else he was an evangelist. Routinely, that statement gets people looking at me in quizzical ways. But for those who are steeped in Dallas's thoughts, they tend to think for a second, and then lean their heads to the side with a smile. They understand why I would make such a connection. For me and many others, Dallas helped us see and experience the good news of Jesus with new eyes, open ears, and clear minds when many of our religious traditions were stuck on the premise that just attaining a golden ticket to heaven will solve every conceivable problem of our lives.

Of course, we have our own ideas about what those problems are, why they exist, and how to fix them. And it is that fact, the fact that we come to the Kingdom of Heaven with our own stubborn and entrenched convictions, preconceived notions, religious interpretations, and demands for our lives, expecting to get what we think and believe is best for ourselves in return, that becomes the hindrance to the abundance of human life as God intended it to be.

Perhaps hell is a place where we can never stop wanting that which is bad for us despite always suffering from what we get. And perhaps heaven is a place where we are able to become the kinds of people who both want and get what is best for us, a place where we can't ever stop benefiting from the result. As an evangelist, one who brings, professes, and manifests good news, Dallas was arguing for, demonstrating, and living in God's factory of goodness, and he was handing out golden tickets for that life to everyone he could find.

The question for us now is to reconsider what we believe these golden tickets will allow us to achieve. The conditions of both heaven and hell primarily center on the nature of our eternal character. I am suggesting that the fulfillment and consequences of what has formed our values, motivations, pursuits, and choices all coalesce to forge the characteristic nature of our individual existence. The effects of our histories do not radically change after physical death if we don't want them to change during our earthly lives. Therefore, our lives today prepare us to face and endure the reality of heaven. One way or another, we all face the realities and conditions inherent to life in an eternal state. Whether this is a tremendous or terrorizing event is up to us.

Here is the good news: Jesus gives us a sure way to achieve the tremendous. He has provided a choice, a way, a life, that is not only good but also great, full of purpose, joy, power, grace, relational unity and intimacy, fearless trust, and genuine truth. All of it must be, and can be chosen, walked into, experienced, learned, shared, and intimately known at the core of our beings—right this very second. Those conditions that plague us, that create areas where we struggle and falter, that have caused us to experience the absence of joy, purpose, and the like must still be faced. The sooner, the better.

I suggest that instead of saving our Willy Wonka golden tickets until we die, we should cash them in, right now, for all they're worth, and settle for nothing less. When we do, I believe we will attain real life, abundant life, the radiant existence we all inherently seek, long before we die. And when we face our earthly death, we will be prepared to experience the closing act of this life as a radiant passing into eternity with expectancy, hope, honor, and grace, all to the glory of God. For truly, truly, we look forward not only to a distant time in the by-and-by, but to the life we have now where we can discover the fullness of life that God has prepared for us that will never end. Such a reality is rich and full of the knowledge and experience of the nature of God's omnibenevolent character. Dallas developed an unflagging assurance that in the end, God can be trusted to do everything for, to, with, and through us for the highest and greatest good forever and ever. All we need to do is get on board with that agenda.

The Banquet

One of the most enjoyable events in my life is celebrating the holidays with my family and friends around a wonderful meal. I enjoy cooking, but I really enjoy cooking the big holiday meals that take a lot of planning and coordination. I usually start weeks in advance, thinking about the main course, the appetizers, what traditional side dishes we'll serve, and what new recipes I want to experiment with. I enjoy hunting down the various ingredients and maybe buying a new kitchen gadget or two. I like visiting the butcher, the baker, and the local grocer, looking for fresh foods and new ideas. I like listening to Bach and Beethoven during the chopping, searing, and stirring. I like the sound of the doorbell ringing and the anticipation conveyed in the words, "The house smells great!" I like it all.

Most of all, I love the assembly, the moments when everyone sits face-to-face around a large table, when loved ones have arrived after traveling long distances, and lifelong relationships are renewed and rekindled. I love hearing my father give thanks to God "for life, and the joy of living it." I love watching guests who are experiencing our family celebrations for the first time. Some are initially overwhelmed, but they soon realize they are more than just welcome; they are essential to our celebration. I love the ritual of reminding the children why we celebrate whatever special occasion has brought us together, why it's important, and what it means to us.

The meal serves as the means wherein we are intimately reminded and are thankful for the abundance of blessing we experience in our lives, both for the provision of our needs and the delight shared in the love and devotion we have for one another. Long after the food is gone, I love to sit and listen to old stories and the telling of new adventures and to watch the children bend their ears to discover where they have come from and what destiny and legacy is theirs to inherit. I don't like the cleanup.

Therefore, it's no surprise that of all the metaphors used to describe heaven, the one that speaks to me most intimately is the image of a banquet. I imagine such a banquet will take a lot of planning, eons of forethought, boundless energy, and amazing levels of devotion. Such a banquet will perfectly quench every possible hunger and thirst. The triune God, the celebration's most glorious participant, will sit at the head of this table. He will offer his blessing. We will radiate his glory as we finally behold him face-to-face. Every longing will cease, for we are wanted and honored around that table. There is a place setting for each of us. Most of us will likely have traveled long distances, and there will be amazing stories to tell. Old friendships and crucial relationships will be restored and redeemed. Faith will fill every cup. Hope will be the music carried in the air, and love's aroma will fill the room as it is lavishly served, one to another. We will experience eternal belonging. We will listen as the elders retell the story of God's glorious deeds, those known and unknown to us. We will serve others while being served by others. We will be delighted in while being delightful. We will celebrate while being part of the celebration. We will be thankful, restful, and peaceful, all at once.

I've started to pack away these invaluable treasures. I'm preparing my life, heart, mind, and soul, for eternal living. I'm endeavoring, with both setbacks and successes, to experience and instill the Fruit of the Spirit into my soul in a way that will make my life in the Kingdom of Heaven blessed, both now and throughout all eternity. I'm also making plans to be at that heavenly banquet table. I wouldn't miss it for anything. I'll be the one in the Husserl cap, laughing and sharing stories with those beloved who arrived before me, learning from Jesus how to overcome whatever unfinished business I will have left to resolve, which may take a while. Yet I am confident I will engage all those realities and much more with Jesus, filled with joy unspeakable, because that is, finally and ultimately, what I want, what I long for, and desperately seek with my deeply flawed heart and soul. What about you? What do you want? What do you seek?

Until then . . .

I pray that you would have a rich life of joy and power, abundant in supernatural results, with a constant, clear vision of never-ending life in God's world before you, and the everlasting significance of your work day by day. A radiant life and a radiant death.

Amen.

And Amen.

Acknowledgments

There have been many people whose expertise, encouragement, and devotion allowed this book to come into being and who deserve my heartfelt appreciation and recognition. First, the professionals at HarperOne, Mickey Maudlin and Kathryn Renz Hamilton, whose belief in this book and devotion to Dallas's legacy gave it its birth. My literary agent, Stephen Hanselman, has been and continues to provide a wise, discerning voice of guidance while also being a devoted friend and lover of Dallas's work. Stephen's wisdom was displayed in partnering me with Julia Roller, a wonderful writer, insightful editor, and lovely person, to refine and shine this text far beyond my abilities alone. Such is the nature of grace.

Walt Zimmer, a longtime family friend and role model, was kind enough to read and offer his unique perspectives on the first draft of this book. As providence would have it, after being apart for decades, we found ourselves together again beside the casket of his wonderful daughter and my childhood friend Kimberly. That event, while sorrowful and tragic, and Walt's willingness to read the book in the midst of his own mourning and loss, provided me with invaluable insights and clarity. For that I am deeply grateful.

My fellow colleagues, friends, and students at Azusa Pacific University have been constant sources of invigoration and inspiration. Specifically Keith Matthews, Tony Baron, Jon Wallace,

Scott Daniels, Barbara Hayes, Jan Johnson, Don Thorsen, Gregg Moder, and Paul Kaak continue to provide thoughtful support and encouragement. Kent Carlson and Mike Lueken are two of the best friends a man could have. I am so privileged to know and learn from them. My dear friends John and Danice Burdett and their family inspire me in ways they may never fully appreciate. I'm so very grateful for the prayers and direction of Rebecca Przybylski who has often reminded me that "how we get there is where we arrive." And then there is Sandy and Morgan Davis, whose hospitality is epic, along with an eager patience, wise judgment, and enthusiastic encouragement that are simply irreplaceable in my life. My hope for all of us is to better experience the realities described in this book in our families, churches, schools, vocations, and neighborhoods.

I have been immeasurably blessed by my immediate family, who have always offered their love, support, and guidance. My parents, Jane and Gary Sr., read *all* my early manuscripts and allow me to see the potential these ideas have in their hopeful and knowing eyes. I also am indebted to my brother Patrick, sister-in-law Donna, niece Peyton, and nephews Jackson and AJ for courageously seeing the benefits of allowing me to share some of our family's historic laundry. I pray our past helps illuminate and bless others' futures.

As always, projects like these require a level of devotion that takes away from time spent with those we love and cherish the most. I pray that the sacrifices paid by my daughters Taylor and Jacy can be somewhat assuaged by using these pages to learn ever more about the nature of their lives and the beauty and power of the Kingdom of God, and to discover for themselves why their parents have devoted their lives to searching out and living in its illimitable beauty. We found the field of treasures. Let's play!

I have dedicated this book to my wife, Susie, whose example

of Christlike faithfulness, love, and character is set ever before me as a testament to the truth and power of the gospel. I have learned more about how to courageously and sacrificially apply love, mercy, and grace from her than from any human being I know. Her love is legendary. I am so very thankful and blessed that her love has landed on me.

Finally, no words can express my appreciation to the Willard family, Jane, John, Becky, Bill, and Larissa, for allowing me the privilege of sharing the most precious of days with their husband, father, grandfather, and friend. I hope this book is yet one more testament to the unquenchable devotion Dallas gave to his work and calling as a disciple and minister of the gospel of Jesus Christ. To God be the glory for all the many things he has done. Amen.

Notes

Introduction: Preparing for Evermore

1. Richard Matheson, *What Dreams May Come: A Novel* (New York: Putnam, 1978).

Chapter One: Beyond the Cosmic Car Wash

1. Dallas Willard, *The Divine Conspiracy: Rediscovering Our Hidden Life in God* (San Francisco: HarperSanFrancisco, 1998), 250.
2. Tritheism is a belief about the Trinity that suggests the members of the Trinity are three distinct and separate persons. "The name is especially applied to the teaching of a group of 6th-cent. Monophysites, the best known of whom was John Philoponus; he taught that the common nature shared by the Three Persons is an intellectual abstraction, and that though the Father, Son, and Holy Spirit have a common nature and substance (are 'consubstantial'), they are as individuals distinct substances or natures and also distinct in their properties. This teaching was condemned as tritheism at the Third Council of Constantinople (680–682 CE)." F. L. Cross and Elizabeth A. Livingstone, eds., *The Oxford Dictionary of the Christian Church* (Oxford: Oxford Univ. Press, 2005), 1654.
3. See my conversation referenced on page 97. These ideas are also discussed in Chapter 2 of *The Divine Conspiracy*, which is followed up by some conclusions drawn on pages 301–6.
4. See chapter 2 of *Divine Conspiracy* for a full description of sin management.
5. Gary Moon, "Getting the Elephant out of the Sanctuary: An Inter-

view with Dallas Willard," *Conversations Journal* 8, no. 1 (Spring/ Summer 2010), 10–19.

6. Others have done so to good effect. Some more current discussions that reassess traditional understandings of heaven and the eternal characteristics of the afterlife come from New Testament scholar N. T. Wright and theologians Paul Enns and Christopher Morse. Certainly, C. S. Lewis's theology on these questions is also valuable in these discussions. Also see N. T. Wright, *Surprised by Hope: Rethinking Heaven, the Resurrection, and the Mission of the Church* (San Francisco: HarperOne, 2008); *How God Became King: The Forgotten Story of the Gospels* (San Francisco: HarperOne, 2012); Christopher Morse, *The Difference Heaven Makes: Rehearing the Gospel as News* (New York: T&T Clark International, 2010); and Paul Enns, *Heaven Revealed*, (Chicago: Moody Publishers, 2011).

7. Ironically, there is no going "up there" in these texts. The new Jerusalem comes "down" from heaven in verse 2. So too, three times in verse 3, God is said to make his abode or dwelling place "with man" or "with them"—another description of God coming "down here" as opposed to us going "up there" to be "with him."

8. For more insight on these comparisons, see G. K. Beale, *The Book of Revelation: A Commentary on the Greek Text,* New International Greek Testament Commentary (Grand Rapids, MI: W. B. Eerdmans, 1999), 991–93.

9. Wright provides a wealth of information regarding the historical, philosophical, biblical, and theological grounds for the existence of an intermediate state and the way first-century Judaism and early Christian writers understood life, death, and immortality. See N. T. Wright, *The Resurrection of the Son of God* (Minneapolis: Fortress Press, 2003), 31. Also see 127–200, specifically 133–34, and pt. 2, sec. 5, particularly 216, 252.

10. A recent book investigating the nature of heaven, hell, and purgatory offered from an evangelical perspective is Jerry L. Walls, *Heaven, Hell, and Purgatory: Rethinking the Things That Matter Most* (Grand Rapids, MI: Brazos Press, 2015). A very good survey of the progression of Protestant thought on the intermediate state

is found in Laurie Throness, *A Protestant Purgatory: Theological Origins of the Penitentiary Act, 1779* (Burlington, VT: Ashgate Publishing, 2008), ch. 2.

11. Dallas and I talked at great length about Lewis's comment regarding our perspectives relating to heaven and hell. Lewis states, "Earth, I think, will not be found by anyone to be in the end a very distinct place. I think earth, if chosen instead of heaven, will turn out to have been, all along, only a region in hell: and earth, if put second to heaven, to have been from the beginning a part of heaven itself." C. S. Lewis, *The Great Divorce* (New York: Collier Books, 1984), ix. Thus, it seems clear that the book goes on to describe what those in a hellish state might experience when encountering a heavenly state. Therefore, neither Dallas believed, nor do I believe, Lewis intended to specifically describe the development of Christ-like character in the intermediate heaven. The benefit of Lewis's fiction is the way it allows us to imagine how durable human character is even when confronted with the realities of paradise.

12. Some may wonder why such a statement is necessary. Dallas believed that the human existence continues beyond the death of the body. Some more recent theological positions have argued that there is no immortality of the human soul or spirit, and thus, human existence in eternity requires the resurrection of the body for the continuation of human life after death. In part, this position stems from the increasing popularity of what is called nonreductive physicalism and its connection to theology through the works of philosophers and theologians such as Nancey Murphy and Joel Green. See Joel B. Green, *Body, Soul, and Human Life: The Nature of Humanity in the Bible* (Grand Rapids, MI: Baker Academic, 2008) and Nancey C. Murphy, *Bodies and Souls, or Spirited Bodies?* (Cambridge: Cambridge Univ. Press, 2006). The alternative and more traditional position is offered by philosopher J. P. Moreland. See J. P. Moreland, *The Soul: How We Know It's Real and Why It Matters* (Chicago: Moody Publishers, 2014) and Matthew Levering, *Jesus and the Demise of Death: Resurrection, Afterlife, and the Fate of the Christian* (Waco, TX: Baylor Univ. Press, 2012).

13. In 2 Cor. 5:1–9, Paul suggests there is some form, or state, of existence in which we dwell or "rest" (also see Rev. 6:11) that is substantial but is perhaps less substantial than the "building" that will be our resurrected, incorruptible bodies, something he calls a "further" or more complete "clothing." Dallas believed Paul was referring to such an in-between existence as the condition when we are absent from the body but present with the Lord, which lies somewhere between the "tent" of our earthly bodies and the more permanent "building" of our resurrection bodies. The "clothing" image is carried forward in Rev. as well. There are several references to white "robes" or "cloaks" that may be attempts at describing some form of personal coverings that we inhabit or "wear" in the intermediate state (Rev. 6:11; 7:9–14; 22:14). It seems in some measure Christ may inhabit or incarnate a similar form (Rev. 19:13–16). The two most important points to highlight here are that, first, human beings are never described in the scriptures as free-floating, disembodied spirits or ghosts. Second, the scriptures give several references, in addition to Jesus's statement to the thief on the cross, that indicate human beings continue to exist and maintain a level of conscious awareness after the death of their bodies.

Two key references are found in the Hebrew scriptures that point to an intermediate state of existence after physical death and before the final resurrection of the body. The book of Job (19:25–27) gives a depiction of an expectation of conscious awareness of one's self and God after death. There is also a depiction of King Saul seeking out a medium or witch (1 Sam. 28) to discuss an upcoming battle with the deceased prophet Samuel. In this passage, Samuel is recorded as having made a postmortem appearance. He is aware of Saul's condition, remembers their previous relationship, and has some degree of foreknowledge regarding Saul's impending fate.

The New Testament offers more insight on the matter. In Luke 20:35–38, Jesus refers to Moses, stating that God *is* (present tense) "the God of Abraham, the God of Isaac, and the God of Jacob." Jesus continues by stating, "He [God] *is* God not of the dead, but of the living; for to him all of them *are alive*." The point appears to be that God is now currently the God (sovereign over or in control) of those who have died physically but who remain alive, awaiting their physical renewal/resurrection. Also, the last part of Jesus's statement uses the present tense of the Greek word ζάω (*zoe* or "live") seemingly to further extenuate the point that at least those who died maintaining their confidence in God (patriarchs of Judaism) are now living with, or are alive to, God. Finally, it is important to realize Jesus is arguing this point with the Sadducees, a group who did not believe in life after death (Luke 20:27). Therefore, Jesus is confronting an established system of belief that the soul dies with the body.

The name "Sadducees" (Hebrew מיקודצ, *ṣdwqym*) derives from "Zadok" (Hebrew קודצ, *ṣdwq*) and refers to that Zadok whose descendants became the authorized high-priestly line in the postexilic period (see esp. Ezek. 40:46, 43:19; Sir. 51:12 [Hebrew]). The Sadducees in the first century seem to have been an aristocratic group of members and supporters of this high-priestly family who had to some extent developed their own distinctive views on matters of faith and practice (see Josephus, *War* 2.165–66; *Ant.* 13.297–98; 18.16–17). They were strongly oriented to the Pentateuch (the view of many of the Church Fathers that they entirely rejected the prophets is probably an overstatement; while they certainly had their own traditions of Pentateuchal interpretation, they were at odds with the authority given in Pharisaic circles to traditional developments), and of particular interest here is their disbelief in the resurrection of the dead. The approval of Jesus's answer, to be registered in v. 39 by some of the scribes, reflects the contrasting Pharisaic affirmation of belief in resurrection (of which Luke will make particular mileage in Acts 23:6–9). From John Nolland, *Luke 18:35–24:53,* vol. 35C of *Word Biblical Commentary,* ed. Bruce M. Metzger (Dallas, TX: Word, 1998), 964. The transfiguration is yet another example of the survival of the person after physical death (Matt. 17:1–13). Here, Elijah, who was taken into the air (a whirlwind) without passing through death (2 Kings 2), and Moses, who died a physical death (Deut. 34), are witnessed discussing (willful intent) current events (consciousness) with Jesus on the earth (in time). Although the text gives no clear physical description of Elijah and Moses, the Gospel writer does seem to indicate they were recognizable to the disciples, as was Jesus, in terms of their "bodily" appearance. Finally, the New Testament description of the slain martyrs in Rev. 6:9–11 and 20:4 depicts those who were killed on earth while remaining faithful to Christ, which carries them directly into a state of soul resurrection *without* physical bodies. Nevertheless, the writer states that these martyrs are alive, their souls are "visible," even seated in some fashion, while conscious, desirous, and aware of the passing of time. It is clear that these departed persons remain alive and are engaging in certain activities of the living.

14. William Hendriksen and Simon J. Kistemaker, *Exposition of the Gospel According to Luke,* vol. 11 of *New Testament Commentary* (Grand Rapids, MI: Baker Book House, 1980), 782.

15. Again, perhaps another strike against the aristocratic religion advocated by the Sadducees.

16. The name Lazarus, who in first-century Palestine would likely have been one of the poverty-stricken and therefore anonymous and forgotten throngs, is a derivative of the Hebrew name Eleazar, which means "God helps," the significance of which "indicates someone dependent on God." See Darrell L. Bock, *Luke Volume 2: 9:51–24:53, Baker Exegetical Commentary on the New Testament* (Grand Rapids, MI: Baker Academic, 1996), 1360–79.

17. Abraham's bosom is a "figure of speech probably derived from the Roman custom of reclining on one's left side at meals with the guest of honor at the bosom of his host (cf. John 13:25). It was used by Jesus in the story of Lazarus as a description of paradise (Luke 16:22, 23). In rabbinical writings as well as 4 Maccabees 13:17, the just were thought to be welcomed at death by Abraham, Isaac, and Jacob. Jesus, probably aware of this, was also alluding to the 'messianic banquet,' an image he used a number of times. Thus, in the world to come, the godly poor like Lazarus would not only be welcomed by Abraham but would occupy the place of honor next to

him at the banquet. Such a picture is presented by Jesus in contrast
to the torment of the rich man in Hades." Walter A. Elwell and
Barry J. Beitzel, *Baker Encyclopedia of the Bible* (Grand Rapids,
MI: Baker Book House, 1988), 15.

18. It is also unclear what differences exist in the Gospels regarding
how and why the words *sheol, hades, hell, tartarus,* and *gehenna*
are used and for what intended effect. Each tends to carry different
degrees of negative connotations. Yet some scholars have separated
these abodes of the dead in more specific fashion. It appears these
differentiations, although perhaps helpful, are difficult to apply
across all usages in the New Testament, since there is debate as to
if or when Jesus used the Greek language in contrast to Aramaic
and Hebrew.

19. Bock, *Luke, Baker Exegetical Commentary,* 1370.

20. As an important aside, during his teaching or lectures, Dallas
would often make specific note of instances in scripture like this
where one's memories or personal identity is maintained, while not
having a working brain to draw these memories or consciousness
from. He routinely took the opportunity to point out where and
how the scriptures speak against the increasingly familiar philosophical and theological position of nonreductive physicalism. For
more detail on this phenomenon and the problems it presents for
Christian life and thought, see J. P. Moreland and Scott B. Rae,
Body & Soul: Human Nature & the Crisis in Ethics (Downers
Grove, IL: InterVarsity Press, 2009), 131 and Moreland's *The Soul:
How We Know It's Real and Why It Matters.*

21. Still, in *sheol,* the rich man is suffering. What causes his suffering is
less clear. But it is important to examine the description Jesus gives
of the rich man's suffering. The word Jesus uses for torment (*basa-
nos*) has been likened to the punishment one may inflict "on a slave
to elicit a confession." Also, the heat of the "fire" is not consuming the rich man "physically." He is able to communicate, reason,
remember, and seek relief. If the torment is cumulative, one would
expect a point when the "burning" would ultimately consume him,
eventually rendering relief. Therefore, the suffering may be more

spiritual pain (nonphysical or nonmaterial) rather than physical pain from which he is seeking any and all possible means of relief. See Bock's *Luke, Baker Exegetical Commentary*, 1370.

22. A second interpretation may proceed from the scriptures' frequent use of the concept of thirst as an illustration or metaphor for desire for God. If the rich man is thirsting for God, and all he can imagine is the comfort even a tiny fragment of God's spirit would provide, then perhaps Lazarus has no means of giving God to those who have chosen in life to separate themselves from God. Perhaps not even God himself is able to overcome such resistance of will. Thus, the status of hades becomes a place where God isn't, yet where God, or the beneficial reality and effect of God's essence, is most desired but never realized. This seems to be at least part of the cyclical, unrequited desire that fuels a teeth-gnashing futility that burns inside the hearts and minds of those truly lost.

23. According to its grammatical form, *parakletos* is a passive verbal adjective from *parakaleo*. It means primarily "called (by someone for something)." When used as a noun, it means "one called upon for support, one called in for assistance," thus an *advocate*. The Latin Fathers, therefore, often translate *parakletos* as *advocatus* (Augustine, Tertullian, Cyprian). Outside the New Testament, one finds "the clear picture of a legal adviser or helper or advocate in the relevant court." Horst Balz and Gerhard Schneider, eds., *Exegetical Dictionary of the New Testament* (Grand Rapids, MI: Eerdmans, 1990), 28.

24. Paul echoes that God has done what needs to be done and that no one has an "excuse" (Rom. 1:20). This is not a result of some burden of duty. This is a product of God's love and the heart of a shepherd who seeks for any and all wandering sheep.

25. Unlike Lewis, Dallas did not believe in the possibility of acquiring salvation after death. The parable gives no indication of a "second chance," as we call it today. The rich man's awareness that his loved ones must be warned reveals his level of understanding and the great priority of preventing others from a similar fate while remaining powerless to changing his own. Perhaps this is the great-

est tragedy of the story. Abraham's response is that everyone the rich man is worried about will have ample opportunity to avoid his condition, the same opportunity, in fact, that the rich man, himself, wasted.

26. It is unclear how fully conscious the rich man is of his lost opportunity. Perhaps the ignorance in what was lost is a form of grace. He does express that his loved ones, or his fellow Jews, need to be warned of what lies ahead. Abraham assures him that if his brothers desire God with their whole hearts, God will find them. God can be counted on for that. That is Abraham's declaration. God's ways and will are readily available for all who desire them.

27. Perhaps the denial is an attempt to save, in some sense, his own victimhood. He desires a bigger sign, a louder word, a clearer vision from God. "If only" is so often the cry of despair from the lost and tormented heart. Abraham rebukes him, well aware that empirical signs and wonders are not the final and best answer.

28. Matheson, *What Dreams May Come*, 178–79.

Chapter Two: A Good Death?

1. Jim Harrison, *Legends of the Fall* (New York: Delacorte Press, 1979).

2. See Andy Court, producer, "The Cost of Dying," *60 Minutes,* November 19, 2009, www.cbsnews.com/news/the-cost-of-dying/.

3. Jonathan Edwards, *The Works of Jonathan Edwards: The "Miscellanies": Entry Nos. 501–832*, ed. Ava Chamberlain, vol. 18 (New Haven, CT: Yale Univ. Press, 2000), 481–84.

Chapter Three: Why We Exist

1. This idea is covered in *The Divine Conspiracy*, 21–29.

2. This vision is outlined in detail in our coauthored book *The Divine Conspiracy Continued: Fulfilling God's Kingdom on Earth* (San Francisco: HarperOne, 2014).

3. As a result, opposing viewpoints clash over the question of the purpose of human life. These clashing viewpoints often result in the development of oppositional worldviews evidenced in political,

economic, religious, and educational choices within the cultures of nearly every people group inhabiting the globe today.

4. The breath of life was and is much more than mouth-to-mouth resuscitation that infuses oxygen into fleshly lungs. God does not breathe as humans breathe. God's nature or essence is spirit, a nonmaterial, nonbodily personal power. Thus, the major issue of creating or animating human beings comes from the act of infusing God's power or Spirit (*ruach*) into the human form. However, we will reengage this subject in more detail in Chapter 5.

5. It is very difficult to lift the human mind to such high thoughts and gain an appropriate appreciation of the potency of human life. In great measure, our understanding of the spiritual nature of human existence has gradually decreased while secular forms of materialism, naturalism, and individual consumerism have increased. As such, the value of human life has progressively been devalued and commoditized. We see this today in the lack of human rights protection provided to the very young, the very old, the very costly, and the economically unproductive. It is quite the paradox that at the same time we engage in dramatic and expensive efforts to keep people from dying, there are many other lives we consistently devalue. Dallas's devotion to the subject of moral knowledge highlighted these dilemmas. He knew that such paradoxes, or hypocrisies, are inescapable when we choose to take upon ourselves the authority to dissect or parse the truth, applying situational ethics and political correctness as our guide instead of trusting, then applying, the wisdom of God universally in every instance and circumstance.

Dallas also discussed the practical side to the depreciation of human life. Too few of us have experienced the kind of power required to do our own little jobs of feeding our families in the easy yoke of Christ. Therefore, he suspected there was a significant correlation between the rise of purposelessness in human life and our sense of impotence, which culminates in experiencing pervasive degrees of futility. Together, impotence and futility join to form a terrible image of senselessness and anger regarding the purpose of human existence, leaving only the hope of survival. Such a low bar carries an assumption that human life is destined to be little more than an enduring slog through a very precarious state where we simply hang on for dear life. All of this is antithetical to the type of life Jesus taught was available in the Kingdom where the God of Abraham, Isaac, and Jacob is king. Lives marked by aimless drifting and habitual skepticism resist any move toward recapturing human dignity, which is the legacy of the sons and daughters of the most-high God. For those interested in Dallas's thoughts on moral knowledge, see a few articles available at www.dwillard.org, including Luci Shaw, "Spiritual Disciplines in a Postmodern World," *Radix* 27, no. 2. (n.d.), www.dwillard.org/articles/artview.asp?artID=56 and Dallas Willard, "Moral Rights, Moral Responsibility and the Contemporary Failure of Moral Knowledge" (lecture, first annual Human Rights Conference hosted by the IPFW Institute for Human Rights at Purdue University, December 10, 2004), www.dwillard.org/articles/artview.asp?artID=107.

6. Barbara Kellerman, "Lessons from Madoff's Minions," *Washington Post,* January 20, 2009, http://views.washingtonpost.com/leadership/panelists/2009/01/learning-from-madoffs-minions.html. Also see Adam LeBor, *The Believers: How America Fell for Bernard Madoff's $65 Billion Investment Scam* (New York: Orion, 2010).

7. *The Wall Street Journal* has opened and maintained a website devoted specifically to the Madoff scandal and the ongoing fallout. See www.wsj.com/public/page/bernard-madoff.html.

8. Christopher M. Matthews, "Five Former Employees of Bernie Madoff Found Guilty of Fraud," *Wall Street Journal,* March 25, 2014, www.wsj.com/articles/SB10001424052702304679404579459551977535482.

9. This is a well-established practice. For example see John W. Howe and Samuel C. Pascoe, *Our Anglican Heritage: Can an Ancient Church be a Church of the Future?* (Eugene, OR: Cascade Books, 2010), 6 and Donald A. McGavran, *Ethnic Realities and the Church: Lessons from India* (South Pasadena, CA: William Carey Library, 1979), 5.

10. For those interested in Trinitarian theology I am not at all trying to argue for a form of modalism here. This is simply a metaphor attempting to describe the different functions displayed within the Trinitarian union. And like all illustrations, it should not be taken too far.

11. This is a major theme in *The Divine Conspiracy Continued* as well.

Chapter Four: The Substance of Spirit

1. When I was working with Dallas on my Ph.D. dissertation, we spent months discussing his views on these ideas. And as a result, I came to better understand how vital and unique his views were of our culture, and how we eventually live our lives is affected by our thoughts. He was able to show me how what philosophers discuss in the ivory towers of universities eventually spills out into the culture. Sometimes the overflows of ideas are beneficial and good, but sometimes ideas can birth the most heinous of crimes. I often heard him say, "The killing fields of Cambodia started in the cafés of Paris." This may be a quote Dallas used that is unattributed. I was blessed to hear from Steve Porter, philosophy professor at Biola University and doctoral student of Dallas at USC, about the exact nature of what Dallas is referring to in this quote. It comes from Dallas's understanding that the idea of "European civilization" is oxymoronic. The horrors of Nazism and Communism, "all arose out of European ideas, political and philosophical, being put into practice. Even the Cambodian genocide had its genesis in the cafés of Paris where Pol Pot got his ideas. Hitler got his ideas in the cafés of Vienna." My thanks to Steve for his insights and recollections.

2. For those interested in such topics and their effects, Dallas has written on the subject of epistemology and phenomenology in his more academic works, and in some fashion has hit a few high points in *Knowing Christ Today: Why We Can Trust Spiritual Knowledge* (San Francisco: HarperOne, 2009). For a list of these articles, see the Dallas Willard Ministries website at www.dwillard.org/articles/phillist.asp.

3. *Theology of Dallas Willard: Discovering Protoevangelical Faith* (Eugene, OR: Pickwick Publications, 2013), 93. Also see Dallas Willard, *The Spirit of the Disciplines: Understanding How God Changes Lives* (New York: HarperCollins, 1988), 60.

4. Pierre Teilhard de Chardin, *The Phenomenon of Man* (New York: HarperPerennial, 2002), 36.

5. *Everything Is Spiritual,* directed by Rob Bell (Zondervan, 2007).

6. *The Matrix,* directed by The Wachowski Brothers (Warner Bros., 1999), DVD.

7. C. S. Lewis, *The Screwtape Letters* (San Francisco: HarperOne, 2015).

8. For those of you not familiar with this lingo, I'm referring to the plot of the first movie of *The Matrix* trilogy.

9. William Arndt, Frederick W. Danker, and Walter Bauer, *A Greek-English Lexicon of the New Testament and Other Early Christian Literature* (Chicago: Univ. of Chicago Press, 2000), 981.

Chapter Five: Choosing Eternal Life

1. This is captured in *The Divine Conspiracy* in relation to Dallas's discussion of the sin-management Gospels.

2. *Surprised by Hope,* 182

3. C. S. Lewis, *The Problem of Pain* (San Francisco: HarperSanFrancisco, 1996), 129–30.

4. *The Divine Conspiracy,* 302.

5. *The Divine Conspiracy,* 302. Richard Foster mentions this idea as well in "Growing Edges," *Renovaré* 13, no. 3 (July, 2003), http://blog.renovare.org/2003/07/15/perspective-on-hell/.

6. There are different ways of defining the philosophical concept of substance. I am using the term as it is connected to the Greek concept of *ousia,* translated "being," which is further translated into Latin as *substantia.* All of which Dallas combined to convey that which stands under or grounds things and forms the foundational or fundamental entities of reality. Thus, spirit, in this definition, is a substance or basic element from which everything is constructed.

Chapter Six: Honesty

1. I first heard the phrase "conflict breeds intimacy" from Nancy Ortberg while coteaching a class together using Patrick Lencioni's book *The Advantage* (San Francisco: Jossey-Bass, 2013). Nancy's insight perfectly describes what I learned that day with Dallas.

2. Augustine discusses the topics of the hereafter, heaven, and hell in his Confessions. Augustine of Hippo, "The Confessions of St. Augustin," in *A Select Library of the Nicene and Post-Nicene Fathers of the Christian Church, First Series: The Confessions and Letters of St. Augustin with a Sketch of His Life and Work,* ed. Philip Schaff, trans. J. G. Pilkington, vol. 1 (Buffalo, NY: Christian Literature Company, 1886), xiii, xxiv, xxxii.

3. Lars Bo Kaspersen, *Anthony Giddens, An Introduction to a Social Theorist* (London: Wiley-Blackwell, 2000), 6, 154–55.

4. These and many other questions are pursued and researched by Andrew Root, *The Children of Divorce: The Loss of Family as the Loss of Being* (Grand Rapids, MI: Baker Academic, 2010), footnotes 7, 155.

5. Anthony Giddens, *Modernity and Self Identity* (Cambridge, UK: Polity Press, 1991), 38.

6. Lewis, *The Great Divorce,* ch. 7.

7. Jesse Jarnow, "Patrick Henry's Liberty or Death Speech: A Primary Source Investigation," in *The Federalist–Anti-Federalist Debate Over States' Rights: A Primary Source Investigation,* ed. Lea Ball (New York: Rosen Publishing, 2005), 50–53.

Chapter Seven: Fearlessness

1. Keith Getty and Stuart Townend, *In Christ Alone* (Kingsway Music: 2001).

2. Roger N. Johnson, "Bad News Revisited: The Portrayal of Violence, Conflict and Suffering on Television News," *Journal of Peace Psychology* 2, no. 3, (1996), 201–16. Ray Williams, "Why We Love Bad News More Than Good News," Wired for Success, *Psychology Today,* December 30, 2010, www.psychologytoday.com/blog/wired-success/201012/why-we-love-bad-news.

3. This is the "motto" printed in the upper-left-hand corner of the front page of the *New York Times*.

4. This quote has an interesting lineage. It is often attributed on the Internet to Ambrose Redmoon, or even to Meg Cabot (see www .goodreads.com/quotes/tag/fear). But a little research proved very interesting. Although this cannot be verified, a Google search turned up this interesting nugget:

> *"Ambrose Redmoon" and also "Ambrose Hollingworth Red-mon" were pseudonyms of James Neil Hollingworth, author and rock band manager. Your main questions about J. N. Hol-lingworth should be answered by this resume of an article in the* Chicago Tribune *of March 29, 2002: "Born in Painesville, Ohio as James Neil Hollingworth. Changed name to Ambrose Hollingworth Redmon. Was a beatnik, hippie, and former manager of legendary rock bank Quicksilver Messenger Service. Spent last 3 decades of life as paraplegic in wheelchair from a car accident outside San Francisco in 1966. Lived in garage apartment in Santa Rosa, Cal. until he died at age 63 (1996?). Was a writer, but found no publishers and was not known beyond a relatively small circle of mystics and fanciers of neo-paganism. According to his daughter, he was seriously radical on every level. The quote about courage is taken from an article entitled 'No Peaceful Warriors!' published in the Fall, 1991 issue of 'Gnosis: A Journal of the Western Inner Traditions'—a defunct magazine about New Age spirituality."*

See "ambrose redmon," question posted by ravsteve-ga, answer posted by scriptor-ga, on Google Answers, September 15, 2002, http://answers.google.com/answers/threadview?id=65200. It is quoted again on a blog called Entersection, managed by Gregory Foster, dated September 3, 2010, http://entersection.com/ posts/1158-ambrose-hollingworth-redmoon-on-courage. There a reference is listed as Ambrose Hollingworth Redmoon, "No Peaceful Warriors!" *Gnosis: A Journal of the Western Inner Traditions*,

Vol. 21 (Fall 1991), 40. There a longer quote is listed. "Courage is not the absence of fear, but rather the judgment that something else is more important than one's fear. The timid presume it is lack of fear that allows the brave to act when the timid do not. But to take action when one is not afraid is easy. To refrain when afraid is also easy. To take action regardless of fear is brave." No verification of this specific reference was possible. The Lumen Foundation does still publish a journal titled *Gnosis* in San Francisco.

5. William L. Lane, *Hebrews 9–13*, vol. 47B of *Word Biblical Commentary*, ed. David A. Hubbard and Glenn W. Barker (Dallas, TX: Word, 1991), 414. Also see *Exegetical Dictionary of the New Testament*, 632.

6. In order to maintain the sanctity of anonymity, the characters discussed and their testimonials were altered in a way to preserve all privacy.

CHAPTER EIGHT: POWER

1. James H. Billington, ed., *Respectfully Quoted: A Dictionary of Quotations* (Mineola, NY: Dover Publications, 2010), 228.

2. Here, I am using the term *sexism* to refer to all the ways and means of objectifying sex.

3. An original citation for Wilde is difficult to find and may be misattributed. However, where and how the statement is currently used is interesting and perhaps telling as well. See Jillian Deri, *Love's Refraction: Jealousy and Compersion in Queer Women's Polyamorous Relationships* (Toronto: Univ. of Toronto Press, 2015), 96. See also Sarah Anne Johnson, *The Very Telling: Conversations with American Writers* (Hanover, NH: University Press of New England, 2006), 14.

4. Nietzsche wrote about the "Will to Power" in *Thus Spoke Zarathustra: A Book for All and None,* trans. Walter Arnold Kaufmann (New York: Modern Library, 1995), and again in *Beyond Good and Evil,* trans. Helen Zimmern (New York: Macmillan, 1907).

5. Friedrich W. Nietzsche, *Beyond Good and Evil*, trans. Helen Zimmern, 227.

6. This is also described in John Ortberg's book, *Soul Keeping: Caring for the Most Important Part of You,* (Grand Rapids, MI: Zondervan, 2014), 146.

7. Richard Selzer, *Mortal Lessons: Notes on the Art of Surgery* (New York: Simon & Schuster, 1976), 45–46.

8. Laura Waters Hinson, *As We Forgive,* Image Bearer Pictures, 2010.

9. Thomas C. Oden, *The Word of Life: Systematic Theology*, vol. 2 (San Francisco: HarperSanFrancisco, 1992), 85.

10. Henri Nouwen is quoted in Dallas Willard's "A Cup Running Over: Why Preachers Must Find Deep Satisfaction in Christ," in *The Art and Craft of Biblical Preaching: A Comprehensive Resource for Today's Communicators,* eds. Haddon Robinson and Craig Brian (Grand Rapids, MI: Zondervan, 2005), 71–73.

11. One mina was the weight of about 50–60 shekels of silver, approximately 25 percent of the annual salary of a migrant worker in the first century. Therefore, ten minas were perhaps two and a half years of wages.

12. Dallas Willard, *The Great Omission* (San Francisco: HarperOne, 2006) 61–62.

13. *Tim's Vermeer,* directed by Teller (Sony Pictures Classics, 2013), DVD.

14. This subject is covered well by J. P. Moreland, *Love Your God with All Your Mind: The Role of Reason in the Life of the Soul* (Colorado Springs: NavPress, 1997) and Mark A. Noll, *The Scandal of the Evangelical Mind* (Grand Rapids, MI: Eerdmans, 1995).

CHAPTER NINE: BENEFICIAL RELATIONSHIPS

1. Both Moses and Jesus manifest a glowing light that emanates from their bodies or around their bodies and that seems to be conjoined with a proximity to God's power or glory.

2. It's also important to note that God places a curse on the serpent and the land that was intended to provide for humanity. There is no mention of a curse placed specifically on Adam and Eve, although they certainly suffer from the consequences of these curses.

3. See ch. 10 of Dallas Willard, *Renovation of the Heart: Putting on the Character of Christ* (Colorado Springs: NavPress, 2002).

4. However, there is some sociological research on the degree to which marriage is affected by religion. See Donna St. George, "Couples Who Share Religious Practices Tend to Be Happier Than Those Who Don't, Study Says," *Washington Post,* August 12, 2010, www.washingtonpost.com/wp-dyn/content/article/2010/08/11/AR2010081101961.html.
5. Brian Lugioyo, untitled lecture (Faith Matters Symposium at Azusa Pacific University, October 2013).

CHAPTER TEN: JOY

1. I like what Winston Churchill said about his depressive moods. He called them "the black dog" that plagued him for much of his adult life. See John Colville, "The Personality of Sir Winston Churchill," (Crosby Kemper Lecture, March 24, 1985), in *Winston Churchill: Resolution, Defiance, Magnanimity, Good Will,* ed. R. Crosby Kemper (Columbia: Univ. of Missouri, 1995), 108–25. See also Martin Gilbert, *In Search of Churchill: A Historian's Journey* (London: HarperCollins, 1994), 209f.

CONCLUSION: FINAL THINGS

1. Peter Kreeft, *Heaven: The Heart's Deepest Longing* (Cambridge: Harper & Row, 1980).
2. Willard, *Renovation of the Heart,* 57–58
3. Willard, *The Divine Conspiracy Continued,* x.

About the Book

This book is the product of conversations between Gary Black Jr. and Dallas Willard during the last few months of Dallas's life.

GARY BLACK JR. is a theology professor at Azusa Pacific University. He is the author of *The Theology of Dallas Willard, Exploring the Life and Calling*, and coauthor of *The Divine Conspiracy Continued*. He was a personal friend of Dallas.

DALLAS WILLARD (1935–2013) was a professor at the University of Southern California's School of Philosophy from 1965 until his retirement in 2012. His groundbreaking books *The Divine Conspiracy*, *The Great Omission*, *Knowing Christ Today*, *Renovation of the Heart*, *Hearing God*, and *The Spirit of the Disciplines* forever changed the way thousands of Christians are experiencing their faith. For more information, visit www.dwillard.org.